HUGUENOT ANCESTRY

Allegorical picture of the excesses committed by the Huguenots. The lion bound and tamed represents France reduced to a deplorable position by the heretics, as much by civil war, pillage, violence and bloodshed as by the impiety of which they left traces everywhere, profaning churches, breaking the sacred vessels and treading under foot the crosses, images and relics of the saints. After a drawing from the 16th-century manuscript 'De Tristibus Franciae', preserved in the Library of Lyons.

HUGUENOT ANCESTRY

Noel Currer-Briggs &
Royston Gambier

Phillimore

1985

Published by
PHILLIMORE & CO. LTD.
Shopwyke Hall, Chichester, Sussex

ISBN 0 85033 564 7

Ak	
Ba	29/4/86
Dt	
O	
R	
U	
Wa	

Printed and bound in Great Britain by
THE CAMELOT PRESS LTD.
Southampton, England

CONTENTS

LIST OF PLATES
(*between pages 22 and 23*)

Frontispiece: Allegorical picture of the excesses committed by the Huguenots

LIST OF TEXT ILLUSTRATIONS

The authors would like to thank the Mansell Collection for permission to reproduce all photographs except plate 11, for which thanks are extended to the John Freeman Group, and plate 20, for which thanks are extended to the British Museum (photographer Ray Gardner). The line illustrations have been supplied by the Mansell Collection (forntispiece and figs. 1, 3, 8 and 9), the Public Record Office (fig. 5, reference R.G. 4/4646) and the Huguenot Library (fig. 6, reference H/D 3/3/1341, and fig. 7, reference MS J28). The authors are grateful for the co-operation of all these bodies.

FOREWORD

THE DUKE OF BUCCLEUCH AND QUEENSBERRY, K.T.

With the wisdom of hindsight, aided by the revelations in these pages, the full significance of Huguenot migration over several generations becomes increasingly evident.

Considering how the countless human tragedies, induced by Roman Catholic persecution of Protestants through France and the Low Countries, were the stuff of which headlines are made today, and considering the still more lasting effect upon France of the greatest 'brain drain' in history, with a corresponding 'brain gain' to Britain, it is quite astonishing how little recognition or acknowledgement there has been of the Huguenot contribution to our national rise to a position of world supremacy through the 18th and 19th centuries.

For the host countries it was most fortunate that so high a proportion of the élite in agriculture, art, commerce and industry happened to be Protestants, when they came in droves between the mid-1550s and about 1700. The exodus only eased off during a 42-year period of somewhat greater religious tolerance; this had resulted from the broadminded liberality of Henri IV with his Edict of Nantes, the revocation of which by Louis XIV in 1685 triggered off the final and greatest spate of refugees. Mercifully the Channel proved to be less of an obstacle than the Berlin Wall, and for several years countless Huguenots, with impressive skills and talents, established themselves as far North as Edinburgh. The warmth and sympathy of their reception must have been enhanced by the coincidental and highly unpopular arrival of the Roman Catholic King James II on the throne, and feelings were manifested by the grass roots support for Monmouth's Protestant rebellion, fruitless though it was, that same year.

Although the impact of the Huguenot settlers was remarkable in so many spheres, it is in the cultural field that their achievements are still most conspicuous today. Many eminent patrons of the arts helped them to find their feet; no one did more than Ralph, Duke of Montagu, who had been Ambassador to Paris in the preceding decade. He, like other discerning connoisseurs, had doubtless spotted the flourishing talent which he used to advantage, so that Boughton House, Northamptonshire today is a strikingly-comprehensive memorial to a wide variety of Huguenot artists and craftsmen.

For 300 years the effects of Huguenot migration have been virtually ignored or taken for granted. It is therefore very timely and salutary that the tercentenary of the climax of the story, the Revocation of the Edict of Nantes, should have provoked this revealing re-assessment of an episode of such momentous historical and evolutionary importance.

ACKNOWLEDGEMENTS

The literature on the Huguenots is very extensive, and to add to it may seem presumptuous, were it not for the fact that this is the first book to deal with the peculiar problems involved in tracing Huguenot ancestries. To do this more easily, it is essential to be familiar with the main features of 16th- and 17th-century French history, and in order to provide our readers with these basic facts we have had to lean heavily on historians who have treated the subject in more detail than we have thought necessary in this work. Their books are listed in the bibliography, and we would urge readers to study them carefully, for we are convinced that they will find them not only instructive but of great assistance in their family research.

In the autumn of 1983 Lady Monson, Chairman of the Huguenot Society Tercentenary Committee, suggested to Royston Gambier that a simple pedigree be drawn up showing the Huguenot ancestry of Prince William of Wales through both the Royal line and the Spencer family. Such was the general interest at the result that the President of the Huguenot Society, Randolph Vigne, M.A., urged that the pedigree be widened to include other notable Huguenot lines. The final pedigree, consisting of 15 principal lines of descent, and now including Prince Henry of Wales, has been checked by Sir Iain Moncrieffe of that Ilk, Bt., and David Williamson, F.S.A. (Scot.), F.S.G. and has been engrossed and illuminated on vellum by David Chesters, F.R.S.A., F.S.A.(Scot.), a Liveryman of the Worshipful Company of Painter Stainers, which illustrates the Royal Coat-of-Arms, the Royal Arms of France and Navarre, and other coats-of-arms of the main families involved. The Prince of Wales approved the suggestion that the pedigree should be displayed at the Museum of London exhibition 'The Quiet Conquest' in 1985, and it will ultimately be hung at La Providence, the French Hospital in Rochester. We are therefore grateful for permission to include the basic pedigree in this book, and wish to record our thanks for the encouragement and help given to Royston Gambier by those mentioned above. We also wish to acknowledge our debt of gratitude to Margaret Audin for her able assistance in the chapter to do with research in France, a subject in which she is a great expert, and to Dr. Robin Gwynn, Fellow of the Huguenot Society and Senior Lecturer in History at Massey University, New Zealand, for reading the typescript and for many valuable suggestions and corrections he made. Finally we would like to thank our publisher, Noel Osborne, for all the help and encouragement he has given us.

NOEL CURRER-BRIGGS and ROYSTON GAMBIER

January 1985

Chapter One

INTRODUCTION

THE FIRST PRINTED EDITION of the Bible was made in Germany in 1455 and a second edition followed seven years later. A number of copies found their way to France where, as the manufacture of paper improved and the method of casting type in quantity was devised, they became accessible to the mass of the people. In spite of papal and episcopal prohibitions, more and more Bibles became available, especially after they had been translated into the vernacular, until it became clear throughout the latter half of the 15th and first half of the 16th centuries that, when ordinary folk could read the Bible and pray to God in their native language instead of through priests in Latin, the authority of the Church itself was endangered.

Bible studies provided thoughtful men with new views about life and death. It impressed them with a deep sense of responsibility, and to the poor it opened up a completely new view of the world. The effect on men like Martin Luther, then a young postulant, was profound, and while reading and studying the Bible they quickly came to realise the need for versions in their own language, so that what they had read in Latin could be made available to the people. By the end of the first half of the 16th century thousands of copies were circulating in Europe with far-reaching effects on the thoughts of men and women.

The printing of Bibles was carried on in the Low Countries, where versions in Flemish and French, as well as copies in other languages, including English, soon became available. Tyndale, for example, had the first edition of his translation printed in Antwerp in 1526, and several translations of parts of the Bible appeared in France before the end of the 15th century, but these were all superseded by the complete version, printed at Antwerp between 1512 and 1530, translated by Jacques Le Fevre (or Faber) of Etaples. His formed the basis of all subsequent editions of the French Bible.

The effects were the same wherever these modern-language versions appeared. There was a reawakening of religious life, a desire for a purer faith and a return to the simpler form of Christianity of the Apostles. Suddenly it was clear for all to see that ecclesiastical abuses, such as the sale of indulgences and the wealth of the clergy and monks, had no biblical authority. The seeds of the Reformation and those of the sanguinary struggles that were to follow in its wake— had been sown.

The first stirrings of the Reformation in France were at Meaux, a town some fifty miles north-east of Paris, not far from the Flemish frontier. It was a typical medieval town, the home of craftsmen, mechanics, wool-carders, clothmakers and similar artisans. Its proximity to Flanders, and especially to Bruges, Brussels and Antwerp, ensured that the new opinions flowing from the printing presses of these cities soon found their way there. Among the most influential of its citizens were Guillaume

1

Briçonnet, comte de Montbrun and bishop of Meaux, and Jacques Le Fevre, a distin-guished scholar and leading professor at the Sorbonne in Paris. The latter's translation of the Bible when he was over seventy had a profound local influence. The bishop had been shocked by the licentiousness of the clergy and their general disregard of religious duty. He consequently invited Le Fevre, and a younger contemporary, Guillaume Farel and others to join him in preaching throughout his diocese and in distributing copies of the four Gospels among the poor.

Alarmed by the spread of the new views, the forces of reaction were quick to launch a counter-attack. The priests and monks of Meaux appealed for help to the Sorbonne, the Faculty of Theology in Paris, and the Sorbonne in turn called upon the king to intervene with a strong hand. The bishop of Meaux was fined and gave no further offence; others were less easily squashed.

Like other important movements in history, the Reformation and the ensuing Wars of Religion were the result of the combination of factors coming together at a specific time. It is thus important to understand these factors for they dominated the lives of most people from one generation to another throughout the 16th and 17th centuries, and until we do, the task of tracing Huguenot ancestry is made much more difficult.

France in the 16th century was the most powerful nation in Europe, not only in manpower and material resources, but also because of its centralised system of government. Through the regional Parlements, the French kings had broken down the independence of the nobles, and the smaller gentry had been forced to retire to their estates. The wealthy merchants and bourgeoisie found that their cities, whose wide privileges were perhaps the most striking feature of medieval European political life, had been divested of many of their civic rights. This meant that regardless of religious beliefs, there were many influential members of the upper and middle classes who were ready to take advantage of whatever upheavals the new learning brought in its wake, to recover their lost position and fortunes.

French academics were likewise in the forefront of the intellectual movements of Europe, both secular and spiritual, and it was in this climate of enquiry that men like Erasmus, Le Fevre, Luther, Calvin and Zwingli proclaimed their thesis for reform. All had hoped to see the Church of Rome reform itself from within, and many regretted the need for a complete break, turning to the establishment of reformed churches with reluctance. So far as the French clergy was concerned, the majority of parish priests were as poor as the peasants that made up their flocks, while the senior clergy were both wealthy and powerful. The influence of bishops and abbots was vast both on account of the large number of benefices they held and the distinction of the families to which they belonged. The large majority had lost all care for the spiritual welfare of their people and many were living lives of luxury and vice. Although this situation had existed for a considerable time, the Pragmatic Sanction of Bourges (1438) exacerbated the problem as it gave the French Church a considerable degree of independence from the king as well as the pope. However, following the battle of Marignano, which established French military predominance in Europe, the Concordat of Bologna (1516) provided for increased papal revenue from the Church in France in exchange for the real control of church affairs by the French monarchy. Conse-quently the majority of church appointments were in the gift of these French kings, and were dispensed as a matter of royal favour rather than in recognition of theological

Fig. 1   John Calvin (1509-64).

dedication. Many a merchant or soldier who had rendered service to the crown found himself a bishop or abbot as a result. Thus, on the eve of the Reformation, the wealth and influence of the Church of France was already at the disposal of the crown, so that the kings had no incentive to change the *status quo*.

Thus it can be seen that this combination of factors precipitated a conflict which began with religious fervour, reached its climax through political aims and ambitions, and ended with a pure adherence to the reformed religion that for many became worth more than life itself.

The origin of the term 'Huguenot' is uncertain. It was first applied as a nickname or term of abuse. Some authorities attribute it to an extension of the name 'Hugues', referring either to Besançon Hugues, a leader of the Geneva Eidgenossen; or to Hugues Capet, founder of the French royal house; or to a legendary King Hugo at whose haunted tower the Protestants of Tours are said to have held secret meetings. Others suppose it to be derived from the obsolete word 'Huguon' meaning someone who walks the streets at night—the adherents choosing this time for their meetings. A more plausible theory attributes the word to the French inability to pronounce the German word 'Eidgenosse', meaning a companion, comrade or partner who has sworn an oath, i.e., a confederate. In Swiss-German 'Eidgenosse' became 'Eignot', and thus 'Huguenot' in French.

Francis I (1515-1547)

The first stirrings for reform in France were felt during the reign of Francis I, and have been sometimes regarded as an offshoot of Lutheranism. Yet Jacques Le Fevre wrote his *Sancti Pauli Epistolae* as early as 1512, and this has been interpreted as the cardinal doctrine of French Protestantism—justification by faith. The new religion was not confined to the north of France, for it quickly spread, especially among those who had grievances against the established order of things. Due to Francis I's alliance with Protestant German princes against the Austro-Spanish power of the Hapsburgs, the reformers had great hopes of his support, but they were disappointed, for the king's vacillating policies gave them no certainty of it. In 1545, for example, a massacre of Waldensians in Provence caused a public and royal outcry which led to a temporary reaction against the excessive zeal of the persecutors, and during the lull in the violence against it, the new religion made rapid headway. Men of rank and learning joined the 'heretics', who soon became so numerous that they constituted a considerable force within the state, where their influence on French political history became an important factor. On the other hand, the king was much influenced by his sister, Marguerite of Angoulême, and by his mistress, Anne de Pisseleu, Duchess of Étampes, who were in favour of toleration; yet he was equally influenced by men like Duprat, Montmorency and de Touron, who were staunch supports of the *status quo*. He gave pledges of support to both parties. In the earlier years of his reign he afforded protection to Le Fevre and Louis de Berquin when, in 1523, through the efforts of the Sorbonne and the Parlement of Paris, they suffered persecution. When Berquin was burned at the stake in 1529 it was without the king's consent.

The political situation during much of his reign suggested rapprochement with the Protestants, though two events in 1534 finally resolved Francis I to guide his religious policy towards the Catholics. An agreement with the pope would allow him to recover Milan if he undertook to stamp out heresy in France; the other was the incident of the Protestant placards. The king had already been angered by the inconoclastic behaviour of the reformers, when they had destroyed statues in 1528 and 1530. Now one of their infamous placards had been nailed to his bedroom door, which so incensed him that he determined to adopt a policy of severity towards these extremists. From this time on, in spite of still courting the friendship of the German princes, and in spite of occasional indulgences shown to the reformers, the king allowed a free hand to the Catholic party who stood for complete repression. The vigour with which this policy was pursued caused many of the leading figures of the reformed religion to seek asylum abroad, the most famous of whom was John Calvin, who settled in Basle in the autumn of 1534. It was here that he is thought to have written his *Christianae Religionis Institutio* which gave the French Protestant movement a cogent ideological basis.

Bernard Palissy

Among the earliest converts to the new religion was a craftsman named Bernard Palissy, whose ability as a writer and philosopher was more than equalled by his fame as a potter. His career is worth describing, not so much because he was a leader of the new religion as because he was typical of so many Frenchmen who embraced it, and whose descendants enriched the life of Britain to such a remarkable extent.

Palissy was born in Périgord in 1510, the son of a glazier from the village of La Chapelle-Biron. At the age of 21, on completion of his apprenticeship as a painter on glass, he moved to Tarbes, where he settled for some years before proceeding through Languedoc, Dauphiné, Alsace and Luxembourg to Flanders. Wherever he went he mixed with the other artists and craftsmen, many of whom had adopted Luther's teaching. Palissy returned to France in 1539 at a time when persecution was severe; when printing had been suppressed by royal edict, and when reading the Bible was punishable by death. The persecution was particularly stringent in and around Paris, so Palissy decided to settle far away in the then remote province of Saintonge in south-western France. There he established himself at Saintes, first as a glass-painter and portrait-painter, then as a enameller. Saintes was already a Huguenot centre, for Calvin had visited it early in his life and left many converts behind him. It is not known whether Palissy ever met Calvin, but he was certainly among his earliest followers. He was also influenced by the teaching of Philibert Hamelin, one of the early Huguenot martyrs in the south of France who had joined Calvin's congregation in Geneva, and who was one of the founders of the reformed church in Saintes. Many of his followers spread the new religion to nearby La Rochelle and Bordeaux, and by 1559 the heresy had become so widespread in this region of the country that a royal edict against it was published making it punishable by death: but this is to anticipate.

During this period, Palissy was perfecting the secret of the enamel he had been looking for all his working life. This brought him to the notice of the duc de Montmorency, who was at that time building a large château for himself near Paris. The duke supported Palissy with funds to enable him to produce the large numbers of tiles needed for the new building, but in spite of this patronage Palissy, whose reputation as an adherent of the reformed religion was well known, was seized and put on trial at Bordeaux. He was only saved by the duke's intervention, for the latter feared that if Palissy was executed the tiles for his château would never be made. Palissy was consequently transferred from the jurisdiction of the Parlement of Bordeaux to that of the Grand Council of Paris and appointed potter to the king. In Paris he re-established his factory at the Tuileries (or tile-works) under the eyes of an increasingly large circle of influential patrons, including the king himself. This change of fortune in no way made Palissy change his religious views, and the last year of his life was spent imprisoned in the Bastille, where he died aged seventy-eight.

Palissy was by no means the only Frenchman of genius to embrace the new faith. Men such as Pierre Ramus and Joseph Justus Scaliger, the philosophers; Charles Dumoulin, the jurist; Ambroise Paré, the surgeon to the royal family; Henri Étienne, the printer; Jean Goujon, the sculptor; Charles Goudimel, the musician; and Olivier de Serre, the agriculturalist, were all Protestants and all members of the bourgeoisie or peasantry. Persecution of men such as these, rather than checking the spread of heresy, tended to extend it. The spectacle of men and women of integrity and talent being martyred only served to arouse the curiosity of the public at large to know what in the forbidden Bible inspired their courage.

In January 1535 an edict had been published ordering the extermination of the heretics. This resulted in the first of many emigrations. In 1538 the first French Protestant church was founded at Strasbourg, then a free city of the Holy Roman Empire, by Martin Bucer who invited Calvin to organise the French community there. It was during this period that Huguenot refugees landed in England in Kent and Sussex, but as their safety lay in obscurity they mingled with the English community and made no attempt to establish settlements or congregations of their own. We have briefly mentioned the persecution of the Waldensians, or inhabitants of the Vaudois as they should perhaps be more correctly described. In 1545 the inhabitants of the villages of Merindol and Cabrières were massacred on the orders of Jean Maynier, baron d'Oppède. This was followed by the massacre of the inhabitants of 22 other villages; of those not slaughtered, 700 were sent to the galleys as slaves.

Henry II (1547–1559)

Francis I was succeeded by his son, Henry II, whose foreign policy was much the same as his father's. He was, however, a bigot and showed far less tolerance towards his Protestant subjects than his father. In the first year of his reign a special court, known as the Chambre Ardente, was set up with the object of rooting out heresy altogether. This was followed in 1551 by a series of laws to the same end, codified under the title of the Edict of Châteaubriant. Its 46 articles provided for a tighter control over the publication of prohibited books and gave additional power to the civil and ecclesiastical courts. Informers were rewarded, the property of convicted heretics was confiscated, anyone who ventured to intercede on their behalf was deemed to be heretic, and only those of proven orthodoxy were able to become teachers or professors. In general, the edict was rigorously applied and as a consequence the flow of refugees increased.

In spite of this increased persecution, the reformers attracted an even greater number of adherents from all sections of society. Until now they had been referred to as Lutherans, but as the main impetus behind their teaching, literature and organisation stemmed from Geneva, it would be more accurate to say that it was Calvinism which was establishing itself in France. It is therefore not without significance that the term 'Huguenot' became to be applied to the reformers at about this time, thus supporting the theory advanced by those who see the term as a corruption of the Swiss-German word 'Eidgenosse'.

In 1555 the first Huguenot consistory was held in Paris, and subsequently similar consistories were formed throughout France. By 1559 their strength was such that they were able to summon the first national synod in Paris, which stimulated many people of the highest rank to come forward and declare their adherence to the new faith. Following the Peace of Câteau-Cambrésis in April 1559, which brought the war with Spain to a temporary end, Henry II determined to exterminate the Protestant sects from his kingdom. Calling himself the Minister of Vengeance, he only waited until the tournament in honour of the double marriage of his daughter, Elizabeth, to the king of Spain, Philip II, and of his sister, Margaret, to the duke of Savoy was over to institute his campaign. However, it was not to be, for in a joust with the comte de Montgomery the king was fatally wounded and died on 10 July 1559.

Francis II (1559-1560) and Charles IX (1560-1574)

The reigns of Francis II and Charles IX were dominated by two events—the regency of their mother, Catherine de' Medici, and the outbreak of the long religious wars in 1562 which lasted for more than 36 years, and which caused not only a massive loss of life but also the emigration of large numbers of refugees to Britain and the Low Countries.

Francis II was a sickly young man of feeble intellect. He had married Mary Stuart, daughter of James V of Scotland, and queen of Scots in her own right, the year before his father's death. Throughout his short reign of barely 18 months, affairs of state were controlled by his wife's uncles, the powerful Guise brothers, Francis, duke of Guise, and Charles, cardinal of Lorraine. Henry II's widow, Catherine de' Medici was too overcome by the sudden death of her husband to put up much resistance to the Guises, whose fanatical Catholicism stimulated them to institute a vicious campaign of persecution against the heretics, in which Anne du Bourge, a prominent member of the Grand Council of Paris, was executed. Of even greater significance was their policy of economies which drastically cut the pensions of many noblemen who were at court in the hope of obtaining employment and advancement, many of whom were Huguenots. It was from this time that the emphasis of the Huguenot cause shifted from the purely religious into the political arena. Personal motives began to loom larger than religious principle. Aristocratic and religious independence on the one hand, and church supremacy on the other became the chief concerns of the protagonists. The Huguenots began to rely on Germany, England and the Netherlands; the Catholics on Spain more heavily than ever before. Not till near the end of the struggle did a national party emerge, which would make political and French interests supreme, leaving the religious questions to be settled by a kind of toleration. This moderate Catholic party

gradually absorbed all but the most bigotted fanatics of either side, but not until
the duc de Mayenne from the Catholic side and Henry of Navarre from the Huguenot
had united under the banner of the 'Politiques'. Eight civil wars in 25 years were to
desolate the country and bring it near to ruin. But all that was in the future.

Compared to Germany, England or Switzerland, France was slow to accept the
Reformation, but when she did, it took a Calvinistic and largely aristocratic and
authoritarian form. This was mostly due to the nature of France itself. It is a very
large, mainly agricultural country with few great cities, and those widely spread. Paris
was bitterly opposed to the new ideas, and then, as even today, somewhat apart from
the rest of the country. Though, as we have seen, many of the earliest converts came
from the towns, they were unaccustomed to independent action or local self-govern-
ment. On the other hand the aristocracy, either because of its more cosmopolitan
culture, or from its spirit of independence, widely embraced the new religion. The
nobles, however, did not commend it to the mass of the people. They were to a large
extent haughty and selfish, and there was among them a love of mockery which went
ill with the meekness prescribed by the Gospels, but was useful when it came to
criticising clerical 'superstition' and obscurantism.

The Court and the monarchy at first liked the reformers, regarding them as a
product of the Renaissance, and it was only when they offended against good taste
and fashionable manners that they turned against the Protestants. Kings and princes
do not like criticism, whether from popes or presbyters. When reforming fanatics
began to break images and hurl insults and anathemas at them and criticise their way
of life, it was enough to frighten them off and persuade them that the old ways were
better than the new. Nevertheless, it has been reckoned that when the civil war broke
out, half the aristocracy, almost all the men under 40, and a considerable portion
of the clergy, including several bishops, were Huguenots. We have already mentioned
the bishop of Meaux, but there were others, such as Odet de Coligny, cardinal de
Châtillon, the archbishop of Aix, and the bishops of Valence, Troyes, Pamiers and
Chartres, all of whom more or less embraced Huguenot ideas and opinions. But no more
than 10 per cent. of the population at large, however, were Protestant, so it can be
seen that the new faith was in no way a broadly popular one, but rather one that
appealed to the intellectuals and the better-off in society.

France had not been subject to papal interference in the same way that England
and Germany had. The kings of France had not been dragooned by turbulent priests
such as Becket. Royal power in France was relatively much greater than in England,
and the kings had for centuries held the popes' authority at bay; indeed, during the
Avignon period, the popes were little more than the vassals of the French king.

The Reformation gave the French aristocracy a new outlook on life. Calvinism
with its emphasis on the elect and on predestination was far from uncongenial to men
and women who already looked upon themselves as exclusive. In Germany the new
religion was supported and protected by independent princes; in France no such help
was possible. French cities were unused to active corporate life; the nobility held no
positions comparable to those of their German counterparts. Although Protestantism
had entered France from the north-east, the new religion established itself more firmly
in the south and west, where for centuries there had been a tradition of heresy dating
from the days of the Cathars and even earlier when Roussillon was an independent

Jewish or Aryan principality. The headquarters of resistance to the reformers lay in Picardy and Paris: the Huguenot power base was roughly south of the Loire, thus following a division which can be traced back to the time in the seventh century and earlier when the north-east was dominated by the orthodox Franks and the south-west by the heretical Visigoths. Thanks to their distance from Paris, the local aristocracy enjoyed greater independence. It was also heir to the long period of independence from Paris dating from the time of the Plantagenets.

Towards the end of his life, Henry II, as we have seen, took a firm line against the heretics, but this had not prevented him from appointing Gaspard de Coligny, the eldest of the three de Châtillon brothers (all of whom had embraced Protestantism even though one of them was a cardinal) admiral of the northern provinces. Coligny's greatest military achievement was the capture of Calais, England's last remaining possession in France (Queen Mary is said to have proclaimed that its loss would be engraved on her heart), so that he became a national hero, and as a Huguenot, found himself in the position of a counterweight to the otherwise overwhelming popularity of the Guise brothers. Because of the disputed succession to the English throne, the Guises had had Francis II crowned not only king of France but of Scotland and England as well. The prospect of these three kingdoms united under one crown was alarming to Philip II of Spain, which accounts for his recognition of Elizabeth as queen of England, and for his proposal to marry her, in spite of the fact that she was his deceased wife's sister and that not so long before the pope had refused to allow Henry VIII to divorce Catherine of Aragon because *she* had been his deceased brother's wife.

Catherine de' Medici

On the death of Henry II, the situation of his widow, Catherine de' Medici was excessively difficult. Diane de Poitiers, the late king's mistress, practically ruled the kingdom. The six sons of Claude, duke of Guise were promoted to all the chief offices of the realm. Although greatly loved by her father-in-law, Catherine was looked down upon by the French aristocracy because of the Medici's bourgeois origin, and when her husband unexpectedly succeeded to the throne her unpopularity increased. In spite of his manifold infidelities, Catherine deeply loved her husband, and for his sake she put up with many years of insults and public slights. Because so many of the opinions about her which have come down to us stem from those who were her enemies, it has been difficult to form an accurate opinion of her character and of the role she played during the religious wars. She was, nonetheless, one of the three great women of her age, ranking equally with Elizabeth I of England and Jeanne d'Albret of Navarre.

During the brief reign of Francis II, Catherine retired from Court, leaving the conduct of affairs in the hands of Diane de Poitiers and the Guises. Under their administration the most violent persecution of the Huguenots set in, resulting from their plot, known to history as the Conspiracy of Amboise, to place the young king under their protection, kill the Guise brothers and substitute members of the House of Bourbon as regents. This ill-fated scheme was led by the Huguenot François de Barry, Sieur de la Renaudie who spoke of a 'greater captain', by whom it was supposed he meant Antoine of Navarre, who remained in the background. The Court was at Blois and it was agreed to converge there on 10 March 1560 to seize the king and get rid of the Guisards. But the conspiracy was leaked and the Court moved to Amboise, whereupon La Renaudie postponed action for a week. As the conspirators began to arrive they were either killed or seized, and 57 leading Huguenots were hanged, including La Renaudie. Although considerable suspicion attached to Louis de Bourbon, prince of Condé, nothing could be proved, and he thus escaped to become leader of the Huguenots at a later date. This leadership was soon to emerge. On the political wing was the prince de Condé and his elder brother, Antoine, king of Navarre, both of whom were no doubt influenced by Antoine's wife, Jeanne d'Albret, who was a staunch Protestant. From among those who were devoted to the Huguenot cause for religious reasons came Gaspard de Châtillon, Sieur de Coligny and his brother, François, Sieur d'Andelot.

Following the conspiracy of Amboise, the Queen Mother, Catherine de' Medici, whose main concern was the safety and security of the royal house, pressed for measures of conciliation. Far from being the bloodthirsty witch as her detractors have tried to depict her, Catherine was a woman of outstanding intelligence and education, possessed of immense patience and great tolerance. From the age of 42 until her death at 70 she worked unceasingly to bring peace to her adopted country. It was her tragedy that she lived at a time when tolerance was unacceptable to large sections of her subjects.

She inherited from her Medici ancestors the gift of pouring oil on troubled waters and she was able to bring together those who were at daggers drawn and persuade them to lay aside their enmity and live at peace. Again and again throughout the long civil wars through which she ruled France, she succeeded in bringing hostilities to an end, sometimes for several years at a time. Herself a loyal Catholic, many notable Protestants owed their lives to her—Condé, Henry of Navarre, Michel de l'Hôpital, her Protestant chancellor, and many more. It was she who defied both pope and king of Spain by refusing to allow the Inquisition to be established in her country. Her strength and untiring energy, her self-control and wisdom were truly admirable. They enabled her to see that the only policy which can give peace to a country in which two opposing religions are equally vehemently supported is to make the two Churches learn to live side by side without conflict. She failed, but she strove mightily. And where she did not succeed no-one else could have done so. Neither in Germany, England nor the Netherlands was it possible to prevent the forces unleashed by the Reformation from lighting similar fires. Her lifelong fight was to bring peace to France by what everyone nowadays, except, alas! in Ireland, knows to be the only means by which peace in such matters can be achieved and preserved. In 1561, she made three attempts to avert civil war: six times in the course of the conflict she made peace.

Her greatest good fortune lay in her choice of chancellor, Michel de l'Hôpital, one of the ablest Frenchmen of his time. He had been recommended to her by one of the ladies-in-waiting, the secretly Huguenot duchesse de Montpensier, and she appointed him in order to find a sure basis for her policy of moderation. L'Hôpital came from the Auvergne, had studied law in Italy, and was a man of great learning, infinite patience like his mistress, and freedom from partisanship. He had a cold, logical and unbigotted mind, and represented all that is best in French legal culture. He was, of course, hated by the fanatics on both sides, and was accused by both of atheism. Simply, he was a man far ahead of his time. After serving Catherine for eight years, he was forced out of office by the clamour of the Jesuits and pressure from the pope. He lived just long enough to raise his voice in protest at the massacre of St Bartholomew's Eve. If anyone could have saved France from civil strife, it was l'Hôpital. Toleration and equity were his means of action; but it was all in vain. Had he been supported by Catherine as Cecil was supported by Elizabeth I in England, much suffering might have been avoided, but her pragmatism sounded the death-knell for his well-intentioned policies.

L'Hôpital's first action as chancellor was to persuade Catherine to refuse to accept the Inquisition in France. In May 1560 the Edict of Romorantin was accepted by the Guises as a compromise. This enacted that the bishops should have exclusive rights to deal with heresy in their dioceses, and it was drawn in such a way that their power was strictly limited in this regard. This pleased neither party. At l'Hôpital's suggestion, Catherine summoned an Assembly of Notables at Fontainebleau the following August to regulate the theological disputes. The king of Navarre and the prince of Condé took no part in it, but Coligny and many leading Protestants did attend, and spoke out in favour of more liberty of conscience. They were supported by the archbishop of Vienne and the bishop of Valence. Surprisingly their advice was accepted, and it was agreed to summon the States General to a meeting at Meaux in December 1560 and an assembly of prelates at Poissy in January 1561 to review the government of State and Church.

The king of Navarre and Condé were particularly summoned to the meeting of the States General, which in the meantime had been transferred from Meaux to Orleans. They came with some anxiety. They were received coolly and at a specially convened tribunal Condé was accused of treason and arrested, but Navarre remained free though under surveillance. Condé was found guilty and sentenced to death on 26 November. The king, who had been ailing since his accession, now became gravely ill and was obviously dying. Catherine, who realised that a political realignment would shortly take place, persuaded Francis to grant a general amnesty to the Bourbon princes. As the prospective king, Charles IX, was only 10 years old, Catherine knew that there would have to be a regency, and as the king of Navarre as first prince of the blood seemed to have as good a claim as herself she decided to act without delay. Summoning Navarre to her study she promised to spare the life of Condé and to protect himself and his kingdom if he would renounce all claims to the regency in return for the title of Lieutenant General of the Realm. His recent anguish, concern for his brother, and natural timidity induced him to agree. The Huguenots, led by Calvin, urged him in vain to seize the reins of government.

With the death of Francis II, in December 1560, the position of the parties changed radically. The princes of the blood and the Huguenots were no longer united; the Guises, on the other hand, had seen their hopes shattered with the departure of Mary Stuart to her own kingdom of Scotland. There remained the Queen Mother and l'Hôpital, who formed a centre party intent on finding some form of compromise in the difficult situation which confronted them.

The States General of Orleans, recognising the parlous state of the new king's finances, also recognised the evils dominant in the Church, and the effect that the persecution of the Huguenots was having on the country's commerce and agriculture.

At its final session the Edict of Orleans was published, embodying, in a moderate form, some of the reforms demanded by the Third Estate—the bourgeoisie. But the Parlement of Paris, a stronghold of lawyers, seeing that some of the most valuable reforms aimed at curbing legal abuses, rejected it out of hand. The Huguenots, for their part, were dissatisfied as well. They threatened to proclaim the king of Navarre Regent of the Realm, but they were frustrated by Catherine's swift action in assuming the regency herself. Huguenot groups in town after town now came out into the open and disputed possession of the churches, many of which they stripped of their statues and ornaments. Exasperated by these events and the apparent favour the Huguenots now enjoyed at Court, three of the chief Catholic leaders, Francis, duke of Guise, Anne de Montmorency, Constable of France, and the maréchal de Saint-André, formed a triumvirate against the Queen Mother, the Châtillons and the Bourbons. The probability of armed conflict thereupon increased dramatically.

There followed a period of almost daily disturbances in Paris, culminating in the proclamation of the Edict of July 1561, which stated that only those who took part in heretical assemblies should be put to death, and all those who were merely suspected of heresy would be brought before the ecclesiastical courts. But no sooner had it been promulgated than l'Hôpital sought to modify it by a convocation of the States General at Pontoise in August. The nobility and the Third Estate were moderates or Huguenots almost to a man. They rallied round the Queen Mother and confirmed her as Regent. They also abolished the Edict of July and called for a reform of the clergy and freedom of worship for the Huguenots, and above all for the exclusion of the Guises from the Privy Council. Although at first sight it looked as if the Huguenots and Catholics would be treated alike, the result was to show that neither side wanted either tolera-tion or comprehension. Instead of healing the breach, Catherine had placed the crown between the disputing factions.

All this provoked great displeasure on the part of the Catholics, and Philip of Spain threatened to intervene. He successfully weaned the king of Navarre away by promising him the kingdom of Sardinia in exchange for the one he lost on the borders of France and Spain. This was a damaging blow to the Huguenots, but l'Hôpital and Catherine did not give up hope of a moderate solution. They invited the presidents and coun-sellors of the eight provincial Parlements, whom they knew to hold moderate views, to attend the king's Privy Council, begging them to support Charles as one who stood above politics for the good of the nation as a whole. The Assembly of St Germain, as it was called, proceeded to draw up a new Edict (January 1562) under which the Protestant worship was allowed in the country but forbidden in towns; all penalties against heretics were to be suspended; the Huguenots were ordered not to disturb the ancient form of worship in any way; in a phrase, the Edict insisted on a fair and equal tolerance for all. It is also notable as the first occasion on which the Huguenots received formal recognition by the State. Had they been more prudent, it might have been the beginning of a great epoch in their history. Alas! they were not. They refused to listen to that part of the Edict which required them to respect their neighbours' faith and forms of worship. They thought their battle won, and many went on the rampage to celebrate, smashing images and pictures, attacking convents and monasteries, and heaping insults on the Catholics. The latter, for their part, were equally determined never to tolerate heretical worship in France. It was the kind of dialogue of the deaf to which we have become all too accustomed in Ulster today.

The spark that set alight the flames of war was of a comparatively minor character. The duke of Guise, who had retired temporarily to his estates now decided to return to Paris. He and his brother, the cardinal of Lorraine, with a retinue of some two hundred retainers, left Joinville on 1 March 1562, a Sunday. As they rode through the little town of Vassy, they chanced upon a group of Huguenots who were holding a service in a barn. Some of them began to insult the Guises and their companions and a riot quickly developed. Being armed, the horsemen broke down the barn doors and attacked the congregation. News of the riot reached the duchess of Guise who was not unfriendly to the Protestants, and she sent word to her husband beseeching him to control his men. As he rode up, he was hit in the face by a brick. This was the signal for his retainers to strike out wildly, with the result that 60 men and women (according to the Catholics only 23) were killed and 100–200 wounded. The barn was utterly wrecked and the neighbouring houses pillaged. When the news reached Paris the duke of Guise was proclaimed a hero by the Catholics, while a howl of anger arose from the Huguenots, whose pent-up fury boiled over. The prince of Condé called the Huguenots to arms; the civil wars had begun.

Historians are divided in their opinion as to who was the aggressor in this case. Samuel Smiles, that arch-champion of the Huguenots, was in no doubt. He places all the blame on the duke. It is certainly true that when the latter entered Paris he was hailed as defender of the faith and saviour of his country. All agree that the Queen Mother and l'Hôpital were powerless to enforce the Edict of January. It was all they could do to prevent themselves from being swept away on the tide of indignation that was swirling round them. The massacre of Vassy was followed by further slaughter at Paris, Senlis, Amiens, Meaux, Châlons, Troyes, Bar-sur-Seine, Epernay, Nevers, Le Mans, Angers and Blois, as well as in many other towns and villages throughout the land. The persecution was especially fierce at Tours and in Provence. Things were now completely out of hand: the struggle could only be decided by war.

Catherine, typically, tried to hold the balance between the conflicting factions, for she knew that war would exalt a soldier to power and make the rule of a woman almost impossible. She therefore named the cardinal de Bourbon as Governor of Paris in the hope that he would be acceptable to both sides as a Bourbon prince and a Catholic. He at once ordered both the duke of Guise and the prince of Condé to leave the capital. Condé, considering his position in Paris vulnerable, made his way to Meaux followed by a growing army; Guise, following his rapturous reception by the Paris mob, decided to stay and brought off a coup that marked a crucial turning point in the struggle. On 27 March 1562 the triumvirate made for Fontainebleau and 'invited' the royal family to join them at Melun. Catherine had no choice but to obey; thus at the very outset of the war the Catholic party had secured both the capital and the person of the sovereign. Henceforth the Catholic cause was the royal cause.

The Wars of Religion (1562–1598)

It is no purpose of this book to follow in detail the civil wars which lasted from 1562 to 1598. This is not a history of the French wars of religion, but some account is necessary to give those of Huguenot descent a broad outline of the events which prompted so many of their ancestors to come to Britain. Consequently we shall set out in broad outline only the main events which culminated in the Edict of Nantes and the Peace of Vervins, with the accession of Henry IV as the first Bourbon king of France. The first period lasted from 1562 to 1570. The massacre of Vassy took place as we have seen on 1 March 1562, and the first battle of the civil war was fought at Dreux on 19 December. The intervening months were occupied by skirmishing and the gathering of armies by both sides, culminating in the siege of the Huguenot city of Rouen during which Antoine, king of Navarre was hit by a stray shot and died of his wounds on 26 October. The following month Condé felt strong enough to march on Paris, thinking that the Catholic army would besiege Le Havre, which was occupied by an English force sent there under the terms of the Treaty of Hampton Court made between Elizabeth I and the Huguenots.

Subsequent delays arising from the negotiations with the Queen Mother allowed the Catholics time to strengthen their forces in Paris, and Condé was obliged to withdraw and endeavour to join the English in Le Havre. The Catholics, sensing that they had the advantage, manoeuvred their forces and met up with the Huguenot army near Dreux on 19 December. At first the battle favoured the Huguenots, who captured Anne of Montmorency and turned to attack the Swiss mercenaries who formed the main body of the Catholic army. They failed, and when the duke of Guise led the re-formed Catholic cavalry against the Huguenot infantry they broke. In the ensuing battle the maréchal de Saint-André was killed and Condé was captured. The Huguenot cavalry withdrew and left the duke of Guise master of the day. It was a disaster for the Protestants although the commanders-in-chief of both armies were taken prisoner.

Coligny, who now assumed leadership of the Huguenots, withdrew his beaten army in good order south of the Loire. He was followed by the duke of Guise as far as Orleans, where the latter was assassinated by a Huguenot named Poltrot de Mère, who under torture confessed that Coligny had instructed him to do the deed. The Guise family firmly believed this to be true and from this time onwards sought revenge. Coligny admitted that he had rejoiced at the news of Guise's death, but denied he had known or approved of the assassination. But Guise's death was a great misfortune for France, for he was a statesman and not adverse from moderation. Both he and his brother, the cardinal, recognised the need for reform within the Catholic Church; some members of his family, including his wife, were not unfriendly toward the Huguenots. If the civil war could have been cleared of its political elements, if the rivalry of the Bourbons and Guises could have been allayed, a moderate settlement might, even at that late stage, have been worked out by Coligny, Guise and l'Hôpital under the friendly eye of Catherine de' Medici. With the Duke's death the situation changed once more, and Catherine again began to negotiate, this time with some hope of success. The Catholics were paralysed, the Huguenots disheartened; no-one had any money; all France was in a turmoil.

In these circumstances Catherine recovered some freedom of manoeuvre which enabled her to negotiate the Pacification of Amboise in March 1563, which allowed the Huguenots liberty of conscience but restricted their right to worship except in certain specified instances. The negotiations had been undertaken with Condé and accepted by him. When Calvin heard of the terms he considered that Condé had betrayed God in his eagerness to be set free, and Coligny was bitter that he had consented to such unworthy terms without his having been consulted or informed. But as usual the Catholics thought too much had been conceded and the Huguenots too little. Catherine now turned her attention to the English at Le Havre and was present at all the assaults on the town. Following protracted and tedious negotiations a peace treaty was eventually signed in April 1564 at Troyes which ended the first English intervention.

Catherine now decided to take advantage of the cessation of hostilities to make a grand tour of France to show the king to his people. The progress began in March 1564 from Fontainebleau and after passing through Dijon, Lyons, Marseilles and Toulouse arrived at Bayonne in May 1565. There she arranged to meet her daughter, Elizabeth, wife of Philip II of Spain, and to have an interview with the duke of Alva. Nothing of consequence came of this, but the Huguenots believed that they must have made some agreement to their disadvantage. From Bayonne the royal party proceeded through Nantes, Angers and Blois, passed the winter of 1565 at Moulins and ended at Saint-Maur in April 1566. When the duke of Alva arrived with a considerable force in the Spanish Netherlands to suppress the inconoclasts who were sacking Catholic churches early the following year, the Huguenots considered their suspicions justified and interpreted this as a co-ordinated plan for their repression as well as of the Protestants in the Low Countries.

The fears raised by Catherine de' Medici's meeting with the duke of Alva go some way to explain the ill-judged scheme initiated by Condé to seize the young king at Meaux during the festivities of St Michael's Eve in 1567. The plot failed, because the Catholics held the only bridge across the Marne which the Huguenots had to cross if it were to succeed and because of the arrival of a force of 6,000 Swiss mercenaries which surrounded the royal party. This combination of factors deterred Condé from attacking, and so enabled the king and Queen Mother to slip away to Paris. The Huguenots then besieged the city from Saint-Denis, and it was not until December 1567 that the Catholics felt strong enough to risk a fight. The ensuing battle of Saint-Denis was inconclusive, for while the duke of Montmorency was killed, the Huguenots were obliged to withdraw. They retreated eastward, where early in 1568 they were joined by a large force of Germans. The Catholics, fearing to attack, proposed to make peace, and the Truce of Longjumeau was signed, which confirmed the Pacification of Amboise and brought the campaign to a temporary end in March 1568. Catherine, who had now lost all sympathy for the Huguenots following the incident at Meaux, planned to protect the king by arresting Condé and Coligny at Noyers in Burgundy. Hearing of her intention, they withdrew to the west of France and established their headquarters at La Rochelle on the Atlantic coast, where they were joined by Jeanne d'Albret, queen of Navarre and her children with an army of about four thousand men.

With the death of Montmorency the command of the royal forces was given to the king's younger brother, Henry, duke of Anjou, who because of his youth was advised by Gaspard de Saulx de Tavannes. In the spring of 1569 they led the Catholic forces towards La Rochelle and met the Huguenot army at Jarnac. The battle was short and sharp, but at the end of it the Catholics had achieved a major victory by the capture of Condé. He had been trying to join Coligny, who was engaged with a detachment of the enemy when he was surrounded by the main body of Catholic troops and his horse was killed under him. With his leg broken and unable to take any further part in the action he delivered his sword to two royalists that he knew, and was made as comfortable as possible in the shade of a tree. At this point a captain of the Swiss guards, baron de Montesquin, rode up, and in a fit of passion discharged his pistol at Condé and killed him on the spot.

Condé's death was not the unmitigated disaster for the Huguenots that it first appeared. It made room for the wiser leadership of the admiral, and gave the party its natural head in the person of young Henry de Bourbon, prince of Béarn, later king of Navarre. Coligny was joined by another German contingent south of Limoges in June, and in the meantime Jeanne d'Albret helped to restore the Huguenot spirits by presenting to them her son and and her nephew, the young prince of Condé. Holding these two boys—Henry of Béarn was 15 and Henry of Condé a few years younger—one in each hand, she presented herself to the soldiers and called upon them to accept her son as their chief. He was received with acclamation and Coligny agreed to serve in his name, while he kept real command. Confidence was restored and the Huguenot and German forces took up a strong position at Saint-Jean-d'Angely on the Charente near Saintes. There followed a period of skirmishing which culminated in the battle of Montcontour (1569) in which the Huguenot army was decimated, largely because the Germans were more intent on booty than on the overall strategy of the campaign. Coligny barely escaped with his life; Niort was taken by the Catholics, but shortage of money and men forced them to halt their advance. Both sides were now ready for peace, and an end to hostilities was signed at Saint-Germain in August 1569. Its terms were the best the Calvinists had obtained so far. Besides the old points of amnesty and liberty of worship, restitution of confiscated goods, and the right to hold office under the State, they got a footing in the Parlements and also won the power to select four cities of refuge in which they might put governors and garrisons of their own. They chose La Rochelle, Cognac, Montauban and Charité-sur-Loire, which Coligny proceeded to make his headquarters.

The Peace of Saint-Germain, though criticised by staunch Catholics, was the best that Catherine could obtain in the circumstances, for she saw no possibility of rooting out the Huguenots from their secure bases in the south-west. It also saw the rise of a moderate party, new in French politics, which became known as the Politiques, who were concerned above all with the peace and prosperity of the country. They included Michel de l'Hôpital, Francis of Montmorency, the late Constable's son, and many of those who resented the influence and power of the Guisards at Court. They received every support from Catherine, who saw her chance to make the royal family once more supreme, and with the help of the Politiques she now ventured on a project which in her opinion would resolve matters entirely to her satisfaction. This project was to propose the marriage of her daughter, Marguerite de Valois, to Jeanne d'Albret's son, Henry of Navarre. At the same time Catherine's favourite son, Henry, duke of Anjou, was sent to England to woo Queen Elizabeth, and though this second proposed marriage never came off, an Anglo-French treaty was signed at Blois in April 1572.

At this time Spain was deeply involved in the Netherlands, and both the Politiques and the Huguenots placed great hopes that war with Spain would unite the French nation. Catherine, however, doubted the wisdom of such a course, and there was also a personal issue involved which coloured her judgement. Since Coligny's arrival at Court late in 1571 as a result of the proposed Navarre marriage, Catherine was becoming increasingly worried by the growing influence he seemed to be exerting over the young king. Catherine was therefore determined to stop Coligny before he succeeded in committing France to a course of action which to her seemed disastrous, and to end his influence which seemed to be alienating the affections of her son. Since power was the ruling passion of her life, she had no wish to see it slip into Coligny's hands. The sudden death of Jeanne d'Albret a few days before the wedding was due to take place, added another uncertainty to the equation.

The Massacre of St Bartholomew's Eve (1572)

The Massacre of St Bartholomew in August 1572 is one of the great mysteries of history: was Catherine de' Medici sincere; were the terms of the Treaty of Saint-Germain intended to lull the Huguenots into a sense of false security; had the massacre been already decided upon; or was it the unpremeditated result of the tensions of the time? It is impossible to tell, but the evidence strongly suggests that it was inevitable. It is, nevertheless, undeniable that the Huguenots were highly suspicious of the favourable concessions they had obtained at Saint-Germain. This is why they withdrew to La Rochelle and grouped themselves around Jeane d'Albret and the young Henry of Navarre.

In 1570, Charles IX was 20 years old, and thought of himself as a man, eager to be rid of his mother's tutelage. It was because she was against it that he made overtures to the Huguenots and Coligny. At the end of 1571 the king was at Blois to meet Jeanne d'Albret, who had gone there reluctantly to negotiate her son's marriage to the king's sister, Marguerite. She liked neither the bride nor the manners of the Court. She was shocked and disgusted at the dissolute courtiers and at the coarse manners of the king. She was accompanied by Coligny and her son, whom the king welcomed warmly. The Court then proceeded from Blois to Paris, where on 4 June, Jeanne d'Albret fell ill and died soon after. The Huguenots, of course, suspected that she had been poisoned, and there is still some doubt as to the real cause of her death. Nevertheless, her demise postponed for a while the projected marriage of her son, who now took the title of king of Navarre. The Catholic party made the most of the interval. Paris was irritated by the sight of so many Calvinists from the south of France, whom they regarded as semi-foreign. Scuffles and riots broke out; the Queen Mother determined to rid herself of the heretics, while her son, the king, continued to cultivate them. At least Coligny trusted him. It has often been suggested that the Queen Mother and her counsellors, feeling that the king was insecure unless Coligny's influence was removed, laid a plot for the admiral's assassination. That, at least, is one theory put forward by her detractors.

Nevertheless, despite these factors, the marriage of Henry of Navarre to Marguerite took place, and the Court, with all Paris, gave itself over to spectacle and fêtes. The marriage had been widely hailed as an act of reconciliation, and the heads of the Huguenot party had come in large numbers to celebrate the event. Some of them were not without fear for their safety, and many had urged Coligny and his family to stay away. But he believed in the good faith of the king and Queen Mother, and insisted on staying until the ceremony was over. It took place on 18 August 1572 at Nôtre Dame, the principal members of both Huguenot and Catholic nobility being present.

As he returned from the Council on 21 August, Coligny was shot at from a window and wounded, the assassin escaping. The wound was slight, but when the king heard of it he swore to bring the assassin to justice and threatened the Guisards, whom he suspected. He visited the admiral in bed and gave him an assurance that his attackers would be pursued. There is little doubt that both the king and Catherine de' Medici were ignorant of the Guises' plot against Coligny, and that the latter, at any rate, was greatly shocked and distressed by it. But this outrage brought matters to a head. In August, 23 secret plots were hatched throughout Paris, both by the Huguenots and Catholics. It was only a matter of which party would strike first. In the event it was the Catholics.

It had been decided to attack the Huguenots between two and three o'clock on the morning of 24 August 1572, the Feast of St Bartholomew. As the church bells rang for early prayer, soldiers of the royal guard rushed into the streets to attack the Protestants in their homes while they slept. The Guises had wished to kill the Bourbons and Montmorencys, but the Queen Mother would not hear of this. The admiral met his death with courage and dignity worthy of the man he was. All those living on the north side of the Seine perished; those living on the left bank were alarmed in time by the din coming from across the river and had time to escape. All the Huguenot chiefs had perished. Paris looked as though it had been sacked by an invading army; corpses littered the streets, houses were looted and burnt. So weak was the central authority that the killing went on for several days. Through the miasma of savagery, isolated acts of generosity stand out. The young duke of Alençon was at no pains to hide his disgust and distress; a gentleman named Vezins, meeting his private enemy, a Huguenot, set him on a horse and let him escape. Here and there in the provinces a commandant refused to sanction disorder and murder; the bishop of Lisieux saved all the Huguenots in his diocese; the nobles of the moderate party—the Politiques—saved all they could. But on the whole, the Church vied with the State in crushing those who had so long opposed them. Between 1,500 and 1,800 were killed at Lyons; 600 more at Rouen; in all of France the total has been variously estimated as between 100,000 and 200,000; no-one will ever know the exact figure. The survivors, at first stunned by what had taken place, were quick to see to their self-defence in those towns and regions where they were in a majority. Many of those who lived near the sea took ship for England, settling in Rye, Southampton and other ports on the south coast.

The two Bourbon princes were offered their freedom if they would hear Mass. Under compulsion Henry of Navarre yielded at once; the young prince of Condé hesitated, but gave way in the end. Most of these sudden conversions only lasted as long as the danger lasted.

Protestant writers have tried to make out that the massacre was premeditated, but this view cannot be seriously sustained. The Spanish ambassador, who was anything but impartial, admitted that with the exception of the murder of Coligny, the rest was due to sudden mob violence. But was Catherine responsible? She certainly had nothing to do with Coligny's death. His murder meant the ruin of all her plans to achieve a *modus vivendi*. This is one of those questions it is really impossible to answer because the evidence is so partisan. Two things only are certain; of those round Catherine at the time, there was not one, French, English or Italian, Huguenot or Catholic, whose word can be trusted; and second, if she was responsible, then it was the only occasion in her life that she resorted to violent measures. The history of her repeated efforts, supported by those of l'Hôpital, to bring peace on terms based on mutual tolerance is far too well authenticated. To have planned and countenanced the massacre would have run counter to her character and to the policy she pursued for nearly 30 years. The true culprits were the fanatics on both sides, embittered by the long years of conflict and cruelty. The country had become by this time so maddened by these furious religious wars that such a massacre was almost inevitable at any time, and in any city. It certainly wrecked all Catherine's plans and hopes for a reconciliation.

The pope and Philip of Spain, on the other hand, were guilty by proxy, for both publicly rejoiced at what had happened. But in the final reckoning the Huguenots were themselves largely to blame. Their arrogance, their armed threats and violent language; their declarations that the king had to choose between war at home or war abroad; their contemptuous treatment of the Paris mob and its prejudices; their intolerance, iconoclasm and unwillingness to compromise; all contributed to their undoing. Those who constantly excite resistance instead of trying to smooth away obstacles, no less at that time than today, usually come to a catastrophic end. The Huguenots were not content to ask for toleration; they involved themselves in the political projects of the discontented nobility and so alienated themselves from Court sympathy. At the same time their unpatriotic spirit made it plain that if, by fair means or foul, they were ever to gain power, the Catholics would not stand a chance of living peacefully alongside them.

The effects of the massacre were not as great as might have been expected. Though their leaders had been killed, as soon as the first shock passed, the Huguenots became as troublesome as ever. On the positive side, the very ghastliness of what had happened proved a stimulus to more moderate views, and we now see the Politiques coming to the fore, and the Huguenots are henceforth only an extreme wing of their party. From the existence of three parties—Catholic, Huguenot and Politiques—there were now two: the Moderates or Politiques, which included most of the Protestants, and the Catholic League. Abroad the atrocity was widely felt, but it is unfair to blame the French entirely. Seven years later there occurred in Ireland a massacre of the Catholic population of Munster carried out by Elizabeth I's Protestant troops which was greater in degree and in no way less revolting than the massacre of St Bartholomew's Eve. While the English were quick to criticise the French, their own misdeeds should not be forgotten. Such was the bitterness and bigotry in England, Germany and the Netherlands, that lurid stories told by the refugees, most of whom were artisans and skilled labourers from the towns, found a receptive audience in the .townspeople amongst whom they settled. It was different with the Huguenot nobility and gentry. They could not or would not abandon their servants and retainers, and most stayed behind in France to face the future as best they could. In the Cévennes, Dauphiné and Auvergne they took to the mountains where they established fortified strongholds to defend themselves. Resistance took place wherever possible. The town of Sancerre on the upper Loire, for example, held out for 10 months against the Catholic troops. La Rochelle likewise withstood a long siege. But neither side had much stomach for war, and the Edict of Boulogne (6 July 1573) gave the Huguenots even more than they had got at Saint-Germain: amnesty, freedom of worship in La Rochelle, Montauban and the other cities; in addition, all feudal possessors of the higher justice were allowed to have Huguenot services in their homes.

In June 1573 the duke of Anjou, in spite of being the leader of the Catholics, on learning that he had been elected king of Poland, abandoned them without a second thought to take up his new possessions. In May 1574 Henry de Montmorency, duke of Damville, who had been sent to bring his provinces of Languedoc to heel, concluded a truce with the Huguenots after a very half-hearted siege.

It is remarkable that the result of the St Bartholomew massacre was not a dynamic cohesion of the Catholics but produced among them a sense of torpor and division. It is apparent that the policy of the Politiques found some favour in Catholic circles, but above all considerations of foreign policy played a great part in this change of attitude. The state of the king's health was another factor. Throughout the spring of 1574 it had become clear that he was unlikely to live, and Catherine, seeing once again a threat to her position should he die, and never lacking initiative, held Henry of Navarre and the young duke of Condé in detention, sent the leader of the Politiques, François de Montmorency to the Bastille, and placed her youngest son, the duke of Alençon under surveillance. When Charles IX died on 30 May 1574, she immediately assumed the regency in the absence in Poland of his heir, Henry, duke of Anjou until such time as he could return to claim the crown of France.

Henry III (1574–1589)

The final period of the civil wars lasted from 1574 to 1598. Within a few months of the new king's accession a dangerous situation arose. Catherine de' Medici had alienated the Catholic Guises and the Politique Montmorencys as well as the Huguenot leaders, all of whom had managed to escape from detention. The new king was a fanatic, licentious and extremely stupid, whose first act had been to order all Huguenots to become Catholics or quit his kingdom. It is no exaggeration to say that during his reign the French monarchy sank to its lowest depths. In the face of the new situation, the Huguenots and Politiques decided to make a common cause and signed what is known as the Confederation of Milhaud (1575), which was answered by the formal creation of the Catholic League the following year. The compact of Milhaud was the first definite agreement between Huguenots and moderate Catholics, and the confederates chose the young prince of Condé as their leader, though he was shortly to be superseded by Francis, formerly duke of Alençon, but on his brother's accession, duke of Anjou. The king found himself powerless to impose his will by force in the face of these new developments, and the Peace of Monsieur (or Edict of Beaulieu) was signed in May 1576 which gave the Huguenots once more full religious liberty along with other concessions and guarantees.

The Catholics were astonished that the crown could not be relied on to destroy the Huguenots, and under the leadership of Henry, duke of Guise, and with Spanish backing, the Holy League was formed. Henry III, fearing a threat to his authority, hurried to place himself at its head. The war was once more resumed. Almost immediately Henry of Navarre escaped from Paris and renounced his enforced Catholicism. His appearance in the Huguenot-Politique camp was the true beginning of his great career. After a few inconclusive skirmishes a peace was signed at Chastency under which the Huguenots once more received freedom of worship throughout the realm except in Paris, some further strong towns in the south, the right to establish schools and hold synods and an equal share in the Parlements. The Politiques secured concessions for their chiefs: Henry of Navarre was given the government of Guyenne; Condé the government of Picardy; and Alençon those of Anjou, Touraine and Berry.

Peace did not last long, and further fighting took place in 1577, much of it inconclusive. Once more a peace was patched up, this time at Bergerac (September 1577) by which the privileges granted to the Huguenots under the Peace of Monsieur were much reduced. In 1579 there was another, somewhat obscure partisan war, which ended in the Peace of Fleix, followed by the Ordonnance of Blois in which more than 350 articles recommended reforms in almost every branch of the country's politics. Although there was little conflict during the following eight years there was no relaxation of tension. The frivolity at Court disguised a morass of bankruptcy both in finance and policy, where Catherine's spirit of intrigue was being tempered by advancing old age and gout. The Guise faction was dominant in the State, but it continued to resent such freedoms as the Huguenots enjoyed. For their part, the Protestants resented the limitations placed upon the practice of their religion, and continued to plot and scheme against the Catholics wherever they thought they could gain some advantage, no matter how transitory.

With the death of the duke of Anjou (Alençon) in June 1584, the situation changed dramatically, for this event meant that Henry of Navarre was now the heir-presumptive to the throne of France should Henry III die without issue, a matter that was extremely probable in view of the king's sexual proclivities. Both Catherine and the king sent emissaries to Henry of Navarre urging him to become a Catholic once more, but he refused, no doubt anticipating that he might lose more than he gained in forfeiting the certain support of the Huguenots for the uncertainties of Catholic backing. It was as well that he hesitated for it would have been premature at this juncture; the Huguenots would without doubt have attached themselves to the prince of Condé and Henry would have lost all hope of their assistance and support.

The Catholic League, and more particularly the Guisards, were quite determined that Henry of Navarre should never rule France. In December 1584, therefore, the Guises signed a treaty with Philip of Spain at Joinville, by which the latter agreed to help them seize the throne on behalf of Charles, cardinal de Bourbon. The scene was now set for the final and longest phase of the civil wars, which turned into an entirely political struggle lasting 10 years. Indeed in the latter part of this phase it ceased to be a civil war and became a European one.

Henry III now found himself between two camps, but in reality he had no room for personal manoeuvre. In July 1585 he agreed to the Treaty of Nemours by which the League leaders received various governments, all the edicts of toleration were to be revoked, and the Huguenots had either to abjure their religion or leave the realm within six months. This reactionary piece of legislation provoked what has become known as the War of the Three Henries—Henry III, Henry of Navarre, and Henry, duke of Guise. The Catholics organised three armies: one to protect Paris, a second to guard the eastern frontier from any incursions by German Protestants; and the third in the south against Henry of Navarre. But by the summer of 1586 nothing much had been achieved, so once again Catherine de' Medici tried to arrange a truce by conferring with the Huguenots at Saint-Brice, near Cognac, in October 1586. Meanwhile a revolutionary government, known as the Seize, had seized power in Paris, and claimed that the king could not be relied upon to crush the Huguenots and advocated his imprisonment. Henry III survived this storm and in the following year sent a powerful army into the south-west under the command of the duke of Joyeuse, who suffered a heavy defeat at Coutras (1587) at the hands of Henry of Navarre's cavalry. The Catholics were routed, Joyeuse was killed, and the Huguenots had won their first great victory since the outbreak of the religious wars 24 years before.

The Catholics were exasperated and vented their spleen on Henry III. The duke of Guise, after defeating a body of German invaders at Auheau in November 1587, encouraged his uncle, the duke of Aumale to ask for the government of Picardy, but the king refused and gave it to the duke of Nevers. Tension rose and plots were hatched to depose the king. The Seize invited Guise to join them in Paris, and although the king forbad him to enter the city, he came nevertheless, and to a delirious welcome. In May 1588 the Parisian mob set up barricades to isolate those who remained loyal to the king, and on 13 May he fled to Saint-Cloud. The duke of Guise was hailed as 'king of Paris', though, in fact, he had no intention of doing away with the king, but merely wished to make him more amenable to the League's demands. This the king was now obliged to be, and by the so-called Edict of Union he agreed to annihilate all heretics, recognise the cardinal de Bourbon as heir-presumptive, and appoint the duke of Guise commander-in-chief of the royal forces. But the Guises had gone too far. For all his faults, Henry III was not so stupid that he did not realise that the only thing which separated the Guises from occupying the throne in all but name was himself. With Catherine de' Medici on her deathbed, and following the defeat of the Spanish Armada by the British climate, no immediate threat from Spain could be expected. He determined to rid himself of the Guises. He invited the duke of Guise and his brother, the cardinal to Blois, where on 23 December 1588, he gave himself the Christmas present of their mangled corpses.

When the news reached Paris there was stupefaction followed by uproar and a tightening of the alliance between the League cities. On 5 January 1589 Catherine de' Medici died; within a few weeks of her death Henry III, having no-one else to turn to, sent envoys to Tours where they concluded a deal with the Huguenots, and together with the royal forces they marched on the capital. They were on the point of attacking the city on 1 August when a Dominican friar, Jacques Clement, believing himself to be a divinely appointed agent, stabbed the king to death. Thus ended the long rule of the House of Valois, and France had to face the fact that the next king would be the Huguenot, Henry of Navarre.

1. Francis I, King of France (1494-1547), from a portrait by Jean Clouet.

2. Henry II, King of France (1518-59).

3. Catherine de' Medici, Queen of France (1519-89).

COL NI NEI   FRATRES

Gaspar chilasiarchus

Odetus Cardinalis   Francisus Ordinum pedestrium præfectus

Abconterfettung dreyer Bebrueder in Wranckreych, des geschlechts Colligny, mit namen Odetus diser war ev
Cardinal Gaspar der Ammiral vnd Francisus dandelot ein obrister über de landsknecht im feldt

4.   The Coligny brothers—Odet (1515-71), Gaspard II, Admiral of France (1517-72) and François (1521-69).

5.   Gaspard de Coligny in 1570.

6. Antoine de Bourbon, King of Navarre (1518-62).

7. Francis of Lorraine, duc d'Aumale and Guise.

MONTMORENCY (ANNE DE MONTMORENCY DUC DE)
143. Connétable de France
par BARTHELEMI PRIEUR

8. (*above*) Anne, duc de Montmorency, Constable of France (1493-1567).

9. (*left*) Louis de Bourbon, Prince of Condé (1530-69).

HENRY DE BOVRBON · PRINCE DE CONDE · DE CONDE

10. Henry de Bourbon, Prince of Condé (1552-88), from an engraving by Mathonier.

11. (*above*) Massacre of Saint Bartholomew, 1572.

12. (*below*) The assassination of Henry, Duke of Guise at Amboise, 23 December 1588.

Henricus Rex Galli.

Monsigneur
Cognac

Henr de Lorrai
ne dux de Guise

1588   23 Decemb.

13. Marguerite de Valois (1492-1549), wife of Henry, King of Navarre, and grandmother of Henry IV, King of France and Navarre.

14. King Henry III of France and King Henry IV of France and Navarre.

19. King Louis XIV (1638-1715), from a portrait by Hyacinthe Rigaud.

20.   Both sides of a French medal of 1685 'commemorating' the Revocation of the Edict of Nantes.

21. French Huguenot refugees landing at Dover in 1685 after the Revocation of the Edict of Nantes.

22. The French Church, Threadneedle Street.

23. Huguenots coming out of the Greek Church, Soho, from a painting by Hogarth.

VUË DE LA ROCHELLE

24. La Rochelle.

Henry IV (1589-1610)

Henry, king of Navarre and prince of Béarn, became king of France on the death of Henry III by right of succession. He was extremely distantly related to the late king; both descended from St Louis, their most recent common ancestor, who had died as long ago as 1270. Henry of Navarre was 10th in descent from St Louis and ninth from the latter's youngest son, Robert, count of Clermont, who had married the heiress to the seigneurie of Bourbon, Beatrix, who had held it in her own right. More than forty different branches of the royal house of France, eight of whom had worn the crown, had died without male issue.

Henry's claim to the throne did not, however, go unchallenged. Charles, duke of Lorraine, put in a claim on two grounds: firstly because he traced his ancestry back to before the Capetian kings came to power in 987; and secondly, because he was the husband of the late king's sister, Claude, who was older than Marguerite, Henry of Navarre's wife. In order to substantiate his claim it would have been necessary to set aside the Salic Law which forbade women to succeed to the throne of France. Philip II of Spain, on the other hand, while he agreed with the duke of Lorraine that the Salic Law should be set aside, claimed that since he had married Henry II's eldest daughter, Elizabeth, his claim was better than either of the others. Added to these claimants were the Guises, a younger branch of the House of Lorraine. They hoped to seize the crown for no other reason than that they were popular in Paris and with the Leaguers. They went so far as to proclaim the old cardinal de Bourbon as Charles X. The prince of Condé was not without hope that in the trouble everyone foresaw, he might land on the throne, but in essence it was the king of Spain, the duke of Lorraine and the cardinal de Bourbon who were the only serious competitors with whom Henry of Navarre had to contend. Of these the duke of Lorraine was neither powerful nor French; the king of Spain was very formidable because he wielded power south of the Pyrenees and along the northern frontier of France. The cardinal, although personally feeble, had the whole force of the Catholic League and the Guises behind him. While he lived, the king of Spain and the Guises made common cause in spite of their differing ambitions, though their general aims, the restoration of strict Catholicism and the exclusion of Henry of Navarre, were the same.

Against this array of force, Henry of Navarre's support was not impressive. The Huguenots were much weakened though their army was well trained and experienced, if small. He controlled a few towns in the south and west and could count on some support from the moderate Catholic party. Most of the nobility went home to their estates to wait and see which way the cat would jump before committing themselves. Henry therefore decided that it would not be either prudent or possible to continue to besiege Paris, so he withdrew into Normandy, where he was able to obtain support from England in the form of money and munitions, yet still menace the capital. As his forces were not above 10,000 men and those of the Catholics under Charles de Guise, duke of Mayenne, numbered more than 25,000, he was obliged to withdraw to Dieppe and defend it by fortifying the narrow defile that guards the approach to Arques. Battle was joined on 21 September 1589, but owing to the nature of the ground, Mayenne was unable to gain a decisive victory, leaving Henry in command of the situation. This was of considerable importance to him, for as a result, he gained the support of both the nobles and the populace alike. Fresh recruits joined him from Normandy, Picardy and England, and with these he made an attempt to take Paris.

He reached the suburbs at the end of October and captured that part of the city which lies south of the Seine. Due to its inner defences, he failed to capture the rest of the city, and was obliged to fall back on Tours in November, from where he swung north capturing Le Mans, Alençon, Argentan, Falaise and Honfleur. With the exception of Rouen he was virtually the master of Normandy and once again able to put pressure on Paris. Poissy fell in February 1590, followed by Nonancourt and then Dreux was besieged. Mayenne and his Spanish allies were not slow to react, and advanced to relieve Dreux. Leaving the siege Henry IV met his enemies head-on at Ivry (March 1590), where he scored a decisive victory. Once again the way to Paris seemed open to him. But in reality the situation was once more deadlocked. The siege of Paris began in April but was relieved in September by the Spanish under the duke of Parma.

Henry IV now changed his tactics and resolved to take Rouen to clear Normandy of the League, but again he was frustrated when the city was taken by Parma, an action which incensed him and induced him to make a determined attack on the Spanish army in force. Coming up against their advance-guard near Aumale (February 1592), he attacked with a cavalry force of 7,000 horsemen against a force of 23,000 infantry, which so confused Parma that he disengaged, believing that the French king had a much larger force at his command than was the case. This did not prevent Parma from relieving Rouen, which presented Henry IV with the choice of pursuing him or renewing the siege of Paris. As it turned out he did neither: sweeping round Paris through Senlis and Épernay he arrived at Provins in September 1592. By this time ordinary Frenchmen were wearied of war and convinced that only a king who was independent of both Spain and the noble factions could restore stable government. But the one impediment to Henry's acceptance as king was his religion. Henry, like so many monarchs, was more concerned with political convenience than religious belief, but he felt unable to desert those who had died and suffered on his behalf.

Early in 1593 the States General, or at least part of them, met in Paris to elect a king. Spanish envoys appeared in order to demand the repeal of the Salic Law so that Philip II's granddaughter, the Infanta Elisabeth, could be recognised as queen. At the same time, Henry IV began to negotiate with the pope, Clement VIII, a man of moderate opinions and conciliatory character. He felt that the time had come for his conversion, and he sought the advice of his supporters, Catholic and Protestant, among them the duke of Sully, who is reputed to have replied, 'To advise your majesty to go to Mass is something you cannot expect of me, a Calvinist; but I can tell your majesty it would be the best way of sending off all those rascally plots and plans into smoke . . . to conform to the wish of the great majority of your majesty's subjects would relieve you from very many vexations, pains and obstacles in this world—but as for the next', he added with a smile, 'I cannot answer for that'. Henry burst out laughing, and not long after took the advice his minister had given him. The moderate clergy, led by the archbishop of Bourges, declared their readiness to receive the king into the Church. Indeed, this seemed to them a fine opportunity for the Gallican Church to assert the kind of independence from the papacy that Henry VIII had secured for the Anglican Church. Fear of Spanish domination, should the Infanta be elected queen, was enough to bring to Henry's side many Catholics whose patriotism was greater than their religious prejudice.

At last on 23 July 1593, after a five-hour conversation with the archbishop of Bourges, the king made up his mind. He signed a profession of faith, and after provisional absolution by the archbishop, 'took the great plunge' as he termed it, and heard Mass at Saint-Denis. The Catholic Leaguers, both lay and clerical, still refused to recognise the conversion, for it was the king's object to find a middle way whereby Catholics and Huguenots could live together. He succeeded because he taught his compatriots that they were first and foremost Frenchmen. In achieving this he was undoubtedly helped by the unpatriotic, pro-Spanish behaviour of the fanatics.

Religiously insincere though his conversion may have been, it was politically wise, and prevented much bloodshed. His genius lay in knowing exactly when the time was ripe for it. Had he converted in 1589 when the force of faction was still so strong, it is doubtful if any great result would have come of it; whereas four years later, France was ready and even Paris welcomed him. Whether or not he really did say 'Paris is worth a Mass', the fact remains that the move led to results which fully justified his action. It took the heart out of the opposition; city after city swore allegiance to him, and by the end of the year the greater part of France was at peace and declared for the king.

In February 1594 the king was crowned at Chartres and entered Paris the following month. He had not waited for the pope's absolution, and the bishop of Chartres officiated in place of the archbishop of Rheims, a city which had not yet come over to him. The ambassadors of only two powers, Venice and England, were present, the latter in spite of Elizabeth's caustic comment on the king's change of faith. She was far too shrewd not to understand his reasons, and renewed her alliance at once. His entry into Paris where he heard Mass in Nôtre Dame was the signal for great rejoicing. He showed his appreciation by allowing the Spanish garrison to depart in peace, and with extraordinary clemency pardoned his adversaries all the excesses of the past 10 years. Genuine loyalty or self-interest, accompanied by bribes, influenced an increasing number to come over to his side.

The chief provincial areas of resistance were in Brittany, Picardy, Champagne, Auvergne, Burgundy, Languedoc and Provence. The history of the next four years is of their progressive submission, for the king's struggles were not ended by his entry into Paris. Spain refused to recognise him, and continued to foment trouble. Clement VIII, after some delay, absolved him, hoping to make him a faithful subject of the Papacy and a counterweight to Spain at Rome, but not without imposing onerous conditions aimed at stamping out heresy in France, which Henry quietly ignored. The pope's absolution ensured that the rest of France acknowledged him. Marseilles, a city fanatically devoted to the ultra Catholic cause, and supported by a Spanish fleet, alone stood out. In May 1595 a Spanish army marched on Dijon in the hope of securing the lines of communication between the Netherlands and Italy. The king hurried into Burgundy and defeated the Spaniards at Fontaine-Française.

This was probably the final blow for the Guises, for in October 1595 the duke of Mayenne began negotiating with the king, and in January 1596 agreed to accept the Edict of Folembray, granting him unconditional pardon. Mayenne's submission was followed by that of young Joyeuse, but all was not yet quite over. While Henry IV was recovering large regions in the south, he was losing towns to the Spaniards on the north-eastern frontier. As soon as he was satisfied that it was safe for him to leave the south, Henry advanced north and took Cambrai, driving the Spaniards back to Ardres and Calais. The duke of Épernon, who had made a treaty with Philip II in November 1595, was forced into submission by the young duke of Guise in May 1596. Of the dissident nobility only the dukes of Mercoeur and Aumale were left in rebellion against the king. Aumale's hatred of Henry IV was irreconcilable, and he retired to the Spanish Netherlands where he eventually died. Mercoeur maintained his opposition and set up an autonomous court at Nantes.

In November 1596 the king called a conference of notables at Rouen to deliberate on the best means of helping the crown. It remained in session until the following January and put forward some useful proposals for financial reforms. In March 1597 news came that the Spaniards had captured Amiens. The king's reaction was immediate. Rallying his forces he laid siege to the place, and in the following September the Spanish garrison, worn down by sheer weight of numbers, surrendered. Both Spain and France were heartily sick of the struggle, and at last Philip II was dying. The pope's mediation was accepted and peace was signed at Vervins in the spring of 1598. Henry IV immediately turned his forces against the duke of Mercoeur in Brittany and forced him into submission. The long wars were almost over. The Huguenots, however, and not unnaturally, resented the favours Henry was showing to those who had formerly been his enemies, but the king was quick to realise this, and determined to do what he could to prevent this resentment boiling over into war. Accordingly, in April 1598, he signed the Edict of Nantes.

Up to now the Huguenots had been treated to agreements which were mere truces, constantly evaded, which led inevitably to war. But the Edict of Nantes was made in good faith by a strong king who intended to see that it worked. It gave them at last the right to worship anywhere they pleased except in a few stated cities such as Rheims, Soissons, Dijon and Sens. It gave them complete civil equality, the right to hold public office, and established a Protestant Chamber in the Parlement of Paris and joint chambers in local Parlements. In brief, it gave them most of what Catherine de' Medici was willing to grant nearly 40 years before, but was prevented by the fanaticism of both sides. After 60 years of persecution the Huguenots were at last given the comparative liberty of conscience and freedom to worship as they wished. They were now admitted to public employment and their children allowed to attend schools and universities. By the Edict of Nantes they gained a quasi-independence. There were at that time about 750 Huguenot churches in France: of these, over 200 were in Burgundy; over 100 in Poitou and Saintonge; 94 in Provence and Dauphiné; and 83 in Guyenne. In the north, there were about 59 in Normandy and a rather smaller number scattered throughout Picardy, Champagne and the Ile de France.

On 2 May 1598, three weeks after the promulgation of the Edict of Nantes, the Treaty of Vervins was signed. Four months later, Philip II, who had done so much to stem the advance of heresy, died, with all his aims shattered—the seven northern provinces of the Spanish Netherlands were defiant, independent and Protestant; France was granting toleration to the Huguenots; and England was triumphant at sea and on the verge of supplanting Spain in large parts of America. It was not only the

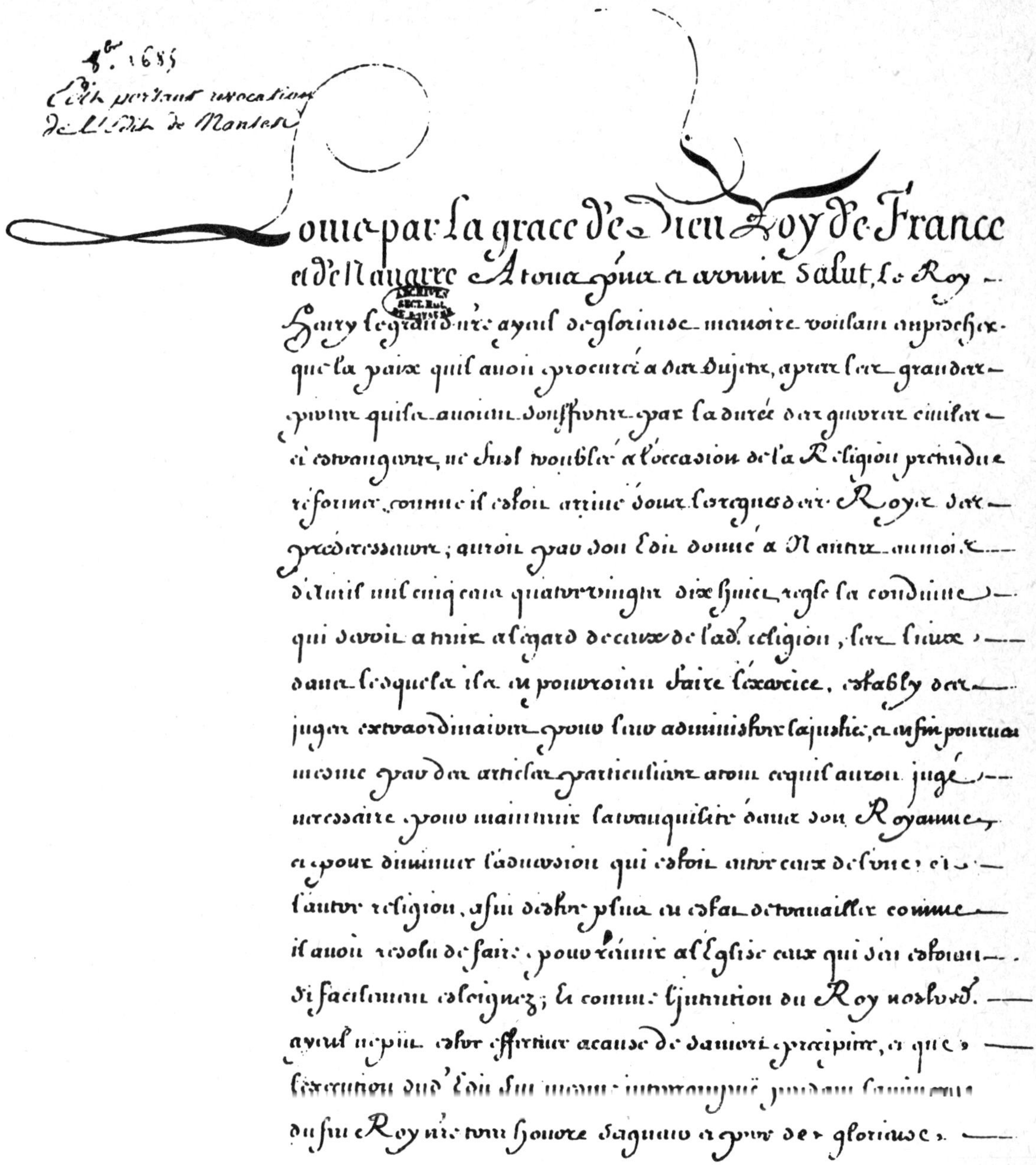

8bre 1685
Edit portant revocation
de l'Edit de Nantes

Louis par la grace de Dieu Roy de France
et de Navarre A tous presens et a venir Salut, Le Roy
Henry le grand nre ayeul de glorieuse memoire voulant empescher
que la paix quil avoit procurée a ses Sujets, apres les grandes
pertes quils avoient souffertes par la durée des guerres civiles
et estrangeres, ne fust troublée a l'occasion de la Religion pretendue
reformée, comme il estoit arrivé sous les regnes des Roys ses
predecesseurs; auroit par son Edit donné a Nantes au mois
d'Avril mil cinq cens quatrevingt dix huict, reglé la conduitte
qui seroit a tenir a l'egard de ceux de lad. religion, les lieux
dans lesquels ils en pourroient faire l'exercice, estably des
juges extraordinaires pour leur administrer la justice, et enfin pourveu
mesme par des articles particuliers a tout cequil auroit jugé
necessaire pour maintenir la tranquilité dans son Royaume,
et pour diminuer l'aversion qui estoit entre ceux de l'une et
l'autre religion, afin d'estre plus en estat de travailler comme
il avoit resolu de faire pour reunir a l'Eglise ceux qui s'en estoient
si facilement esloignez; et comme l'intention du Roy nostredit
ayeul ne pût estre effectuée acause de sa mort precipitée, et que
l'execution dud. Edit fut mesme interrompue pendant la minorité
du feu Roy nre tres honoré Seigneur et pere de glorieuse

Fig. 2 Facsimile of the Revocation of the Edict of Nantes, signed at Fontainebleau, in October 1685 by Louis XIV.

end of a century but the end of an era: the new century was in every way to be a new beginning.

The reign of Henry IV, the first of the five Bourbon kings of France, marks the beginning of modern France. He laid the foundations for a centralised monarchy, but based on complex policies, which often appeared illogical, contradictory and cynical to outside observers. For example, the erstwhile leader of the Huguenots repressed Protestantism at home, yet encouraged the new religion abroad. He sought to make France the head of the Latin countries in Europe in secular antagonism to the German, mainly Protestant, princes, yet stood between the Latin and Germanic nations, thereby obtaining an overwhelming influence in the councils of Europe. The French people themselves were decidedly Catholic in temper, but the spirit of doubt and enquiry persisted, at first among her Huguenot population, but towards the end of the Bourbon period in the almost atheistical cult of Reason propounded by Voltaire and the thinkers of the Revolution. Such a policy was bound to create martyrs and refugees.

Henry IV not only fulfilled the pledges he had given to the Huguenots in the Edict of Nantes, but by allying himself with the Dutch, English and Germans he contributed to the great victory over the Spanish at Nieuport in 1600, by which Spain was henceforth completely crippled in the Netherlands. His chief minister and Huguenot friend, Maximilien de Bethune, duke of Sully, had ambitious, advanced views of how the Europe of his day should be reconstructed to take account of the new religions that had developed over the past century. Although nothing came of these in practice, the Christian Republic, as Sully called it, is worth mentioning, for it foreshadowed the Europe we have come to know today. Sully realised that poverty was the main weakness of the crown, and made it his main objective to increase the royal revenue. He did not attempt to revolutionise the French fiscal system, but was content to remove some of the worst abuses and to make the existing system more efficient. His success was considerable, for the country which had been almost bankrupt in 1598 was in a position to enter a major war in 1610. Whatever the underlying defects of the French economy may have been, Henry IV and Sully gave the kingdom a much needed period of order and prosperity.

Sully's Christian Republic was to consist of 15 states, at whose head were to be the Holy Roman Empire and the Papacy. There were to be three elective monarchies—Hungary, Poland and Bohemia; and four republics—Switzerland (comprising Franche Comté, Alsace, Tyrol and some Alpine districts of Italy), Italy (a ducal republic comprising Genoa, Florence, Mantua and the central Italian duchies), Venice (a seigneurial republic combined with Sicily), and Belgium (a provincial republic of 17 provinces). Next came six hereditary monarchies—France, England (which was to rule over certain dependencies in the Low Countries such as Limburg, Brabant and Malines), Spain, Denmark, Sweden and Lombardy. These powers were to be guided and kept in check one versus the other by a Grand Council. The scheme paid great attention to the religious differences of the time, for Sully considered there were basically three religions in Europe—the Roman Catholic Church, the Lutheran and what he termed the 'Reformed', but which we would call Calvinist. Italy and Spain were purely Catholic; France was mixed, but would be tolerant; Germany was mixed, comprising all three forms, which were required to co-exist in peace; and the rest were for the most part Protestant, though not without infusions of Catholicism. Each area was to be secured in the faith it had chosen; toleration would be granted only in those states which were mixed.

Sully's grandiose scheme was widely discussed and supported by, among others, Elizabeth I and James I of England. It failed to materialise mainly because Henry IV and most of his contemporary monarchs had no intention of seeing it succeed, dismissing it as romantic and impractical. Notwithstanding this, Sully did succeed to some extent in his grand design through the formation of an anti-Hapsburg coalition of powers which was aimed at ending that family's domination of central Europe and the Spanish peninsula, and so free France from the threat of encirclement. Treaties of friendship were signed with Venice, Florence and Savoy as well as with the Dutch. In 1609 the disputed succession to the duchy of Cleves threatened the outbreak of a European war. Sully prepared to throw the armed strength of France into the contest in alliance with the Protestant powers, and on 11 February 1610 made a formal alliance with the Evangelical Union of Schwabisch and prepared for war against the Imperial forces. But fate intervened on 14 May 1610 in the person of a fanatical Catholic schoolmaster, François Ravaillac, whose narrow mind was disturbed by the possibility of a Catholic king fighting side by side with the heretics. As Henry's coach, coming from the Louvre to visit Sully in the Arsenal, was halted by a cart carrying a load of straw, Ravaillac stabbed the king. Thus ignobly died one of the noblest kings of France. His sudden death plunged the country into a crisis which lasted from 1610 to 1624 and which was alarmingly reminiscent of the situation in the 1560s at the outset of the religious wars. The price was renewed persecution and emigration for many Huguenot families.

Louis XIII (1610-1643) and Richelieu

Henry IV was succeeded by his nine-year-old son, Louis XIII. Henry and Marguerite de Valois had been divorced by mutual consent, and in 1600 the king had married Marie de' Medici, a distant cousin of Catherine, largely on account of the huge dowry she brought with her. She was as devoid of brains as her kinswoman had been endowed with them. She was good-natured and moral in a time when immorality was rife, but unlike most of her family, she was entirely lacking in humour, wit or intelligence. She objected to the king's numerous illegitimate children being educated with the princes and princesses. Under her regency the French Court became the scene of constant dissension; quarrels, rivalries and battles-royal were incessant. It has been said that the nine-year-old Louis was as fit to rule France as his mother. Marie de' Medici had five children by Henry IV—Louis XIII, Gaston, duke of Orleans, Elizabeth, later wife of Philip IV of Spain, Henrietta Maria, later the wife of Charles I of England, and Christine, wife of the duke of Savoy.

As Queen Regent Marie was entirely under the thumb of her minister, Concini, and her mistress of the robes, Leonora Galligai, whom she had brought with her from Florence. She immediately reversed Henry IV's foreign policy by contracting a marriage between Louis XIII and Anne of Austria, the daughter of Philip III of Spain. The Huguenots, unable to forget what they had suffered at the hands of Spanish allies of former kings of France, were equally horrified by the trust Marie appeared to repose in the papal nuncio and the Jesuits. Furthermore, the high French nobility grabbed control of the provincial governments and bullied her into squandering Sully's hard-gained treasure among them in the form of pensions and sinecures. Sully, needless to say, was soon dismissed.

In 1612 war seemed imminent and Sully's son-in-law, the duke of Rohan, became one of the leading figures among the Huguenots. In an assembly held at Saumur he attacked the Catholic and Spanish policy of the Queen Regent and prepared to raise the standard of rebellion at La Rochelle. However, calmer counsels prevailed; the government made some concessions, Rohan's position as Protector of the Huguenots was recognised and the danger of war passed. It was at this point that Armand-Jean du Plessis de Richelieu, bishop of Luçon, makes his appearance on the stage of France.

Born on 9 September 1585, Richelieu became bishop of Luçon in 1607 at the age of 22, thanks to family influence. His diocese, a small, unimportant town in the fens not far from La Rochelle had a huge Huguenot minority, and from the beginning of his career, he had to confront squarely the problem of reconciling the two religions. The situation at that time was highly fluid and the wars of religion had covered the deep differences of opinion within the Catholic Church—between those who believed in a revived papal authority and those who believed in a purely French Catholicism; between those whose religion had a mystical meaning and those whose approach was rational. Thus Richelieu was faced with not only the major debate between Protestantism and Catholicism, but also with these internal questions within the Gallican Church, which carried with them deep political implications.

In his own way, Richelieu was devout: the critical problem of his life was the uneasy interplay of public activity on the one hand and religious, moral standards on the other. His religion was intellectual rather than heartfelt; his political ambition, boundless. In 1618 he published *Principal Points of the Faith of the Catholic Church*, a detached, tolerant and conciliatory work. In it he rejected the idea that heresy could or should be totally extinguished as well as the notion that the monarch's religion should be that of his subjects. At the same time, there had to be limits to toleration, and these he defined as the line where religious liberty leads to political action.

Richelieu regarded the Protestant thesis that biblical authority is the bedrock of religion as inadmissible, because the majority could not read, and therefore had to be guided. The interpretation of the Bible by ministers in the reformed religion had taken over the Church's interpretation handed down from above. How, he asked, could one man's judgement and interpretation be superior to the accumulated wisdom of the Church handed down from centuries of experience? On the basis of free interpretation, the Protestants claimed powers and knowledge greater than those they denied to the pope. The Protestants regarded this as unfair, pointing out that Luther had upheld the civil power and that to accuse Protestants of viewing the law of the Church and the State with contempt was to accuse them of political disloyalty. But, in fact, Protestantism conceived of law as externally binding, though it need not internally encumber a man's conscience. Coupled with the thesis that the sovereignty of the people is greater than that of the monarch, the Protestant argument, if taken to its logical conclusion, would lead to anarchy. Richelieu's book was an enormous success among Catholics, and made a deep impression on many Huguenots, especially among those of the aristocracy who had embraced the reformed faith, many of whom were converted back to the old religion after reading it.

But Richelieu regarded the Huguenots, not without reason, as a state within a state. In enclaves throughout the southern half of France they exerted an independent authority which no other state in Europe would have tolerated. At Milhaud in 1573 they had established their own political organisation, and an administration which functioned independently of the king's. The Edict of Nantes had given them a privileged position, guaranteeing them liberty of conscience and worship under very precise conditions, and regulating among other things the probate of wills, burials, and the constitution of Protestant churches and the payment of their clergy. Its secret clauses granted the Huguenots the right to retain for eight years all the fortified castles and towns they were occupying at that date. These conditions expired in 1606, but during those eight years the Huguenots were in absolute possession of 150 strongholds scattered over the country, each one of which was in a position to defy royal authority. The size of this privileged group can be estimated by the fact that at that time there were probably 3,500 Protestant nobles who could raise 25,000 troops; though in all there were only about a million Huguenots in a population of 15 million.

The States General of 1614 chose Richelieu to compose an address to the throne, which brought him to the attention of Marie de' Medici, who gave him a place in the Council of State as minister of foreign affairs. In the following year the discontented aristocracy and, to a lesser degree, the population at large began to mobilise and civil war once more threatened, only to be narrowly averted by the Treaty of Loudun in May 1616.

France took no part in the opening stages of the Thirty Years War, and friendly relations with England—something always of help to the Huguenots—was maintained throughout the negotiations for the marriage between Henrietta Maria and the prince of Wales. But the Huguenot party was becoming disunited and torn by internal dissension. The aristocracy was drawing away and many became Catholics, including Henry, duke of Condé, which turned the movement by degrees in a more populist direction, increasing the influence of Calvinist ministers. The Huguenots began to seek an even larger measure of independence for their cities, especially for those where they were in a strong position, and there was talk of a Protestant representative body for the nation as a whole, which should be for France what the States of Holland were for the Dutch. This caused friction not only between the different classes of society, but also between regions of the country. When Richelieu spoke of the Huguenots as a 'state within a state' it was demands such as these that justified his words.

While Richelieu was feeling his way to power, Louis XIII was coming increasingly under the influence of his favourite, Charles d'Albert, duke of Luynes. At the latter's instigation he arrested and executed Concini and Leonora Galligai and banished Marie de' Medici from Court and later from the country. Thus Luynes became first minister and the king assumed the reins of power. The fall of Marie de' Medici was potentially dangerous for Richelieu, who had enjoyed her favour and protection, but he played his cards carefully, and was used in the end to effect a reconciliation between the king and his mother.

The French part of Henry IV's kingdom of Navarre, known as Béarn, refused to apply the Edict of Nantes in reverse to the Catholics who were in a minority there.

In 1512 four-fifths of Navarre had been seized by the king of Aragon, which left a rump on the northern side of the Pyrenees. Because Navarre was an independent state there was nothing to restrain Protestant assaults on the Catholics. Catholicism was banned and church property seized, and, as in England, sold to the gentry. When the crowns of France and Navarre were united in Henry IV, the anti-Catholic laws remained in force there. When Henry was converted to Catholicism, one of the conditions imposed upon him by the pope was the obligation to repeal these acts and restore its seized lands to the Church, or grant it equivalent property from crown lands. Henry failed to do this before he was assassinated. This led to interminable wrangles, for once the two countries were united, Béarn became, in theory, subject to French law, including the Edict of Nantes. There was, however, a snag. The Salic Law had never applied in Navarre, so it was theoretically possible that at some future date a daughter of a French king might succeed, although not in France, as Jeanne d'Albret had done. The two crowns, therefore, might one day devolve on different heads.

In 1617 matters came to a head when the Estates of Béarn refused to accept a royal proclamation incorporating the province into France. The Huguenot Assembly of La Rochelle declared the following month that the cause of Béarn was the cause of all Protestant France. This only served to stiffen the resolve of Louis XIII, who had meanwhile succeeded his father as king of France and Navarre, and in June 1617 he decreed that all ecclesiastical property in Béarn was to be restored to the Church, and that those who had been dispossessed would be compensated by the crown. There was an uproar on the part of the Béarnais, and in May 1619 they managed to persuade the Huguenot Church to issue an ultimatum annulling the Decree of Restitution. The king took up the challenge and went to Pau where he saw to it that the Catholic clergy took possession of the church of St Martin. In December that year La Rochelle resolved to support the Béarnais and throughout France the Huguenots began to raise troops. It was civil war once more. Richelieu saw immediately that this would give an excuse for Spain and Austria to intervene unless it was stopped at once. Peace with the Huguenots, not their destruction, was what the situation demanded. Saumur and Saint-Jean-d'Angely were captured, and the question arose whether La Rochelle should be attacked. It was decided to bypass it and to march south, where Montauban was besieged, but the royal troops suffered an epidemic of typhoid from which the duke of Luynes, their commander, died, and had to retreat. Carcassonne, Narbonne and Béziers fell to the king in the early part of the following year; the duke of Soubise, the Huguenot commander was defeated with heavy losses and Huguenot nobles such as the dukes of Sully, La Force and Châtillon withdrew from the contest. The duke of Condé now led the royal army to lay siege to Montpellier, but the royalists were harried fiercely by the duke of Rohan, and the city held out.

The struggle in Europe now began to take on a character which boded ill for France, and Richelieu became anxious to end the struggle with the Huguenots so that all the country's strength would be concentrated for the broader struggle. Richelieu was not yet master of France, but his advice prevailed and the king decided to abandon the siege of Montpellier and to make peace with the Protestants. Rohan was advised by the English to accept the terms he was offered, and peace was signed in October 1622 by which the Edict of Nantes was confirmed, but the position of the Huguenots had suffered a severe setback. They had lost about half their fortified towns, and though they were promised their political and municipal independence, this was only on condition that they laid down their arms. In Montauban and many other towns in the south they maintained their defiance: the Peace of Montpellier was no more than a truce. The duke of Rohan was much criticised by the more volatile members of his party for accepting these peace terms, but he defended himself by pointing out how little support he had received from the Huguenot aristocracy, cities and congregations, and how this had resulted in the extremities to which the garrison of Montpellier had been reduced.

With the death of Luynes, Louis XIII entrusted the affairs of the nation to Sillery and La Vieuville. They were no more fitted to rule France than the king himself, and the problems that had been created by the regency of Marie de' Medici were, if anything, aggravated. In April 1624 Richelieu was given a seat on the Council and 11 days after the fall of Vieuville, on 24 August 1624, he was appointed chief minister to the crown. Richelieu set himself four tasks: to check the power of the nobility; to destroy the political privileges of the Huguenots; to exalt the authority of the king; and to make France respected abroad. Fortunately for him, the Huguenots posed much less of a threat than they had in the preceding century. They were less numerous, less ardent, less cohesive, and less ably led.

The Peace of Montpellier was short-lived. Fighting began again in January 1625 when Soubise precipitated war by seizing the Ile de Ré, which lies some 10 miles off La Rochelle, and which commands the entrance to its harbour. Next he seized seven royal ships which were anchored in the River Blavet in Brittany, near Lorient. He went on to capture the Ile d'Oléron which commanded the mouth of the Gironde and the entrance to Bordeaux, while Rohan collected troops in Languedoc and prepared for war on a grand scale.

Richelieu knew that an all-out attack on the Huguenots would be welcome at Court, but was determined to avoid it if he could. In the face of considerable opposition, he succeeded in opening negotiations, which were nearly wrecked by the improvident attack by the royal garrison of Fort Saint-Louis against La Rochelle. It was only the mediation of the English and Dutch that enabled him to sign the Peace of La Rochelle in February 1626. But no sooner had he done so than war broke out with England, which immediately led to a further Huguenot uprising, forcing Richelieu to the view that the only solution was the complete annihilation of the Huguenot strongholds on the Atlantic coast. The issues became more complex through the machinations of the duke of Buckingham on behalf of the princess Henrietta Maria and his imagined infatuation with Marie de' Medici. But the fundamental causes of the war were to be found in the commercial rivalries of England and France not only in Europe but also in Canada, about which we shall have more to say later.

Richelieu desired to make France a strong naval power, and England was not slow to see and feel the threat that this posed. She therefore decided to embark on an aggressive war. Grandiose plans for the invasion of France were drawn up, with one expedition to land near Bordeaux, another in Normandy, and a third to join up with the Huguenots at La Rochelle. Rohan agreed to raise a Huguenot force in the south once the English had actually landed in France. The reduction of La Rochelle became the focus of Richelieu's strategy, for with its fall, the rest of this grand design could not hope to succeed. He made no attempt to launch a direct assault on the city, but drew a line of trenches and towers round the landward approaches, leaving only the seaward approaches open for the city's support. Until the harbour mouth could be cut off from the Huguenots on the Ile de Ré, the city could hang out indefinitely, so it became necessary to construct breakwaters from either side of the estuary to prevent the entry of shipping. Before these works were completed, Lord Denbigh arrived with an English fleet of 60 ships. He managed to get a message into the city telling the defenders that they must clear a passage for his ships to enter the inner port. But owing to their lack of ships and equipment the Huguenot defenders could not assist him. Denbigh then attempted to force a passage by bombarding the breakwaters, but it was a desultory, half-hearted attack and in the end Denbigh, believing discretion to be the better part of valour, decided to take his fleet back to England. The Huguenots felt that Denbigh had betrayed them, and it is indeed hard to acquit him of the charge.

When the English fleet departed on 19 May 1628 the Huguenots felt that their chances of survival had been seriously jeopardised. But a new council of war, made up of 19 members led by Jean Guiton, the legendary hero of the siege, resolved to hold out regardless of the consequences. There were occasional sorties and one or two vessels managed to slip through, but they brought little relief to the beleaguered city. With a royal army of more than 25,000 men surrounding them, the Huguenots were soon reduced to less than half that number, and could only hope that the landing of a powerful English supporting force could save them from destruction. Before help arrived the breakwater and its supporting works were finished and the trap was closed.

The Duke of Buckingham fully intended to bring an expedition to the relief of La Rochelle, and was on the point of embarking at Portsmouth, when he was assassinated by John Felton, who believed it was his God-sent duty to rid the country of this unpopular royal favourite. Buckingham's death did not prevent the expedition from setting sail, for the honour of England was at stake, and the fleet appeared off La Rochelle in September 1628 under the command of Lord Lindsay. This time the attack was pressed with more vigour, but the naval bombardment made little impression on the French breakwater and defences. The fleet withdrew, but this time it remained on hand with the intention of acting as mediator between the royal forces and the besieged Huguenots.

Inside the city the situation was desperate. There was little or no food, and Richelieu knew that he only had to wait until starvation did its worst. The siege had already lasted 14 months and Guiton, the mayor, now saw that their plight was hopeless. Richelieu, however, refused to allow the English to mediate, insisting that this was an internal matter that had to be settled between the French king and his rebellious subjects. On 18 October 1629 terms were agreed and a treaty signed by which the king allowed the defenders their lives, the possession of their property and the free exercise of their religion within the city. On 30 October Richelieu entered La Rochelle, and although he would not treat with Guiton, the latter was pardoned and later joined the French navy. In this hour of victory, Richelieu was neither vindictive nor cruel. He ensured that provisions were quickly made available and that all possible medical aid was afforded to the survivors. When the armed men of La Rochelle were ordered to leave the city, 90 Englishmen and 64 Frenchmen marched out. Of the rest of the inhabitants it has been estimated that out of a population of about 25,000 at least 10,000 had perished.

Richelieu now encouraged individuals to surrender and many prominent Huguenots came in and received the king's pardon. The duke of Rohan, however, was still at large in the south, and he again appealed to England for help. Then, when this was clearly not forthcoming, he turned to Spain, France's chief enemy. A treaty was made by which the Huguenots received a large subsidy in return for supporting Spanish interests at all times. This compact with the devil had no effect other than to turn the Huguenots into permanent traitors to their country. But before Spanish help could be effective, the Protestant forces were defeated. Privas was taken and Alais besieged. At first Richelieu refused to treat with the party as a whole and insisted on the surrender of individual towns and noblemen. But this was a slow process and he was in a hurry to be free for the great European crisis he saw looming ahead. He therefore allowed a General Huguenot Assembly to be held at Anduze, near Alais, and there dictated the terms for peace, which were signed on 28 June 1629. Under its terms the Huguenots were compelled to destroy all their fortifications and an end was made of the guarantees to individual towns. At the same time, most of the Edict of Nantes was reaffirmed, allowing them freedom of conscience and civil liberty.

From now on, the Huguenots ceased to exist as a political party, and were distinguished from the rest of the population by their religion alone. The duke of Rohan withdrew from France and fought in the Thirty Years War; Soubise went to England where he died and was buried in Westminster Abbey. Many aristocrats reconverted to Catholicism, though large numbers of the smaller gentry, merchants, craftsmen and artisans continued to worship as Protestants.

Three years after the Peace of Alais and the Edict of Pardon the duke of Montmorency and the king's brother, the duke of Orleans, sought for factious reasons to reawaken the religious passions of Languedoc of which the former was governor. Their appeal failed and the inhabitants of Montauban even offered to march against them. This reaction was all the more welcome to Richelieu because the rebellious dukes had found considerable support among the Catholic clergy of the south, and he expressed his gratitude to them accordingly. The long-term benefits of Richelieu's policy were great, for the loyalty of the mass of the Huguenots to the crown fully justified the toleration he had granted them. The next 30 years were the most peaceful the Huguenots had ever known, and even though there was a degree of tension and the occasional outbreak of violence, they became a religious body which took little part in the politics and wars of the country at large. But the government could, if it wished, interfere with them at any time. Fortunately it did not, and the Huguenots were able to devote themselves to commerce and industry, which worked to their own and the country's great material benefit. They had their own schools and colleges at Nîmes, Saumur and Montauban among other places.

The Catholic Church during this period was more vigorous and less fanatical than it had been in the past, and the presence of the Huguenots was a stimulus to thought and controversy. The Jansenist movement began to spread within the Catholic Church, claiming the allegiance of intellectuals and writers like Pascal, but at the same time causing some concern among certain members of the hierarchy, which ultimately denounced it as heretical.

After the fall of La Rochelle, Richelieu can hardly have contemplated the permanent presence of more than one state religion. At the same time, he hoped for the peaceful conversion of the Huguenots and made some effort to bring this about wherever he could. He planned to win over leading Protestant ministers by discussion, concessions and reunion and then to hold a conference in the presence of the king. A number of ministers were won over by these means to the prospect of a peaceful conference, but when the plan was presented to the provincial synods it was utterly rejected and the project was dropped. Notwithstanding, Richelieu did not give up hope, and despatched missioners or convertisseurs throughout the Protestant areas, but the results achieved were small. The king had sworn to uphold the Edict of Nantes, but its meaning was sometimes obscure and its implications not always easy to determine. The Catholic leaders and lawyers tended to interpret it as unfavourably to the Huguenots as they could, and never ceased to find ways of whittling away at the privileges it had granted them.

In the meantime, Richelieu, having destroyed the political power of the Huguenots, set out to do all he could to strengthen the power of the crown in the person of the king and his immediate advisers. To forestall rebellion he changed the provincial governors at frequent intervals and made special provisions for the trial of rebels with whom the ordinary courts were powerless to deal. The often fractious provincial Parlements were brought under stricter control, and by the use of *intendants* direct links were forged between the crown and the provinces, thus cutting down the power of feudal dignitaries. He expanded the army and modernised it and the French navy can be regarded in many ways as his special creation. Before he died he had established effective Atlantic and Mediterranean navies which dramatically altered the balance of power at sea.

It is hard to underestimate Richelieu's contribution to the creation of France as the leading power in Europe, for the Treaty of Westphalia in 1648 and the Treaty of the Pyrenees 11 years later were made possible only by the groundwork he had done. By the summer of 1642 he was clearly dying, and the end came in Paris in November. He was followed to the grave by the monarch he had so nobly served six months later with the death of Louis XIII in May 1643.

Louis XIV (1643-1715)

Louis XIV succeeded his father at the age of five and the Queen Mother, Anne of Austria, like her Medici predecessors, immediately assumed the regency. As a Hapsburg princess, she was unpopular, and her position was not enhanced by the appointment of Giulio Mazarini as her chief minister. Fortunately for France and for the young king, Mazarin, as he was known in France, departed little from the policies of his own predecessor, Cardinal Richelieu, especially in regard to internal affairs. Like Richelieu, Mazarin showed unrelenting determination to keep the nobility in check by occupying them in wars against Spain and the Holy Roman Empire, Anne of Austria notwithstanding. But the mounting cost accompanied by a series of disastrous harvests led to agricultural depression and widespread famine. The resulting economic and political unrest led to the uprisings known as the Fronde, which lasted from 1648 to 1653.

The Fronde began as a protest against the loss of their rights and privileges by royal officials and was supported by the Parlement of Paris. The Paris mob rioted but the

Parlement, fearing that it might bring down the government, came to terms in 1649 with Mazarin. By this time the Thirty Years War was over, and the aristocratic officers who had been fighting abroad turned the discontent they found at home to their own advantage. Seizing what they saw as an opportunity to regain some of the power and influence that Richelieu had so successfully deprived them of, they chased Mazarin out of the country and the king and his mother out of Paris. Many of them hoped to dismantle the centralised authority established in the last reign and to turn France into a mosaic of sovereign princely states similar to the Germany they had come to know during the war. For three years their private armies roamed the country, tilting against one another as if in some gigantic feudal tournament. None of this did anything to endear them to the population at large and when the king, in 1652 at the age of 14, declared himself of age, he was welcomed back to Paris enthusiastically. Mazarin followed him in 1653; the rebel nobles retired to their estates or disappeared into exile. The Fronde was over. Throughout the troubles the Huguenots had sided with the king—even the inhabitants of La Rochelle supported the regent against their own governor. Mazarin frankly acknowledged their loyalty and the king formally thanked his Protestant subjects for their support.

Louis was still too young to take personal charge of affairs and Mazarin resumed their direction, reaping the rewards of Richelieu's sound policies. Despite his preoccupation with the Fronde, Mazarin was able to secure advantageous terms at the Peace of Westphalia, which brought France the provinces of Alsace and Lorraine. The war with Spain continued for a decade more, though both contestants were largely engrossed with domestic matters. It was finally concluded in 1659 by the Treaty of the Pyrenees, by which Mazarin secured further territorial advantages in Artois adjoining Flanders and in Roussillon bordering Catalonia in the south. The Bourbon-Hapsburg feud was papered over by the marriage of Louis XIV to his cousin, the infanta Maria Theresa, through whom he established strong claims to the inheritance of all the Spanish Hapsburg possessions in Europe and America, and could thereby hope to create a new dynastic empire greater even than that of the Emperor Charles V.

Although the king had declared in 1652 that he would observe the provisions of the Edict of Nantes, the Catholic clergy resented it, and their efforts were continually directed towards obtaining its revocation. During Mazarin's lifetime they were unsuccessful, but when the Italian cardinal died in 1661 Louis took the reins of government into his own hands, in which he held them for the rest of his long life. The king regarded Protestantism as the product of egotism and obstinacy, and believed it could be eliminated without much difficulty provided certain pressures were brought to bear on those who practised it.

The years 1660 to 1679 were the most prosperous of the king's reign, and during this period Jean-Baptiste Colbert, as his chief minister, made use of the Huguenots as his agents and clerks. He also encouraged the French to extend their manufactures and at the same time held out inducements to skilled foreign artisans to settle in the kingdom and establish new industries. Many of these were Dutch and Walloon Protestants who settled as cloth manufacturers in the northern provinces. With the king's policy of constant war abroad, in which he sought for and obtained alliances with the Protestant powers of England, Prussia, Denmark and Sweden, the situation of the Huguenots was a favourable one, as it made any attack on them unlikely and politically inexpedient. Nevertheless, these years saw a decline in their influence, and they found themselves faced with an increasingly hostile Catholic majority, jealous of their wealth, supported by the king. The Edict of Nantes, which was part of the law of the land, might seem to offer them protection, but the Catholic clergy and the lawyers found ways of getting round many of its provisions by insisting on its literal observance. It was by no means a well-drafted document, and contained many loopholes through which clever legal and ecclesiastical minds could find a way of making life difficult for the Huguenots. What the clergy demanded one day, the king performed sooner or later, and there was no shortage of those who were calling upon him to use his authority to extirpate heresy from his kingdom.

The Peace of Nijmegen in 1678 brought to an end the long war which had preoccupied Louis XIV and his government for so many years. It enabled them to concentrate their attention on domestic matters which had for too long been neglected, the most pressing of which, in their minds, was the elimination of heresy. It was also the ill-fortune of the Huguenots that there had been a change in the life and character of the king. This change is usually attributed to the influence of Madame de Maintenon, who, ironically, was the granddaughter of Agrippa d'Aubigné, one of the most prominent Huguenots of the time of Henry IV. She had been appointed governess to the king's children, which brought her often into his company. Her conversation was a welcome change from the frivolity he was accustomed to, and they talked much of religion. Under her influence Louis was reconciled to his wife, and the Court took on a religious and moral tone it had hitherto lacked. To love the Catholic faith was to hate heresy; to hate heresy was to seek to destroy it.

From 1679 attacks on Protestantism increased. During the next six years more than 126 decrees were issued curtailing Huguenot liberties and inflicting penalties on them. They reveal a carefully-worked-out plan of persecution. There were few martyrdoms, no victims invoking the name of Christ, just a series of ever more onerous burdens, as privileges were withdrawn, means of livelihood removed, the stigma of social inferiority attached in such a way as to make Huguenots feel and appear to be an untouchable caste. For a community of above-average intelligence and education, industry, thrift and self-reliance, life became more and more intolerable. One of the most subtle and successful ways of obtaining conversions was to billet soldiers on Huguenot households, who were made responsible for their board and lodging, and for their pay and maintenance. In one year alone more than 30,000 reconverted to Catholicism to rid themselves of this onerous imposition, known as the dragonnades.

The year 1685 opened inauspiciously for the Huguenots. They could expect no help from any foreign power, least of all England, where the accession of the Catholic James II removed whatever hopes they may have looked for from that quarter. Appeals to Louis to maintain the rights granted to them by his grandfather, Henry IV, fell upon deaf ears. Their defence of the monarchy during the Fronde and against the Catholic League counted for nothing. With or without the king's knowledge the final attack was being prepared. Laws and penalties, bribes and rewards had done much, but the soldiery had done most and they were used for the *coup de grace*. The final assault took place in Béarn. Once again there was tension on the Spanish frontier, and a considerable force was despatched to the south-west in order to be ready for any attack across the Pyrenees. When the danger of war passed, this force was turned against the Huguenots with the intendant, Foucault, directing operations. Conversions were reported by tens of thousands; other provinces were not slow to copy the example of Béarn. Troops marched into Languedoc and Guyenne, where it comes as no surprise to learn that vast numbers pronounced the formulae and signed the documents necessary to save them from brutal ill-treatment and even murder. Whole towns surrendered to the religious demands of the troops.

The Edict of Nantes was still maintained—in theory at least—though it had long since ceased to afford any protection to life, liberty and property. To all intents it had become a dead letter. It would obviously be easier to treat all Frenchmen alike if there were no legal Huguenot body left in France. The chancellor, Le Tellier, drew up an edict for the revocation and submitted it to the king, who made a few changes, and sent it to the Parlement of Paris for registration. From 18 October 1685 there was to be only one religion in France under this Act of Revocation.

The historian Lavisse has described the Revocation of the Edict of Nantes, not without reason, as a shameful page in the historical documents of France. In essence it stated that Henry IV had granted the Edict to give peace to the country and to allow mutual animosities to cool 'in order that he might be in a better position to labour for the reunion of those to the Church who had so lightly separated from it'. His death had prevented him from doing anything and Louis XIII had been too constantly engaged in foreign wars. Louis XIV, too, had found no time sufficiently free from troubles until now. All he had been able to do for the advantage of religion had been to diminish the number of Protestant temples and abolish the divided chambers—'which had only been set up provisionally. But now we see with thankfulness to God that our cares have had the end proposed for them, since the better and larger part of our subjects of the Reformed Religion have embraced Catholicism. Wherefore the Edict of Nantes is hereby revoked entirely'.

All temples were to be destroyed; no Huguenot services would henceforth be permitted in any public or private place; ministers who accepted conversion were to be granted salaries one-third larger than their former stipends and could be admitted to the legal profession on easy terms; children of Huguenot parents were to be baptised by Catholic priests and brought up as Catholics; Huguenots who had fled the country were invited back, but if they did not return their property would be confiscated; Huguenots were absolutely forbidden to leave the country or send out their property on pain of imprisonment or the galleys. Those who refused to abjure Protestantism could remain in the country on condition they did not hold any services or meet for any religious purposes.

The Revocation was greeted with wild enthusiasm by courtiers and writers whose habit of flattery had dimmed their sense of justice to the point of extinction. But heresy could not be banished so simply and painlessly as this. The clause in the Act that appeared to give freedom of conscience had been welcomed by many as meaning that persecution was over, if only they abstained from public worship. Many of the forced converts believed it was safe to withdraw the abjurations they had made under duress and to return to their former faith and religious practices. They soon found out their mistake. Louis XIV believed that there were practically no Huguenots left in his kingdom, for his agents had conspired to confirm this belief. They were, of course, wrong, and the persecution and cruelties began all over again with renewed

Fig. 3   Louis XIV revoking the Edict of Nantes, 1685.

force. There still remained hundreds of thousands of Huguenots in France. Large numbers of them found life no longer tolerable in their native land and joined the many who had fled before the Revocation. No-one puts the numbers of emigrants at less than 100,000; some believe it was as high as half a million, but the generally accepted figure is about a quarter of a million, many of whom were among the country's most skilled artisans and manufacturers, and all among its most useful citizens if the progress of French civilisation and prosperity was to be maintained.

What France lost her neighbours and rivals gained. Huguenot refugees poured into Switzerland, the Netherlands, Germany and England. They also made their way, as we shall see, to the English colonies in America and South Africa, though they were, of course, excluded from the French colony of Canada. Into all these lands they brought their energy, skills, language and culture. In the field of international politics the Revocation produced a profound change in French military fortunes and foreign policy. Since the 16th century France had usually been in alliance with the Protestant powers. She had contributed to the rise of Holland; and the entente with England, with a few lapses, had been a constant feature; she had usually been on excellent terms with Prussia. From this time onward she encountered opposition from England, Prussia and Holland until the reign of Louis XIV ended in the disasters of the War of the Spanish Succession. In France itself, the financial, political and economic consequences were unmistakably adverse, and in the religious field there were many who were shocked by the draconian nature of the king's policy.

Though the Revocation destroyed the Huguenot's religious freedom, French Protestantism survived the century that followed. In 1702 there was a Protestant uprising in the Cévennes which lasted until 1711. On 8 March 1715 Louis XIV again announced that he had put an end to Protestantism in his country, but in that very year, on 21 August, while the king lay on his deathbed in the Palace of Versailles, there assembled at Nîmes, under the presidency of Antoine Court, a conference devoted to the restoration of the Protestant Church in France. This was the first 'Synod of the Desert' as it became known. As the 18th century progressed, public opinion began to revolt against the persecution of Protestants, especially during the period between 1745 and 1754 when there had been an outbreak of oppression in Dauphiné, the Cévennes and Languedoc, which led to the efforts of pastor Paul Rabaut, Malesherbes and Lafayette in 1787 to restore some of their civil rights to the Huguenots. In December 1789 during the Revolution, the National Assembly affirmed the liberty of religion and granted Protestants admission to all offices and professions. Full civil and religious equality was finally granted and guaranteed by the Code Napoléon in 1802.

Among modern historians the Revocation of the Edict of Nantes by Louis XIV has few, if any, defenders, and French historians are no less vehement in their condemnation than English or Americans. The age of the Sun King has many admirers, and the character of the king is now regarded with more sympathy than heretofore, but there are few who admire his religious policy. The Revocation of the Edict of Nantes may be regarded as inevitable in the context of the age, but no-one can refuse to admire the patience and endurance of the Huguenots or their abhorrence of a policy which turned such a large number of talented Frenchmen into exiles and which deprived the country of so much of value to its intellectual, economic and industrial life.

Chapter Two

AREAS OF HUGUENOT SETTLEMENT IN BRITAIN

WE MUST NOW TURN to an examination of the history of the early French and Flemish refugees who came to England in the 16th and 17th centuries, and of the churches and congregations they established there, for it is among their records that we must search to find our Huguenot ancestors.

After the Edict of Nantes had been signed the flow of refugees dried up for a time. While their number was small, the refugees were content to meet for worship in each others' houses, but as their number increased they sought permission to set up their own places of worship. Under Edward VI existing church buildings were set apart for them in London, Glastonbury and Canterbury. In Norwich, for example, baptisms according to Dutch rites were conducted in St Michael Coslany; St Andrew's Hall and St Mary Tombland were used by the French. In Canterbury, part of the cathedral crypt was set aside for the French. The earliest foreign Protestant church in London was known as the Temple of Jesus in Austin Friars. This was licensed in 1550 under the superintendence of a Polish refugee named in English records as John A'lasco. Two Flemish and French pastors took it in turns to conduct services there in their respective languages, but soon a second church, for French refugees, was licensed at St Anthony's Hospital in nearby Threadneedle Street. At Sandwich the old church of St Peter was set aside for their use, and had a flourishing Dutch congregation well into the 18th century.

The Southampton church, St Julian, or the 'Domus Dei' was licensed by Edward VI and still exists. The registers begin in 1567 and continue until 1797. The first list of communicants reveals a congregation of just under 60, whose professions included a doctor, weavers, bakers, cutlers and brewers. Their places of origin were given as Valenciennes, Lille, Dieppe, Guernsey and Jersey. (It is interesting to note that at this period, although they were English subjects just as they are today, the Channel Islanders were French-speakers and worshipped with their Huguenot brethren rather than with their English compatriots.)

Before new refugees could join a congregation, they had to show evidence of their genuine Protestant beliefs. Phrases such as 'Avec attestation', 'Témoinage par écrit' or simply 'Témoinage' are found attached to a number of names. Close contact was kept with the events on the Continent, and fasts and feasts took place according to how the fortunes of the Protestant cause was faring there. For instance, there was a fast in 1570 following the prince of Condé's defeat at Jarnac, and prayers throughout September 1572 following the St Bartholomew massacre.

The date of the establishment of the Canterbury congregation has not been firmly established, but it was thriving early in Elizabeth's reign. Its members came mainly from Lille, Nuelle (Belgium), Tourcoing, Waterloo (Belgium), Armentières, and other places on the borders of Picardy and Flanders. Dover and many other ports and towns in south-east England were chosen as places to settle by the refugees. Many of them arrived destitute, especially from France after the St Bartholomew massacre. They were of all ranks and professions, including gentlemen, merchants, doctors, clergymen, students, schoolmasters, tradesmen, mechanics, artisans, shipwrights, mariners, and labourers. Such landings continued for many years, but as might be expected, the majority gravitated towards London. Here they found communities established by earlier generations of immigrants in, for example, the suburban village of Tottenham, which accounts for the presence of a French church in Soho Square today. These refugees were for the most part industrious and hard-working, peaceful and well-educated. They may have been poor, but they were also thrifty and self-reliant. Had they been weak they would have conformed: but they were brave and conscientious, and determined to make good in the country of their adoption.

One of the circumstances which gave offence to the kings of France and Spain was the free asylum Elizabeth I offered in England to Protestant refugees. They were looking for conformity not depopulation, and all attempts at flight were, as we have seen, forbidden on pain of condign punishment. But the contribution the Huguenot refugees made to the economy of England, let alone the sympathy their sufferings aroused in the hearts of a people who have always tended towards an insular distrust of foreign monarchs, especially French and Spanish ones, were powerful factors in favour of their protection by English governments. Bishop Jewell, for example, testified that 'the poor exiles from Flanders, France and other countries . . . are our brethren; they live not idly. If they have houses of us, they pay us rent for them . . . They beg not in our streets . . . they labour truefully, they live sparingly. They are good examples of virtue, travail, faith and patience. . . .'

National feeling throughout the 16th century was intense: even Elizabeth's Catholic subjects were unwilling to be bullied by Frenchmen and Spaniards. The political and religious issues thus became confused in the minds of most people, and herein lay Elizabeth's greatest strength. The St Bartholomew massacre had a powerful influence in determining the sympathies of the English people, just as 350 years later the Nazi outrages at Auschwitz, Belsen, Dachau and Sachsenhausen removed and submerged whatever anti-semitism there may have been in those areas of the country where there were large, immigrant Jewish populations from an earlier generation. It is interesting to speculate whether the attitude of the contemporary man in the street would have been more ready to accept coloured immigrants had they come as refugees from persecution rather than of their own free will.

In attempting to assess the contribution the Huguenot refugees made to the cultural and commercial life of England, it is, perhaps, worth comparing the reign of Philip II with that of his great political rival, Elizabeth I. The former ascended the throne of Spain in 1556 as the most powerful monarch in Europe; Elizabeth succeeded her Catholic sister, Philip's wife, two years later, and found an impoverished country, an empty exchequer and a divided nation. Philip died in 1598, the year that Henry IV of France promulgated the Edict of Nantes, defeated and nearly bankrupt. Elizabeth survived him five years and left a prosperous, united kingdom, where the intellect and industry of her people had produced a literature unsurpassed since, a sense of enterprise which led to the foundation of a vast empire, and the first glimmerings of what ultimately led to the brilliant advances in science and technology which continue even now. It is too easy to see in all this, as some writers such as Samuel Smiles have done, the triumph of freedom over tyranny. Elizabeth certainly encouraged freedom of enterprise, but can hardly be said to have encouraged toleration of religious opinion— certainly not in the way Catherine de' Medici or Richelieu did. Philip repressed freedom of thought and supported repression on a vast scale, but that was not the cause of his financial downfall. Elizabeth's was more the triumph of a materialistic pragmatism than anything else, but that does not alter the fact that her welcome to Protestant refugees was one of the wisest acts of her reign. The long-term benefits of her policy towards the victims of religious persecution have been enormous. Up to the 14th century, the English were a pastoral and agricultural people. The wool they produced was sent to Flanders, France and Germany to be made into cloth. Thus whenever there was a major interruption of free cross-Channel trade, both sides suffered. Invitations to Flemish artisans to come and settle in England were issued as early as the reign of Edward III, and a substantial number settled in London, Kent, Norfolk, Devon, Somerset, Yorkshire, Lancashire and Westmorland.

A similar policy was adopted by successive kings down to Henry VIII, who encouraged skilled craftsmen of all kinds to settle. From the reign of Edward VI onwards, religious persecution in Europe no longer made invitations necessary— the influx of refugees saw to that. It became in time a threat to the employment of native Englishmen, who then with characteristic shortsightedness began to complain and threatened riot against the foreigners.

For those of Huguenot descent, therefore, it is useful to know something about this movement of peoples into England and where they settled and when. Large numbers made their home in Soho and the east end of London, but others settled in the suburbs, such as Southwark and Bermondsey, where they established industries, some of which survived into the 19th century. One area of Bermondsey became known as the Borgeny, or Petty Burgundy, because of the many refugees it housed from that part of France. Joiners Street in the same district took its name from the Flemish carpenters who almost wholly occupied it. Hats and beer were two other products made by the Flemings and French in this part of London. There was a French dye-works at Bow (it is interesting to notice that right up to the present day dyers and cleaners are frequently called 'French Cleaners', a title that dates from that time). There was a French felt factory at Wandsworth, a tapestry works at Mortlake started, or at least staffed, by tapestry workers from Aubusson and Brussels.

Many of the foreigners established themselves as city merchants. Several had been distinguished in their own countries, and they brought with them an enterprising spirit which had the profoundest effect on the history of English colonisation in the following century. The contribution of merchants descended from such families as the Houblons, Palavicinis, Corsellis, Van Peynes, Vassals, Delabars, Courteens, to name but a few, to the establishment of the American colonies and of overseas long-distance trade is so great that we shall devote a whole chapter to them.

It is hard to give any accurate figure for the number of Protestant refugees in London during the second half of the 16th century, but in 1571, the year before the St Bartholomew massacre, there were in the City of London (which did not, of course, include the outlying suburbs we have already mentioned) 889 foreigners belonging to the English church; 1,763 to the Dutch, French and Italian Protestant churches; 1,828 scattered among the various city wards but not adhering to one of the above-mentioned churches; and a further 5,224 'strangers' who had recently come in search of work, making a total of 9,704 persons in all. In another return of about the same date, we can get an idea of the respective nationalities of the refugees. Out of 4,594 'strangers' resident in the City, 3,643 were Dutch (i.e., Flemish), 957 were French, 233 were Italians, and 53 were Spaniards and Portuguese.

Fifty years later, in 1621, there were about 10,000 'strangers' in the City carrying on 121 different trades. Although Norwich was originally among the most popular places for immigrants to settle, the natives of that city were among the first to turn against them. The jealousy of the Norfolk workmen against the Flemish in particular compelled them to move elsewhere. A number settled in Leeds and Wakefield in Yorkshire; others returned to the independent United Provinces of the northern Netherlands. As a result of this obscurantism Norwich declined from its position as the second most important city in the land to the comparatively humble status of a country market town. About 1570 there had been over 4,000 foreigners there; 10 years later this figure had increased by a further 700; 50 years later this number had declined drastically.

Relatively few Huguenots fled to England during the 16th century, and the major influx only began after the St Bartholomew massacre in 1572, and then was largely confined to those from Brittany, Normandy and Picardy, the provinces nearest the English Channel. The great majority settled in areas where French-speaking communities were already established, such as London and Canterbury. Norwich was not the only place where anti-French disturbances took place, however. The employment of foreign artisans caused discontent in London, too, where tradesmen sought help from the City Corporation and Parliament against what they thought of as unfair competition. The fact of the matter was that the foreigners worked harder. In 1592, for instance, the London freemen and shopkeepers complained to Parliament that the immigrants were spoiling their trade and a bill was brought in to restrain them, but it failed to be passed because Parliament was dissolved before it could be.

The policy adopted by earlier English kings and carried on by Elizabeth I throughout her reign to give help and protection to refugees was continued by James I. It is true that Archbishop Laud in the following reign tried to compel them to conform to the Anglican liturgy which, since most were Calvinists, they did not take to kindly, but when they appealed to the king to confirm them in the privileges granted them by Edward VI and Elizabeth, he did so, though with some provisos. Those who were born abroad might still enjoy the use of their own churches and languages, but their children, if born in England, were to attend Anglican services regularly. Even this concession was limited to the French congregation at Canterbury, and measures were taken to enforce uniformity in other dioceses. Many of the refugees felt that they were under much the same threat as they had been in their native country, and many families preferred to leave rather than give up their own particular form of worship. Some went to Holland, where they were received hospitably, and where they were given free accommodation, and were exempt from taxation for seven years if they would agree to instruct native artisans in the art of woollen manufacture and other crafts. The majority, however, went to America, especially to New England.

The outbreak of the Civil War and the subsequent Commonwealth checked this trend, and foreign refugees were welcomed once more and permitted to worship according to their consciences. Up to 1680 the majority of Protestant refugees came to England from the Low Countries. In 1660, when Charles II regained his throne, the relationship between France and England changed dramatically. English people often forget that Charles II, James II and Louis XIV were all the grandsons of Henri IV, and of these Charles II most resembled his grandfather, not only in temperament, but also in his policy of toleration—some call it cynicism—with regard to religious questions. Both Charles II and James II had been brought up in the French Court during part of their exile, and both felt themselves closely tied to their French cousin. Though English public opinion forced Charles II to renounce the French alliance, the friendliness between the two cousins was hardly affected. When James II embarked on his attempt to increase the power of the monarchy at the expense of Parliament, and to remove the unjust disabilities under which Roman Catholics were suffering in England, he was encouraged by his cousin, even though he may have resented the patronage and offers of help which reached him from Paris.

From 1680 when Louis XIV's anti-Huguenot policy began to bite, refugees poured into England in ever larger numbers. They were generally welcomed both out of religious sympathy but also because it was soon realised that their arrival could benefit English trade and manufacture. In 1681 a collection was made for needy French refugees and a royal proclamation granted them all privileges and immunities for the liberty and free exercise of their trade and crafts. This declaration was greeted warmly.

James II, an honest and convinced Catholic, found himself in a dilemma when the flow of refugees turned into a flood after the Revocation of the Edict of Nantes. He had come to the throne advocating toleration in the interests of his fellow Catholics; now he found it hard to repudiate this when the same toleration was claimed by Huguenots. At the same time, their presence and the stories they told of French atrocities against them made it even harder for him to admit English Catholics into the body politic of the realm. His reactions were accordingly equivocal. He allowed collections to be made for them in all churches, but he ordered Claude's book on their sufferings to be burnt and he encouraged the French ambassador to induce them to return to their native country.

The Revolution of 1688 which put a Calvinist on the English throne completely altered the political and religious situation. Once more French refugees who had sought shelter in the Netherlands were welcome in England with equal enthusiasm. The migration never lost its religious character, of course, and churches, consistories and ministers were to be found wherever they settled. Every rank in French society was represented, from members of the highest nobility down to the humblest labourer, but the great majority came from the artisan and mercantile classes. Their favourite places to settle were Spitalfields in the east of London, and Leicester Fields and Soho in the west. Spitalfields had long been a centre of political and religious disaffection and a stronghold of nonconformity. Silk weaving had been established there for more than 30 years, so it was a natural place for Huguenot artisans to go to, particularly those from the silk-making areas such as Lyons and Languedoc. The reason for the popularity of Leicester Fields and Soho were historical in the case of the latter, but there had been a French congregation in Westminster in the 1640s, and in 1682 they were granted the lease of a Greek chapel in the neighbourhood. Furthermore, just as artisans had been attracted to the east end of London, so the proximity of the Court of Whitehall and St James's attracted those of bourgeois or noble origin to the west end.

These were not the only areas in and around London where places of worship were set up, for there were French chapels in Greenwich, Hoxton, Wapping and, as we have already mentioned, Wandsworth. There were also churches or chapels at Chelsea and Hammersmith, and it is probable that some refugees settled in Battersea, Paddington and St Pancras as well as Streatham and Tooting, even though there were no separate Huguenot churches or chapels there. A considerable number of families settled elsewhere in the London region to be close to others of the same profession, business or trade.

Outside London the majority of refugees settled in the south-east and south-west of England. We have already mentioned Canterbury and Norwich; in 1626 there was a colony of foreigners at Sandtoft in Lincolnshire, who came in the train of Cornelius Vermuyden, whose contribution to English land reclamation we shall be considering later. These were not so much religious refugees as foreign workers imported for the specific purpose of fen drainage. In Cambridgeshire there were similar settlements at Thorney in 1652, and at Whittlesey in 1654, which merged with Thorney later. However, a true refuge was established at Soham, which lasted from 1687 to 1690. In Suffolk there was a foreign congregation in Ipswich in 1681, where the refugees seem to have been engaged in the manufacture of linen, though later they were superseded by silkworkers. In Essex there was a settlement at Colchester which was founded by those who had branched off from the Maldon settlement of 1686. Another group settled at Thorpe-le-Soken between 1681 and 1683 and were distributed over several villages in the district.

The earliest mention of a foreign congregation in Canterbury is contained in a letter from the prominent refugee Utenhove. It was originally a Walloon congregation, but some of the names of those who escaped the St Bartholomew massacre begin to appear in the registers in 1581. This congregation increased in numbers up to about 1690 after which it declined, according to some authorities because of internal dissensions, but the names of Huguenot families continue to occur in substantial numbers in the Anglican parishes of the city up to the end of the first half of the 19th century. There was also a Huguenot settlement at Dover associated with the foreign church there which was founded in the 16th century. Other Kentish groups settled at Faversham in the 1600s, and at Boughton Malherbe in 1682, though members later moved to Hollingbourne. At Rye in Sussex there are records of refugees from the 16th century, but there is little trace of any after about 1650. There was, however, a further settlement of mainly poor families in about 1681 in Rye.

In the south-west, we have already mentioned Southampton, but there was also a settlement in Exeter, where there were two churches, one founded about 1682 and the second a few years later. Dartmouth settlement was formed in the 1680s, but the largest Huguenot congregation in the south-west was at Plymouth, where the first refugees arrived in about 1681. Two churches were established there and a few years later a third was established at Stonehouse. There were settlements at Barnstaple and Bideford dating from soon after the Revocation, and a group of lace-makers from Antwerp settled at Honiton, where French and Flemish names such as Stocker, Murch, Spiller, Genest, Maynard, Gerard, Rochett and Kettel are still common. While on the subject of lace, we should mention another group from Valenciennes who had settled at Cranfield in Bedfordshire in 1568 which was followed by others who went to Buckingham, Stony Stratford and Newport Pagnell, from where lace-making gradually spread into Northampton and Nottinghamshire.

Huguenots are known to have landed at Falmouth in 1685, but the church they established by 1687 was closed four years later. The first Huguenots arrived in Bristol in December 1681, but many stayed only long enough to catch a boat for Ireland. A French church was founded in 1687, and though there may have been a considerable number of refugees attending it, it is probable that it was a transitory congregation, for many intended taking themselves and their families to America. The district of Bristol known as Frenchay is a memorial to them. The only reference to a French church at Taunton is that associated with Jacques Fontaine, whose son was born there in 1691, and when he left for Cork late in 1694 all reference to worship in French ends. Finally there was Salisbury where a church was established by 1689 but did not last more than six years.

As with London, it is quite likely that many individuals and family groups settled in numerous other places and were prepared to worship at the local parish church. In fact, as we have seen at Canterbury, it was often within the lifetime of the first generation refugees and certainly within that of the second that most joined Anglican or nonconformist congregations either locally or elsewhere. This and inter-marriage with their English neighbours ensured their effective integration with the native population, even if some of their manners and customs persisted here and there until the 19th century.

It would be tedious to enter into a detailed account of all the foreign Protestant settlements throughout the country. They were spread widely as we have seen, and more particularly wherever wool was to be woven into cloth and garments to be made. Places such as Kidderminster, Stroud and Glastonbury had sizeable colonies; so did Manchester, Bolton and Halifax. Calvinist Scotland had a considerable appeal for many Huguenots and small groups settled in and around Edinburgh at the end of the 16th century. Their number was increased after the Revocation and they established factories in Edinburgh and Leith for weaving Colchester baizes in 1693, and in 1694 for the manufacture of linen, with which the name of Nicholas Dupin is linked. This colony is said to have used the French language until the middle of the 18th century. A group of metal-workers from Liège settled at Shotley Bridge, near Newcastle-on-Tyne, where they introduced the making of steel, an industry which has endured thereabouts to the present century. Another group of Flemish iron and steel workers went to Sheffield under the earl of Shrewsbury's patronage: a number of fishermen from Holland established a fish-curing industry at Yarmouth which gave the English nation one of its favourite dishes—the kipper.

Besides the numerous settlements in England and Scotland, a substantial number of Huguenots went to Ireland. The situation and character of Ireland made their treatment more questionable. In the early years of James I's reign many Flemings and Frenchmen obtained grants of naturalisation in Ulster, and the government in Dublin was happy to welcome them in the southern parts of the island, but the great mass of the population had no special sympathy for them or their sufferings. Ireland was the scene of much fighting and the disturbed state of the country made it unattractive to the immigrants. On the other hand the troubles of the 17th century had left much of the country desolate, and the English government saw in the settlement of Huguenots a means of giving Ireland prosperity and strengthening the Protestant element within the population. The earliest settlements of Flemings were in Dublin, Belfast, Waterford, Limerick and other towns, but the unsettled state of affairs did little to encourage industry. In spite of this they got a foothold in Irish society and began to prosper. After the restoration of Charles II more refugees were sent to Ireland at the expense of the government, and in 1674 the Irish Parliament passed an act offering letters of naturalisation to the refugees and free admission to all corporations. Under the duke of Ormond's vice-royalty, colonies of Huguenot refugees were planted at Dublin, Cork, Kilkenny, Lisburn and Waterford, with the settlement of Portarlington under the special protection of the marquis de Ruvigny.

With the Revolution of 1688 Ireland was once more thrown into chaos. Irish Catholics remained loyal to James II, who landed at Kinsale in 1689 intent on reclaiming his lost kingdoms. The country flocked to his standard, and with the substantial help he had received from his cousin, Louis XIV, he was able to raise an army of 40,000 Irishmen. The best troops of William III had by this time been sent abroad or, like the Huguenot regiments, been disbanded. However, as soon as the news of James's landing reached London, measures were taken for their re-embodiment. The Huguenot regiments were hastily despatched to join the army of about 10,000 men sent into the north of Ireland. Their first operation was conducted against the town of Carrickfergus, which fell after a siege of one week, but not without losses on the part of the Huguenot regiments who led the assault and suffered heavily in consequence. Soon after, a Huguenot cavalry regiment arrived from England and was joined by three regiments of infantry, the Enniskilliners. They marched south through Newry and Carlingford to Dundalk where they set up camp.

James II's army was at Drogheda, where it waited inactively giving William III time to bring over from Flanders his best English and Dutch regiments. So far as he could he tried to match Frenchmen with Frenchmen and despatched agents to all countries where Huguenot soldiers had settled, inviting them to take up arms with him against the enemies of their faith. This had the effect of attracting a large number of Huguenot veterans to his standard and along with men sent from England, Holland, Denmark and Germany he assembled an army of 36,000 men. He arrived at the River Boyne in June 1690 to find the combined French and Irish armies drawn up on the other side with the standards of Louis XIV and James II flying side by side. On the morning of 1 July the Battle of the Boyne began and after fierce fighting, in which the renowned Marshal Schomberg was killed, the combined French and Irish armies were heavily defeated. Undoubtedly a considerable number of Huguenot soldiers who had taken part in the Battle of the Boyne settled in Ireland, and apart from anything else have contributed to the Protestant presence there to this day.

Before the 15th century England had been almost entirely dependent on the Continent for its manufactured goods. Only gradually did the English monarchs foster the establishment of a native manufacturing industry for cloth, glass, iron and suchlike, and for that they encouraged artisans to immigrate from northern Europe. The best armorers, cutlers, miners, brewers and ship-builders came from Flanders and northern Germany, and long before these people were subjected to persecution on account of their religion, groups of them had come to settle in parts of England. After the middle of the 16th century the skills and origins of immigrants changed, for we begin now to see more gentlemen, merchants, doctors, students and scholars among those flying from persecution in France as well as the Low Countries. The flow of other tradesmen and artisans did not dry up, but the refugees tended to come from a broader spectrum of society. Bruges and Antwerp provided cloth-workers, Valenciennes was a centre of lace-making, Cambrai gave its name to cambric cloths. Paris was a centre of glass-making and there were stuff-weavers from Meaux.

Many settled in Sandwich, which since the silting up of the river had declined in importance as a port, and gave it a new lease of life by installing looms for weaving sayes and bayes. Potters from Delft and millers from other parts of Holland added two further industries there. Perhaps the skill to have had the greatest physical effect on Britain as a whole was that of horticulture and gardening. The Flemish had long been famous for their gardens and one of the first things they turned to good account was the excellent soil they found in Sandwich. Cabbages, carrots and celery found a ready market in London and other cities, and soon colonies of gardeners came to settle in the suburbs of Battersea, Bermondsey and Wandsworth. Others introduced the art of paper-hanging, which rapidly replaced the more expensive fashion of covering walls with tapestries. Cutlers, jewellers and makers of mathematical instruments, the latter so useful in navigation, found ready markets for their wares.

We have already mentioned the conflicts that arose in Norwich between the immigrant and native populations. This did not prevent the duke of Norfolk importing and settling a body of Flemish workmen in the city in Elizabeth's reign. This did much to restore the city's prosperity, for the refugees began manufacturing serges, arras and bombazines and introduced the striping and flowering of silks and damasks, which soon became one of the most thriving branches of the city's trade. Beaver and felt hats, too, previously imported, were made in Norwich, and here, as at Sandwich, the Flemish introduced the art of gardening with beneficial results for the diet and wealth of the county. In spite of renewed mutterings on the part of the local population, the refugees were granted the queen's protection in 1570 and the foreign community continued to prosper and increase. Flemish weavers gradually spread throughout those parts of the country where sheep grazed and wool was grown, until gradually the native population learned to practise these arts and new sources of employment were opened up to them. It was not long before England ceased to depend on foreign imports of cloth and was able to satisfy demand for home-made products, as well as export large quantities abroad.

Although immigration continued throughout the 16th and 17th centuries it was not until the Revocation of the Edict of Nantes that the trickle became a flood, and, moreover, a French, rather than a Flemish or Walloon flood. The greater number were Calvinists and wished to continue as such; some were more amenable and were prepared to conform to the Church of England, and there were a few who were not so much Protestants as philosophers and scientists and as such refused to be hypocritical about their beliefs. But no matter how lightly their religion rested on their shoulders, they were no more ready than Calvinists to be dragooned into popery. One of these was Solomon de Caux, a native of the town of the same name in Normandy. He had studied architecture in Italy, was an engineer and mechanic and a natural philosopher. After seeking refuge in England he was employed at Court for a time, and among other things designed and built the hydraulic works for the palace gardens at Richmond.

Still more distinguished was Dr. Denis Papin, one of the early inventors of the steam engine and probably also the inventor of the steamboat. Born at Blois in 1647 he graduated in medicine at Angers in 1669. Six years later he emigrated and spent the rest of his career in England, apart for a short period of seven years in the 1690s when he was professor of mathematics at Marburg. He constructed a boat with paddle-wheels on the Weser, but there is nothing to show that it was driven by steam, though it is hard to imagine how it was propelled if not.

John Theophilus Desaguliers was born in 1683 at La Rochelle and fled to England in 1685. He became a Fellow of the Royal Society in 1714 and invented the planetarium, published numerous works on physics, astronomy and mechanics, and also a controversial book entitled *The Contributions of the Freemasons* in 1732. His son, Thomas, became a lieutenant-general and commandant of artillery who invented a method of firing small shot from mortars and an instrument for verifying the bores of cannon.

Pierre Desmaizeaux, born in the Auvergne in about 1673, came to England in 1699 and was made a Fellow of the Royal Society in 1720. He co-operated with Joseph Addison and David Hume on their political and philosophical works and published numerous biographies of his own.

David Durand, a French Protestant minister born at Sommières in 1680, was first a pastor at Rotterdam and, after being taken prisoner fighting among French refugees at Almanza in 1707, came to England where he was successively pastor at the French church of the Savoy and St Martins Lane. His history of painting in antiquity, published in French in 1725, was highly regarded.

Abraham de Moivre, born at Vitry in 1667, educated at Sedan and Namur, came to London in 1688, and was made an F.R.S. in 1697. He was appointed commissioner to arbitrate on the claims of Newton and Leibnitz to the invention of infinitesimal calculus, wrote on fluxions and the doctrine of chance, and in 1730 created by his method of recurring series what is known as 'imaginary trigonometry'.

Among the literary men were the brothers du Moulin, Louis and Pierre, the sons of Pierre (1568-1658). The father was professor of philosophy at Leyden after studying at Cambridge and although he spent much of his life and, in fact, died, at Sedan, he was appointed a prebendary of Canterbury in 1615. His elder son, Pierre, became an Anglican divine and a chaplain to Charles II, and his younger son became

Camden Professor of History at Oxford and published violent attacks on Anglican theologians.

Henri Justel, born in Paris in 1620 succeeded his father as secretary to Louis XIV, but left France before 1675 in which year he was made a Doctor of Civil Law at Oxford in recognition of his gift of valuable manuscripts to the Bodleian Library. He was librarian at St James's Palace from 1681 to 1688 and published his father's *Bibliotheca Juris Canonici veteris* in 1661.

Pierre Antoine Motteux, born at Rouen in 1660, was a translator and dramatist. He came to England in 1685 where he soon became editor of *The Gentleman's Journal* and brought out a translation of Rabelais. He wrote numerous comedies and was a clerk in the foreign department of the post office from 1703 to 1711. In 1712 he became an East India merchant.

Michel Maittaire was a scholar and writer on typography. Born in France, he was educated at Westminster School, where he became Second Master in 1695, a post he held for four years before devoting his life to publishing editions of the Latin classics.

Jean Gangier was an orientalist, born in Paris in 1670 or thereabouts. After studying Hebrew and Arabic at the College de Navarre he came to Cambridge, where he took a master's degree in 1703, but eventually settled in Oxford. He best-known work is a translation of an Arabic treatise on smallpox.

Abel Boyer, from Languedoc, came to England in 1689, where he obtained the post of French teacher to William, duke of Gloucester. Between 1711 and 1729 he edited a periodical entitled *The Political State of Great Britain*.

Hubert François Gravelot was a draughtsman and book illustrator who came to England in 1732 at the invitation of Claude du Bosc, who made a reputation for his engravings of the Raphael cartoons at Hampton Court. He in turn was brought over by Sir Nicholas Dorigny, a Parisian painter and engraver who came to England in 1711 and was knighted in 1720, but returned to France, where he died in 1746.

If one opens the *Dictionary of National Biography* at almost any page, one can find there a record of some French Huguenot refugee who has added to the cultural and business life of Britain; the list is enormous.

We shall consider the contribution of Huguenot businessmen in greater detail later, but it is worth remarking here that their contribution to English industry was of the greatest importance. When Huguenot employers shut up their works in France it was not unusual for many of their employees to follow them into exile. They converted what they could into money, regardless of loss, and brought it with them. Papermakers from the district round Angoulême and silk-makers from Touraine left their factories; vine-dressers and farmers from Saintonge, Poitou and Vendée left their vineyards, farms and gardens, but not their skills, behind them. The whole Protestant population of Coutances in Normandy left, and brought the fine linen industry they had created there to England.

There were similar mass migrations from Elboeuf, Alençon, Caudebec, Le Havre and other northern towns. Nantes, Rennes, Morlaix, Le Mans, Laval, Amiens, Abbeville and Doullens were all deserted *en masse* by emigrant workers in the clothing industry. The printing of calicoes was introduced by refugees who established themselves near Richmond; other print works started at Bromley in Essex. A Huguenot refugee named Passavant bought the tapestry factory at Fulham, which had been originally established by Walloons, but had fallen on hard times, and revived it in Exeter by importing Protestant workers who had escaped from the Gobelin works in Paris. Whereas before this immigration silks and taffetas, velvets and satins, ribbons and gloves, laces and buttons had all been imported, henceforth they were made in England. Featherwork, fans, girdles, pins, needles, combs, soap, aquavite, vinegar, and many other household goods that had been imported before were now made at home, with untold benefit to the English economy.

Although the manufacture of glass had been introduced into England before the advent of the Huguenot refugees, it had made comparatively little headway since the Middle Ages until the immigrants developed it. The first glassworks in London was set up in 1564 at Crutched Friars by Venetian immigrants, and a second was established three years later by Flemish refugees at Greenwich. The first Huguenot glass-makers started up at Savoy House in the Strand, but soon moved to Sussex where the availability of fuel made it easier and cheaper. These factories were soon so productive that large quantities could be exported to Holland and other European countries. Angoulême had long been recognised as the centre for fine paper-making in Europe, and when refugees from that part of France arrived in England in 1685, they soon set up mills in Maidstone and along the Darent River on the borders of Kent and Surrey.

The list of industries to which the Huguenots brought their skills is so large that it would be tedious to examine all of them in detail. Enough has been said to show that for anyone tracing their Huguenot ancestry, a knowledge of the traditional trades in which their ancestors engaged is a great help in establishing their origin in France, for there, many of these industries were strictly local, and thus a knowledge of the nature of the immigrants' trade or profession can often give a clue as to where to start the search in France or the Low Countries. It should also be mentioned in passing that many sons of both noble and bourgeois families joined the armed services, and that this tradition of service with the crown has persisted to the present day. Air-Chief Marshal Sir Philip Joubert de la Ferté and Major-General Edward de Fonblanque are two such who come to mind. Others made careers for themselves in the Church and the law.

In addition to the Huguenot soldiers who settled in Ireland after the Battle of the Boyne, mention should be made of one in particular—Samuel Louis Crommelin, who was born at Armandcourt in Picardy in 1652. There had been other refugees who had settled in and around Dublin, where they began the manufacture of what is now known as Irish poplin. The demand for this cloth grew to the point where a number of French masters and workmen left Spitalfields and took up residence in Ireland. Louis Crommelin (who gave his name to the road in Belfast now the scene of so much trouble) arrived in Lisburn in about 1697 under the aegis of William III, who had sent him there to enquire into the state of the linen industry in Ulster. Crommelin had been living in Holland and brought over other French refugees with him, and in time he became overseer of the royal linen manufacture in Ireland. His work was appreciated, for in 1701 he was formally thanked by the Irish Parliament, and 10 years later was the head of a number of settlements devoted to the manufacture of hempen sail-cloth as well as linen.

Some of these early French–Irish settlers became leading merchants and rose to wealth and distinction. It is said that the houses of the strangers were distinguished by their neatness and comfort, and their farms and gardens were patterns of tidiness and good cultivation. They introduced new fruit trees from abroad, including the black Italian walnut and the Jargonelle pear. They also introduced the 'espalier' with great success, and their fruit became widely known and appreciated. In spite of all this, and in spite of the fact that they had helped to establish the Bank or Ireland, the main area of Ireland in which the Huguenots left their mark was in the north, where the industries they founded took root and continue to this day.

In an age when the population of Great Britain is nudging 60 million it seems incredible that 300 years ago when it was less than 10 million, Englishmen should have been complaining that land shortage made it hard to support the population. All the same, there were good reasons for believing this. Animal and arable farming were far less productive than they are today; transport of foodstuffs from the countryside to the towns was slow and costly, and there was an acute unemployment problem arising indirectly from the economic upheavals brought about by the suppression of the monasteries in the previous century. At the same time, there were large numbers of wealthy gentlemen seeking profitable ways to invest their money. Fen drainage and colonisation were two solutions to these twin problems. Both provided extra land upon which to employ more labour: both were risky, but for different reasons, and in both the French and Flemish refugees had an important part to play.

The drainage of the fens was first mooted as early as 1585, but it took 15 years for the necessary Acts of Parliament to reach the statute book. At that time no-one in England had any experience of co-operative drainage schemes, nor of the financial means to undertake them. In the Netherlands the co-operative method of land reclamation or 'onderneming' was commonplace by the end of the 16th century. Ironically one of its leading proponents was Humphrey Bradley of Bergen-on-Zoom, a Netherlander of English descent. He submitted a grandiose scheme to Lord Burghley for the drainage of the East Anglian fens estimated to cost £5,000 and to bring in a revenue of £40,000. It sounded too good to be true, and the queen would not entertain it; the local fenlanders were likewise hostile to the idea, for it would have meant the end of their particular way of life which depended on the snaring of wildfowl which found a ready market locally.

The great reclamation projects of the 17th century are always associated with the name of Cornelius Vermuyden. Born in 1590, he was a native of St Maartensdijk in the island of Tholen, part of the province of Zeeland in the United Provinces. The Vermuyden family had long been established there and occupied a position of some importance. Of equal, or greater importance was the Liens family, of which the brothers Joachim and Cornelius were respectively 'rentmæster' and town councillor of St Maartensdijk. (Another prominent Tholen family were the Roosevelts.) The Liens had made their fortune from embanking the neighbouring island of Schouwen and constructing the port of Zierickzee there. Joachim Liens had married Cornelia Vermuyden, one of the Cornelius's sisters, in 1610.

In 1606 Cornelius Liens submitted proposals to James I for the drainage of the Great Level of the fens in Cambridgeshire, Lincolnshire and Norfolk. While these met the same fate as Bradley's 20 years earlier, they are significant because they represent the first real impact on the English fens of the town of St Maartensdijk and its citizens.

Although his major scheme was not accepted, Liens was asked to draw up less ambitious ones for the drainage of the Yorkshire fens of Hatfield Chase and for Sedgmoor in Somerset. In 1620 he was knighted by James I, after he had begun to drain the Isle of Axholme as the first step towards the complete drainage of the marshlands between Goole and Gainsborough.

In the following 20 years Vermuyden and Liens, together with a number of other Dutch merchants, were responsible for the drainage of marshes on both sides of the Thames estuary and in south Yorkshire and Lincolnshire. Most of these enterprises were financed by the City of London establishment. Many City merchants looked upon fen drainage as a less risky investment than colonial trade, since it brought them land and status in England. They were joined in these enterprises by members of the immigrant Flemish community as well, which included Sir Philibert Vernatti, John Corsellis, Sir William Courteen, Sir Lucas Corsellis, Lucas and Matthew van Valckenburg, Pieter van Peenen and Jan van Diemen, a member of the family which gave its name to Van Diemen's Land, or Tasmania as we now know it.

Dutch and Flemish influence in the City was not confined to the financing of fen drainage. Many of these merchants were part-owners of ships and consequently interested in overseas and colonial trade. During the first quarter of the 17th century English trade to North America, the West and East Indies was developed by government-protected monopoly chartered companies. Individual members traded for themselves under rules laid down by the corporations. By the end of the 1630s this system involved the designation of the times and distances of company shipping and the limitation of trade to company ships as well as the setting of maximum prices and quantity restrictions on the purchase of produce. The chartered companies' control of the market was supported by restrictions on the size of membership. Entry into the trade was regulated by a strict system of admission based on apprenticeship and nepotism. Since the price of apprenticeship was high, only the sons of wealthy merchants could afford it, so it is understandable that a great many recruits were kinsmen of company members. Between one-third and a half of all active Levant traders had fathers, fathers-in-law, or brothers who were already members of the company at the time of their admission. Much the same applied to the London and Plymouth Virginia Companies, the Massachusetts Bay Company, the Providence Island Company, the Canada Company, and others concerned with colonial development. In fact, the core of most companies' membership could trace family connections back to those leading merchants who had established England's overseas trade in the 16th century, a circumstance of the greatest importance to those who seek to trace the ancestry of early emigrants.

A system based on such exclusiveness soon became unacceptable to ambitious men who happened not to have been born within the magic circle. These included many immigrant merchants, whom we now see making marriages with established mercantile families, but also striking out on their own in defiance of and in opposition to the established corporations. These men became known as the interlopers, the most successful of whom was Maurice Thompson. An emigrant to Virginia when he was a little over 17 years old, by 1627, when still in his early twenties, he was regularly exporting tobacco from Virginia to Holland through the port of London. In the 1630s he turned his attention to the Canadian fur trade, which led him in time to come into conflict with both the Canada Company and with powerful Virginia merchants, among them Lord Baltimore. In later life he had trading ventures in West Africa, Madagascar and the Far East, and ended his life as one of Cromwell's financial advisers and an architect of the Navigation Acts of the Commonwealth period. Maurice Thompson's son, John, married a daughter of John Corsellis, and his daughter married Nicholas Corsellis. Among his closest business associates were John Delabar and William Pennoyer. It would be possible to cite many examples of similar alliances between native-born English traders and French or Flemish immigrants and their families throughout the 17th century. We shall consider this in more detail in Chapter Three.

Chapter Three

HUGUENOTS IN NORTH AMERICA AND SOUTH AFRICA

ONE OF THE GREATEST of Richelieu's achievements was the establishment of French colonial expansion. The Articles of Association of the Company of One Hundred Associates of Morbihan, for example, is a remarkably enlightened document, which contrasts strongly with the contemporaty English Virginia Companies in the way it approached the matter of natives of colonial territories. The fact that so many French colonialists were Huguenots who did not share Richelieu's enlightened views has been important for the subsequent history of North America.

'The descendants of the French who colonize these countries', said Richelieu, 'together with the savages who will be brought to a knowledge of the Faith and make profession of it, shall henceforth be considered native-born Frenchmen, and as such may come to live in France when they wish, and acquire property there, make wills, succeed as heirs and take gifts and legacies in the same way as true nationals and native-born Frenchmen, without being required to take out letters of denization or naturalization.' How different would the history of the British Empire have been if such had been the policy of English colonisers.

The development of the French Canadian colonies was based on Brittany, that of the Caribbean on Normandy, the main ports of departure being St Malo, Le Havre and Dieppe. The Morbihan Company did not make a great impact on French colonial development because of the provincial jealousies on the parts of the Bretons and Normans, so the exploitation of Canada got off to a bad start. The activities of English interlopers and their Huguenot associates was a contributory factor of great importance.

By the beginning of the 16th century, sailors from all the French ports between Dieppe and Bordeaux were regularly fishing off the Newfoundland Grand Banks. There is evidence as early as 1504 of Basque, Breton and Norman fishermen visiting these waters, and some of them may have been there before Cabot's voyage of 1497. In 1506 Jean Denys of Honfleur explored the Gulf of St Lawrence, and was followed in 1508 by Thomas Aubert of Dieppe, who brought back seven Indians to show the king of France.

Many attempts to found settlements were made in the early decades of the century, the best known of which was Jacques Cartier's in 1534 and 1535, but it was not until 1541 when Jean François de la Rocque, Sieur de Roberval and the Vicomte de Beaupré accompanied Cartier to establish forts near Quebec that a constant French presence in Canada was felt. The outbreak of the religious wars in the 1540s meant that it was 60 years before France attempted once more to found a permanent settlement in North America, though there were many expeditions of a more ephemeral nature during this period.

In 1555 Coligny decided to establish a Huguenot colony in the New World. His purpose was threefold: to establish a sanctuary for French Protestants; to have a base for colonial expansion; and to weaken the Catholic power of Spain and Portugal in the Americas. Coligny intended to send his settlers to Rio de Janeiro, but this failed, and it was not until 1562, when Jean Ribaut, a staunch Dieppe Huguenot, sailed from Le Havre under Coligny's orders, that there were any further attempts by the French to break into the Spanish empire. Ribaut aimed to establish a Huguenot colony at St Augustin in northern Florida, and he succeeded in settling 30 families at Port Royal about 240 miles up the coast, not far from what was later Charleston, South Carolina, though the Spanish thwarted his attempt to establish the more southerly settlement. Two years later, Coligny sent René de Laudonnière to make another attempt to settle in Florida, and he succeeded in founding a settlement at Fort Caroline near the mouth of the St John River, not far from the modern city of Jacksonville. This led to Charles IX claiming the coast of North America for France because it had been discovered by Frenchmen over a century previously. He christened it La Terre aux Bretons. In September 1565 the Spanish attacked Fort Caroline, killing 147 men, women and children. About 30 escaped, including Laudonnière and Jacques Ribaut, the admiral's son. They returned respectively to La Rochelle and Swansea.

In 1567 Dominique de Gourgues set sail from the Charente in three ships to avenge the massacre of Fort Caroline. He arrived in April 1568 and recaptured the fort from the Spanish. But it was not for another 30 years that there was anything like a permanent French or Huguenot presence in North America. In 1598 Henry IV commissioned the Marquis de la Roche to establish a settlement on Sable Island off the coast of Nova Scotia, and the following year Chauvin de Tonnetuit, a Norman merchant from Honfleur, and Aymar de Chastes of Dieppe obtained a trading monopoly and instructions to found a permanent colony. In 1600 François de Gravé, Sieur de Pont (known as Pontgravé) founded a small colony at Tadoussac on the northern shore of the St Lawrence. Four years later Pierre du Guast, Sieur de Monts, a Huguenot, was named Viceroy of New France. He was granted a fur-trading monopoly in Acadia (Nova Scotia) on condition that he established 100 settlers a year in the area of coast from Cape Breton to New York. He organised a commercial company among the citizens of Rouen, La Rochelle and St Jean de Luz, and was joined by the Sieur de Poutrincourt and Samuel de Champlain. Four years later Champlain founded Quebec.

Following the assassination of Henry IV a great Catholic missionary drive by the French clergy was set in motion in French North America, as a result of which many of the Huguenot settlers left and went to join the Dutch on Manhattan Island. There in 1614 Jean Vigné became the first Huguenot child—indeed the first European child—to be born on the island.

Among the Pilgrims on the *Mayflower* in 1620 was Priscilla Mullins, daughter of Guillaume Molines, a Huguenot. She married John Alden, the ancestor of the well-known New England family of that name, who was also of Huguenot stock. The following year, Philippe de la Noye arrived at Plymouth, Massachusetts, on the *Fortune*. Among his descendants was Franklin Delano Roosevelt. In 1623 the *Nieuw Nederlandt* sailed with 30 families, including Walloons and Huguenots. They landed and spread throughout Connecticut, Delaware and New York. Two years later the duke of Ventadour, viceroy of New France, banned all but those of Catholic faith from the French Canadian colonies. He was greatly hampered in this by the Huguenot merchants of La Rochelle, who refused to help the Catholic missionaries he sent to North America. In 1626 Peter Minuit arrived in New Amsterdam. Of Huguenot origin, he bought Manhattan Island from the Indians and became the first 'Dutch' governor of the New Netherlands.

Anglo-American commerce was founded on the fur trade but soon came to depend on tobacco as its staple product. The development of plantations was undertaken by the very men who marketed their produce, for plantation economy needed constant injections of capital and labour to start and maintain it. As already mentioned, colonial trade was supposed to be restricted to members of the great chartered companies, but by 1630 these monopolies were being seriously threatened and eroded by interlopers, of whom a substantial number were of French or Flemish origin. Samuel Vassall, the son of Jean Vassall, was a London merchant and shipbuilder of French descent, typical of many others. His trading operations lay in the American plantations, the West Indies, West Africa and the Levant. As a wholesale clothier he traded cloth for colonial products; salt and currants from the Middle East, and tobacco, hemp and flax from the plantations. He was one of the original incorporators of the Massachusetts Bay Company and one of Charles I's most stalwart opponents in the London merchant community. He spent many years of his life in New England and Virginia, but returned to live in retirement at Bedale in Yorkshire, where he died in 1667. His career illustrates the way in which such men could gravitate in and out of the establishment, for his association with the Massachusetts Bay Company was of only a temporary nature and undertaken to develop his large schemes for colonial trade. His brother, William Vassall, was an assistant in the Massachusetts Bay Company and had been in America for five years when John Winthrop's fleet arrive there. After a short stay in Scituate, he left New England and moved to Barbados, where he died in 1655. He was survived by a son, John, who was a soldier, first in North Carolina, then in Virginia, and finally in Jamaica.

Samuel and William Vassall had a sister, Rachel, who married Captain Peter Andrewes, brother of Thomas Andrewes, the regicide lord mayor of London. In the 1640s he was a partner of Maurice Thompson and others in the Assada scheme to establish a trading settlement in Madagascar. Their competition was so great that the English East India Company was forced to buy two of their ships then operating on the Malabar Coast of south-eastern Africa. The power and influence of the City of London at this time was based on trade with Russia and northern Europe. However this changed rapidly, first to an emphasis on Middle Eastern, Far Eastern and Chinese trade; then it became dominated by the colonial trading companies. By 1650 their privileges were being seriously challenged by men like Maurice Thompson and his associates, William Cloberry, Simon Turgis, the Vassall brothers and William Pennoyer, the last four of whom were all of Huguenot stock.

Between 1618 and 1650 English colonisation and the capital required to further it were supplied by men of the 'middling sort', who were usually born outside London, many outside England, often the younger sons of country gentlemen or of French and Flemish refugees. They differed radically from those who had held office in the City previously, for they were neither customs farmers, patentees nor directors of the chartered trading or livery companies. There were a few merchants like William Courteen, the son of a tailor from Menin in Flanders, who established himself in business with his stepson, Peter Boudeau, in Abchurch Lane, where he manufactured French hoods. His son, Sir William Courteen, became a leading City merchant and a prominent backer of fen drainage schemes. Other leading businessmen of Huguenot origin included Thomas Bonnell, a gentleman of good family from Ypres, and his son, Daniel, and grandson, Samuel.

Laurent des Bouveries came to England from Lille in 1568 to settle in Sandwich from where he moved to Canterbury to set up a silk-weaving factory. His son, Sir Edward Des Bouveries was a Turkey merchant; his grandson, William was made a baronet, and his great-grandson a viscount; *his* son became the first earl of Radnor. Peter Chamberlayne, a Parisian physician who fled to England after the St Bartholomew massacre, was the father and grandfather of City businessmen and colonial traders. Daniel Chamier, who helped to draw up the Edict of Nantes for Henry IV, has several descendants who settled in England; his eldest son and namesake emigrated at the end of the 17th century to Maryland. Peter Houblon, another refugee, came to England in 1568. His son became a prominent City merchant, and his grandson, James, one of the founders of the Royal Exchange.

Matthew de la Pryme, another refugee from Ypres, settled with many of his compatriots in South Yorkshire in and around Hatfield Chase following a period in London where they partook of colonial trade before backing Liens and Vermuyden's drainage schemes. There was Jan van Acker of Lille who became a London merchant. His grandson, Nicholas, a Turkey merchant, was later created a baronet. John van Sittart of Juliers was born in 1552 and fled to Danzig in 1598 to avoid persecution. His great-grandson, Peter van Sittart, a merchant adventurer, came to England in about 1670 and became a director of the East India Company and the ancestor of a family which has distinguished itself in literature, colonial administration and the diplomatic corps. The Vanneck family, ancestors of the Barons Huntingfield, descend from Cornelius Vanneck, paymaster of the land forces of the United Provinces, whose son, Joshua, came to London in the 18th century and became a City merchant and a baronet. Peter van der Putt of Antwerp, another 1568 refugee, was also prominent in London mercantile affairs and was likewise created a baronet.

It would be possible to increase this list almost indefinitely, but to sum up, these and others like them, many of Huguenot origin, were the men responsible for the large-scale speculative enterprises of the period. Many had their roots in the families of refugees who first came to England in 1568, and who settled at Yarmouth, where they earned a living as fishermen. Up to that time most of the fish off the east coast was caught by Dutchmen who cured them in Holland and brought them back to England for sale. Shortly after its establishment, the Flemish fishery at Yarmouth could almost entirely supply home demand. Some of their descendants moved to London, where 50 years later they were to be found in influential positions as merchants and entrepreneurs. With the inauguration of the great fen-drainage schemes upward of 200 Flemish families settled on the reclaimed land in the Isle of Axholme, and a lesser number on Sedgmoor and in the Lincolnshire fens.*

*For a more detailed account of those families who took part in the fen-drainage, see *English Adventurers and Virginia Settlers*, by Noel Currer-Briggs, Phillimore (1969).

Less well-known, but in its consequences almost as productive, was the illegal exploitation of the fur trade by Maurice Thompson, William Cloberry and William Claiborne in the 1630s. This exploitation contributed to the broader political and economic conflicts which led up to the outbreak of the English Civil War. These men and their interloping colleagues first came into contact with the colonising aristocrats of whom the earls of Warwick, Lincoln and Southampton were the leaders, during the second decade of the century. Together they provided the political and financial leadership for the Parliamentary revolution. Because they are typical of many similar enterprises, but also because they shed light on an otherwise obscure incident in Anglo-American history, the events of these years are worth describing in some detail.

The year 1629 was an important one in the history of the North American colonies. In March, following a number of meetings the previous year, the Massachusetts Bay Company was granted its charter. A few months later, Sir Robert Heath was granted a charter to settle the Carolinas, and in October, after two uncomfortable winters in Newfoundland, Lord Baltimore arrived at Jamestown and announced to a startled Virginia that he intended to establish a Catholic colony in the balmier climate of the Chesapeake. All these events led to increased commercial activity. The first to make a move was Samuel Vassall, acting on behalf of Sir Robert Heath. In October, he and his brother-in-law, Captain Peter Andrewes, fitted out the *Suzan* of London, which reached Virginia in December. They intended to trade but at the same time to look for a suitable place to found a new settlement south of Cape Hatteras. The following year, in defiance of the recent peace treaty signed between Charles I and Louis XIII, which stipulated that all conquests after 24 April 1629 would be negated and returned to their former owners, Englishmen continued to trade in Canadian waters. In March 1630 two expeditions set out from the Thames: the smaller commanded by Thomas Kirke and Richard Brereton was financed by the Canada Company and made for the St Lawrence; the larger was the Great Migration of John Winthrop bound for Massachusetts.

Thomas Kirke was one of the six sons of Gervase Kirke, an English merchant of Scottish extraction, who had married a French wife from Dieppe about 1595 and set up business there. David, the eldest son, was born in Dieppe in 1596, and on reaching manhood became a wine merchant, a business in which many Huguenots were engaged. By 1620 persecution in France drove Gervase and his family to seek asylum in England, where their French and Canadian contacts (Gervase had been associated with the pioneers from Dieppe and St Malo who founded French Canada) led him into partnership with Sir William Alexander, later earl of Stirling. In 1621 Sir William had been granted Nova Scotia and nearly all of eastern Canada south of the St Lawrence, and his charter was confirmed by Charles I when he came to the throne in 1625. In that year Sir William fitted out an expedition of three ships commanded by David Kirke, with Thomas and Louis Kirke. The Kirkes first attacked Tadoussac, which they burnt, and then sailed on to Quebec, where they demanded and obtained Champlain's surrender. While they were there a fleet of transports laden with provisions arrived from France, and was beaten off and captured.

Besides gaining a significant victory, David Kirke brought home a substantial cargo of furs to add to the commercial success of the venture. This enterprise in some measure was seen as a compensation for the disastrous failure of Buckingham's attempt to relieve the siege of La Rochelle, and was greeted with mixed feelings in England. Although it enjoyed the whole-hearted approval of most Englishmen, it was nevertheless a flagrant defiance of both the wishes of Charles I and his government, for while the Kirke brothers were attacking Quebec, the king was trying to negotiate peace with France. Notwithstanding, Sir William Alexander succeeded in obtaining a further grant in 1628 under the Signet of Scotland for monopoly trade in Canada. This was in spite of the recently signed treaty with France, which specifically secured all Canadian trade to the French. In 1629 this was followed by another expedition of nine ships. The Kirke's captured Quebec in June and a garrison under the command of Louis Kirke was installed.

When Sir George Yardley had been appointed governor of Virginia in 1626 he was authorised to grant commissions for discovery and trade between the 34th and 41st parallels of latitude. This included permission to establish plantations and trading posts as appropriate, and among the first to apply was the young and energetic secretary to the colony, William Claiborne.* On 3 April 1627 he was given leave and a commission to 'go . . . and discover any rivers or creeks within the Bay of Chesapeake to the head of the same, and to trade with the Indians for corn, skins or any other commodities . . .'

Sir George Yardley, acting on behalf of the government in London, and in an attempt to secure all the Chesapeake's resources for Virginia rather than allowing the interlopers to take them, gave his particular blessing to the enterprise. Claiborne set sail within a week of being granted his commission and soon arrived at a large island near the head of the bay which he named Kent Island. This was an excellent place from which to trade with the Indians of the Susquehannah River. The expedition surpassed his wildest expectations, for Claiborne effectly planted his own settlement in this hitherto unexploited region, taking for himself the bulk of the northern Chesapeake trade.

In 1628 Claiborne undertook a second voyage in the course of which he penetrated even farther north, returning with a request for another grant to enable him to establish a settlement by the Susquehannah River. He was granted this in January 1629. Claiborne fitted out a third expedition in the course of which he established a trading post on Palmers Island between the 39th and 40th parallels so, by the time Lord Baltimore arrive in Jamestown from Newfoundland, he had already gained a foothold in what was later to form part of the latter's domain of Maryland. Baltimore's arrival caused consternation in Virginia, as the Virginia Council had no desire to see a Catholic colony on the south side of the James River, which was where he was going to settle. He was left in no doubt that he must look elsewhere, whereupon he turned his attention towards the land which lay immediately north of the Potomac up to the Susquehannah, and succeeded in getting a grant from the king for this territory. This was not much less unpopular than Baltimore's first idea of a colony to the south, and early in 1630 Claiborne returned to England to drum up support for the Virginia Council and for those, like himself, who objected to Baltimore's presence among those members of the old Virginia Company who still hoped

*For further details of William Claiborne and his career, *see The Search for Mr. Thomas Kirbye, Gentleman*, by Noel Currer-Briggs, Phillimore (1985).

that their charter, which had been taken away from them by James I, might one day be restored.

While he was in England, Claiborne joined Maurice Thompson, William Cloberry and a Huguenot refugee, John Delabarr, in a joint stock company, whose purpose was to trade with eastern Canada, but by way of the Hudson River and northern Chesapeake. This route escaped the threat of attack from the French, which they would have risked had they approached Canada from the St Lawrence. Claiborne was granted a commission under the Signet of Scotland similar to the one granted to Sir William Alexander for Nova Scotia and the south bank of the St Lawrence in 1629, 'to trade in corn, furs and any other commodity in all seas, coasts, rivers, creeks, harbours, lands, territories in or near the parts of America for which there is *not already granted a patent to others for sole trade* [authors' italics]. He was given no authority by this commission to take possession of any islands other than Kent Island, which he already held, and which he had occupied and settled as a 'planter of Virginia'. As Kent Island was regarded at that time as a Virginia hundred, Claiborne was within his rights as a Virginia planter to take possession of it since it was inside the assigned territorial limits of the colony as then defined. He encouraged the government of Virginia to issue warrants for the arrest of any who trespassed on the island, which was something he could easily arrange as secretary for the colony. So secure did his position appear that in February 1631 Nicholas Martiau, a Huguenot emigrant to Virginia and an early associate of Claiborne's, was registered in the General Assembly as a burgess for Kent Island.

In 1631 Maurice Thompson, John Delabarr and another trader named Eustace Mann succeeded in upsetting the market in Canadian furs by offering the Indians three times as much as the French or the Canada Company's representatives were prepared to offer. This led to lawsuits, the outcome of which in no way clipped the interlopers' wings. The evidence from these extensive cases, which were heard in the High Court of Admiralty and in the Court of Chancery, is a valuable source of information for those of Huguenot and colonial descent.

Claiborne had made it clear to his partners while he was in London that he could not undertake more than one voyage for their joint enterprise, because a longer absence from Jamestown would jeopardise his position as a government servant there. Unhappily a serious fire broke out soon after the settlement on Kent Island had been established, which proved to be a severe setback to his plans. Claiborne was consequently obliged to seek help for his larger ventures where he could find it, and one source lay in an extension of his association with Thompson and Cloberry. Not only might he expect further financial help from them, but there was a chance that Cloberry might be able to get a broader patent from the king than the one he already had, which would make Claiborne independent of the Governor of Virginia, Sir John Harvey, and of his salaried post as colony secretary. Although Cloberry failed to get this broader patent, in March 1632 Claiborne persuaded Sir John Harvey to issue him a commission to visit the Dutch settlements on the Hudson River. With this end in view, Cloberry, Delabarr and a new partner, David Moreshead, despatched the *William* to the Hudson River and from there to New England and Virginia.

Dutch and Flemish cloth bought several times more weight in furs than common English trade goods, especially in the Chesapeake where the Indians were becoming choosy. Claiborne was in special need of such cloth because the Susquehannah Indians had become used to it from their close contact with the settlements farther north in what is now New Jersey and New York State. But the *William's* voyage was primarily designed to attempt to avoid a confrontation with both the French and the Dutch by obeying the strict letter of the recently imposed embargo on trading in the Gulf of St Lawrence, while at the same time operating into Canadian territory by the back door. However, in spite of English claims to all the American lands between Cape Hatteras and Maine, this expedition found the Dutch settlers along the Hudson every bit as hostile as the French along the St Lawrence. They attacked the *William* and frustrated the expedition, with the result that Cloberry and Claiborne suffered heavy loss and damage.

Cloberry had not been entirely unsuccessful in his attempts to obtain an enlarged patent from the king in 1631. Under the articles of association of the joint stock company, Cloberry had two shares, Delabarr, Thompson, Turgis and Claiborne one each. Claiborne was put under contract to establish trading posts on Kent and Palmers Islands, provided Cloberry got a patent from the king to carry on this trade independently of Virginia. This he had obtained in May 1631. It stated that Claiborne, in addition to trading with Sir William Alexander, could make discoveries for the 'increase of trade', but that he was not authorised to take possession of any other islands beyond the two he already held. Claiborne's disregard for this proviso by his occupation of Popeley's Island in 1631 and his settlement of Palmers Island, which had hitherto been a temporary trading post only, shows that he exceeded his instructions. Having got this commission, which appeared to be adequate for their purpose, Cloberry hired the *Africa* and placed her under the command of Claiborne. Before she sailed, Claiborne and Thompson came to a private agreement from which it is clear that the former committed himself to one voyage only, and that thereafter he would be free to pursue his own trade and profession alone.

Meanwhile Lord Baltimore's negotiations with the Council of Virginia and the crown concerning the location of his projected colony dragged on. In the end its northern boundary was pushed to the 40th parallel and westward to the source of the Potomac, and following that river to its mouth eastward across the Eastern Shore to Watkins Point on the Atlantic. Thus it was not until nearly a year after Kent Island had first been settled that Baltimore finally got his grant (June 1632). Furthermore, it was carved out of lands granted to the Virginia Company 11 years before. Not only Claiborne and his associates, but the whole Virginia Council were furious and did all they could to frustrate it, even to the extent of delaying Baltimore's departure from England by a year. Claiborne accused Cloberry of failing to fight Baltimore's claim with sufficient vigour, and Thompson agreed with him, and both withdrew from the joint stock company. This did not prevent Thompson and Delabarr sending another expedition to Canada in 1633 to forestall the Kirkes, which they did successfully.

Meanwhile in England Claiborne's quarrel with Baltimore came before the High Court of Admiralty and the case hinged upon the validity of their respective grants. Claiborne's, like Sir William Alexander's, was given under the Signet of Scotland, whereas Baltimore's was given under the Great Seal of England. Which had priority? The issue rapidly became bound up with the wider dispute between England and Scotland which led to open war immediately before the outbreak of civil war in

England. It also became another cause of friction between the Catholic Marylanders and the Protestant Virginians, while at the same time reflecting the English disputes with France and Holland over trading rights in the St Lawrence and Hudson rivers.

The case dragged on until 1638 when the matter was referred to the Lords Commissioners for Foreign Plantations, which found that Claiborne's commission under the Signet of Scotland was 'of no virtue or power' because it had been got under false pretences, and that Kent Island belonged absolutely to Lord Baltimore, and that no trade or plantations could be carried on there without his permission. The false pretences to which they referred were the inaccurate descriptions of the location of Kent and Palmers Islands, for Claiborne had consistently stated that Palmers Island was on latitude 41 deg. 30 min., which is, in fact, the latitude of Rhode Island, whereas it is at the mouth of the Susquehannah River on about latitude 39 deg. 40 min. He had also tried to make out that Kent Island was north of the 40th parallel though, in fact, it is south of the 39th. All attempts at mediation failed, especially after Baltimore had seized Kent Island and installed his own people there. And so, while in England John Hampden was about to be tried for his refusal to pay ship money—an act regarded by many as the symbolic beginning of the civil war—the first shots in that struggle were being fired in the Chesapeake. The Marylanders sent a troop of 40 men to Kent Island; Claiborne's men resisted as long as they could—long enough to compel Baltimore to send a second expedition against them—but after a few days' resistance, the island surrendered and passed under the jurisdiction of Maryland.

The alliances and conflicts among the various religious, mercantile and political factions in England and America during the two decades leading up to the outbreak of the civil war in England in 1642 are complex and confusing, but an understanding of them helps to identify ancestors who lived at this period, if only because animosities were such that people tended not to cross dividing lines in society. It is too easy to describe the revolutionary crisis in terms of a political confrontation between king and Parliament, for alongside this constitutional struggle raged commercial as well as religious conflicts. When Charles I was forced to summon Parliament in 1640 for the first time in 11 years, Puritans on both sides of the Atlantic drew together in a common cause. Many New Englanders, especially the more far-sighted and better-educated, returned home to help Parliament in the forthcoming struggle. The mercantile community was ideologically sympathetic to the Huguenots in France and hostile to the policies of Richelieu and Louis XIII. Charles I on the other hand had been rebuffed by the king of Spain in his attempt to marry a Spanish infanta, so was emotionally hostile to that monarch and favoured war with him. However, English shipping interests were totally opposed to war with Spain because this meant that the port of Dunkirk in the Spanish Netherlands would be a base for hostile attacks on English vessels. By the same token, Charles I was personally well-disposed towards Louis XIII, to whom he looked for financial help to rid him of dependence on his subjects. The attitude of large sections of the English mercantile community towards the Protestant Dutch was ambivalent on account of the long-standing commercial rivalry between them, especially in the East Indian, African, West Indian and North American trades. The Prince of Orange, Charles I's brother-in-law, claimed the Hudson River Valley and Delaware Bay, which was part of the territory James I had claimed and granted to the Plymouth and London Virginia Companies in 1606. Added to this, the Scots, traditional enemies of the English for centuries, had always looked to France for support against their southern neighbour.

In 1633 the arch-foe of Calvinism and Puritanism, Archbishop Laud, had thrown the full weight of his authority into a crusade against them, not only in England, but in the colonies too. When in the following year he was appointed to head a commission for regulating plantations he was given power to remove disloyal governors, recall and revoke patents, and to hear colonial complaints. In Scotland his attempt to foist episcopalian government on the Kirk brought about, among other things, an alliance between the Edinburgh Calvinists and the Puritans and Huguenots in London, among whom were numbered some of the wealthiest men in the land. The second of the two decades before 1642, therefore, saw the birth of some strange coalitions.* Linked to leading Parliamentarians were prominent city merchants and influential Scots laymen and churchmen; to the royalist cause a large number of wealthy, Anglican landowners adhered, many of whom were related by marriage and attached by financial interest to City merchants. In no way was the movement inspired by the masses as some Marxist writers would have us believe. The majority of the English masses had an overwhelmingly strong prejudice against and distrust of papists and all that Catholicism stood for; many rural areas were royalist, especially the north, where Catholicism was strongest, but this was not by any means confined to the labouring classes. Cromwell himself came from a long-established, highly influential landowning family in a predominantly royalist area. Many well-established City merchants supported both the king and the Laudian Church of England; just as many members of Parliament were sympathetic to the king.

This complex confusion was mirrored in the colonies. All the religious, political and commercial factors in the debate were as hotly discussed in America as they were in England. The colonies did not exist in a cultural vacuum. The activities of men like Maurice Thompson, Samuel Vassall, John Delabarr, the Kirke brothers and Baltimore must be seen in the framework of a complicated political and commercial picture. Thompson and Claiborne were puritans and came from East Anglian mercantile families; the Kirkes, born in Dieppe, were the sons of a Scottish father and a French mother, and exiles in England; Samuel Vassall and John Delabarr came from Huguenot families who had settled in London a generation before they were born. Cloberry came from Devonshire and was a royalist and an episcopalian. John Winthrop, born in the year of the Armada, belonged to the newly-rich Suffolk gentry whose fortunes derived from Henry VIII's dissolution of the monasteries. Lord Baltimore's family, the Calverts, were Catholics from Yorkshire, staunchly royalist, and bore an Irish title. Maurice Thompson, the most astute businessman of them all, became in time the architect of the anti-Dutch Navigation Acts of 1651, yet was the father-in-law of one of the leading Huguenot merchants of the day, John Corsellis.

After the fall of La Rochelle, the baron de Sauce, one of its defenders under the duke of Rohan, took refuge in England. In 1629 he asked permission to establish a colony for Huguenot refugees in Virginia 'to cultivate vines and to make silk and salt' there. His request was favourably received and he was granted letters of denization

*See The Civil War Politics of the London Merchant Community, by Robert Bremner. Past and Present, February 1962.

for himself and his son so that he might return to France in safety to get his family and property. Careful preparations were made, and in due course the expedition sailed for Virginia, settling in Nansemoni county on 200,000 acres then known as Southampton hundred. All records of this colony have been lost, and its fate is a matter of conjecture, but some people must have survived, for Huguenot names are found in early Norfolk county records. Among the leading families of Virginia today many of these names (either obvious or in disguise) can be found, among them Battaille, Durand, de la Mundaye, de Bar, Dabney (D'Aubigné), Jourdan, Martiau, Noel, Flouvier, Ravenell, Rigault, Sully, Vicomte, Vasker, Fantleroy (Faunt le Roi), and Tagliaferro (Tulliver). Many French names were anglicised, and many early Virginian records perished in the American civil war, so it is very difficult to trace Huguenot ancestry in this part of the United States, but enough have survived for it to be stated with some degree of certainty that the Huguenot contribution to the colonisation of the Chesapeake was considerably greater than it might at first sight appear from the meagre list of French and Walloon names.

Some confusion arises from the double migration of many Huguenot families, first to Holland, Germany or England, and then to America. Historians of the state of Maine have failed to notice that the founders of Dresden, the earliest settlement on the Kennebec River, were French, not German. They were Huguenots who had fled first to Germany after the Revocation of the Edict of Nantes, and then migrated in company with a few German families in 1752 to America. They had originated in the eastern provinces of France closest to Germany, and of the 46 emigrants who left Frankfurt in 1752, 28 were of French origin and only five of German. Another example of double migration can be found among the settlers of New Rochelle in Westchester county, New York. In 1689 some Huguenots from New York were joined by others from the West Indies where they had hastily sought refuge after the Revocation. However, the majority came from England and were Rochellois who had left the city four years before and fled to the Ile de Ré and from there to England, where they found a ship to take them to America.

Prior to the grant to William Penn of the region now known as Pennsylvania in 1681, there were many French refugees amongst its inhabitants. Some of their names took on a Dutch or Swedish flavour, thus adding to the difficulties of genealogists, but the majority of them lost their French identity, because they did not come directly, but through Germany or Holland, where most of them had long resided, and where many of them had been born. The names Kieffer and de Witte do not immediately suggest the original French names of Tonnellier and Le Blanc, and the famous 'Dutch' Peter Minnewit is in reality Pierre Minuit, which he found an easier name for the English to pronounce so reverted to an approximation of the French original.

The majority of the French settlers in the Delaware region came over at the time of the first general influx between 1654 and 1664. Among the records of Christ Episcopal church in Philadelphia there are many Huguenot names dating from as early as 1709. More than a century after the failure of Coligny's attempt to found a French colony in Florida, William Sayle, an Englishman, established the first permanent settlement near the site of Port Royal in 1670. The earliest settlers were a mixed lot. From England came both royalists and republicans; a group of Dutch settlers came down from New Amsterdam after the English had turned it into New York; and in 1679 Charles II sent a group of French refugees there under the leadership of the Rev. Elias Prioleau, who had brought a considerable part of his French congregation with him. In addition to these Huguenots who came direct from France, a considerable number of refugees who had first gone to New York and New England came to Port Royal to enjoy a warmer climate. A considerable number came from Acadia after it became British as Nova Scotia, for it was English policy to disperse the French there among other colonies as a precautionary measure. About 1,500 of them were sent to Charleston, South Carolina. In 1764 another colony of Huguenots came from France by way of Plymouth in England to a settlement named New Bordeaux after the capital of the province from whence most of them came. It was they who introduced the manufacture of silk into South Carolina.

Louis XIII banned all foreigners and Huguenots from settling in Canada and the other French North American colonies in 1632, which only served to ensure that Protestant Frenchmen settled in the Dutch or English colonies. Johannes La Montagne became the first physician to practise in New Amsterdam, and Isaac Bethlo, who emigrated from Calais in 1652, anglicised his name to Bedloe and gave it to Bedloe's Island in New York harbour, on which the Statue of Liberty now stands.

By 1656 the French population of New Amsterdam was so large it was necessary to issue all government proclamations in French and Dutch. Between 1657 and 1663 large numbers of French Protestants continued to arrive in the New Netherlands, and in 1658 New Haarlem was founded by Walloons and Huguenots. The next year saw the foundation of the first Huguenot church in New York, and in the census taken two years later it was found that half the inhabitants were of French origin.

In July 1621 Jesse de Forest had addressed a petition to Sir Dudley Carleton, the English ambassador at the Hague, for permission for French and Belgian Protestants to settle in English-speaking colonies in America, but it was not until 40 years later, in 1662, that Jean Touton was given leave to establish a Huguenot colony in Massachusetts. He was joined eight years later by Philippe l'Anglois, who settled at Salem as Philip English to become one of that settlement's most influential merchants. He was responsible for bringing other Huguenot families to Salem, including Jean Touzel, Jean Le Brun (John Browne), Nicholas Chevalier, Peter Morrall, Edward Feveryear, John Voudin, Rachel de la Close, and the Valpy, Lefavor and Cabot families. (It should be noted that the New England Cabots were not related to the great explorers, John and Sebastian Cabot, whose Italian name was Cabotta.)

In 1677 a group of Huguenots bought a tract of land and founded New Paltz in New York state and in 1679 Charles II urged the Huguenots of England to migrate to South Carolina to grow grapes, olives and silkworms. This was one of many attempts to grow these crops in the southern colonies, and French vignerons from the Bordeaux region, and silkworm cultivators from Lyons had been brought to Virginia in the 1620s, though none of their names are known. In 1680 there was a large Huguenot emigration to Charleston, South Carolina, which grew to a flood after the Revocation. This movement included the following families: Bayard, Bonneau, Benoit, Bocquet, Bacot, Chevalier, Corde, Chastaquier, Dupré, Deslisles, Dubose, Dutarques, de la Coursillière, Dubouxdieu, Faysseaux, Gaillard, Gendron, Guignard, Horry, Huger, Legare, Lauren(t), Lausac, Marion, Mazycq, Manigault, Mallichamp, Neuville, Peronneau, Porcher, Peyre,

Ravenel, Saint-Julien, and Trevizant. They were sent to produce wine and silk, many of them travelling on the frigate *Richmond*.

The bishop of London in 1682 sent the Rev. Pierre Daillé to minister to the French Protestants in the New World. His mission was so successful that it earned him the name of the 'Apostle of the Huguenots'. Three years later a French church was established at Boston, Massachusetts, which maintained its separate identity until 1748. Following the Revocation about 15,000 Huguenots emigrated to America in the course of the next 65 years. Most of them settled in South Carolina, but large numbers also landed in Pennsylvania, Virginia, New York, Rhode Island and Massachusetts. Though small in number, they wielded a considerable influence, as they did in England, because most of them were merchants, professionals and craftsmen. One of them was Pierre Jay and others included ancestors of the Faneuil, de Lancey, Boudinot, Badouin and Beron families. Etienne de Lancey, a native of Caen, settled in New York and became a leading merchant and the ancestor of a prosperous New York family. He imported the first fire engine into America. About the same time 15 French families arrived in New England, including the Cazneau, Sigourney, Fréneau and Allaires families. Another 30 Huguenot families settled at Oxford, Massachusetts, on the Manexit, or French River, led by Gabriel Bernon, Daniel Boudet and Isaac Bertrand de Truffeau.

In 1687 a Huguenot church was founded at Charleston, South Carolina, and there were six other Huguenot settlements in that colony at Goose Creek, Orange Quarter, French Santee, St John's Berkeley, Purysburg and New Bordeaux. David Bonrepos founded a colony on Staten Island and in 1689 founded New Rochelle. By 1694 there were over 20 families living there, and in 1727 the population numbered more than four hundred. Michel Boudin, the last French minister, died in 1766. Among many illustrious Americans to receive an education in the school there were Philip Schuyler, John Jay and Washington Irving. Its first schoolmaster was Jean Cottin, who was appointed in 1689.

Unhappily, due to their thrift and energy, the Huguenot settlers tended to find themselves the victims of discrimination by their English neighbours. In 1693 there was an outburst of anti-French feeling in South Carolina, as well as in Rhode Island, but this did not prevent the arrival of 700 Huguenots in Virginia in 1700 under the Marquis de la Muce and Charles de Sailly. They were given 10,000 acres of land along the James River, 20 miles north of Richmond, and because the land was once owned by the Manikin Indians, the settlement was named Manikintown. Nine years later Madame Ferée led a group of settlers to found a plantation in Lancaster county, Pennsylvania, with which the story of Huguenot migration to North America more or less comes to an end.

Huguenots in South Africa

With the annexation of Portugal by Spain in 1580, the many Portuguese possessions in southern Africa became prey to English, Dutch and French Huguenot pirates. The Dutch took over the Portuguese trade to India and the Far East, and in the process, their settlement at the Cape of Good Hope, which was the one point, coming and going, at which ships of the Dutch East India Company could conveniently make landfall. The English East India Company nearly anticipated the Dutch, for in 1615 Sir Thomas Roe, on his way to become James I's ambassador to the great Moghul, put in at Table Bay with four ships. In the succeeding 30 years Dutch and English ships put in more or less regularly for fresh water, and it was not until the Dutch ship *Haarlem* was wrecked in Table Bay in 1647, which compelled the crew to remain there a year, that the Dutch East India Company decided to make the Cape a strongly-held rendezvous in place of St Helena, which they had used up to then as their chief staging post. The task of founding a refreshment station on Table Bay was entrusted to Jan van Riebeck in 1650, and he established a permanent colony there two years later, thus beginning the history of Cape Colony.

The activities of the major London colonial merchants were not confined during the 1640s to America. Their growing commercial interests led them to challenge the Levant and East India establishment on their own ground. In the 1630s, Sir William Courteen had been granted a licence to trade within the East India Company's sphere of interest, but by the time the civil war broke out, his son had been obliged to give up control of the venture to some of his partners, among whom was Maurice Thompson. These men were busy at that time developing the sugar trade in the West Indies, but they were still ready to pursue projects which defied the East India Company's monopoly patent. They began colonial operations off the east coast of Africa by founding the settlement of Assada on Nossi-Be, an island off the north-west tip of Madagascar. Maurice Thompson determined to create there a second sugar-producing Barbados, which would also become a central staging post on the route to India and the East Indies. A more ambitious plan envisaged ousting the Dutch from the clove and spice islands, and establishing colonies on the coast of India. None of these ideas materialised due to the savagery of the Madagascar natives and harrassment by the Dutch.

A third ambitious plan launched by Thompson was in the field of government contracts. He developed a lucrative saltpetre trade to India with the Huguenot William Pennoyer, with whom he also became the largest provisioner of the army in Ireland. As for government offices, Thomson became a Treasurer of Customs, Collector of Loans for Holland and England in return for suppressing Irish rebels, and a Prize Ship Commissioner. As a member of the Committee for Trade, which drafted the Navigation Acts of 1651, as business associate of its chief publicist and as a brother of George Thompson, a member of the Council of State, he was able to realise his interests in national policy. He could also rely on the support of his fellow Customs Commissioners, amongst whom was another of his brothers, Robert, as well as William and Samuel Pennoyer, Thomas Andrewes, the regicide lord mayor and a third Huguenot, Samuel Moyer. As a leading shipowner, Maurice Thompson was an elder brother of Trinity House; his third brother, William, was an alderman of the City of London in 1653 and succeeded Maurice as Governor of the East India Company, and his youngest brother, Edward, captained one of his ships.

The company of Guinney and Binney obtained an order from the Privy Council in 1638 prohibiting Maurice Thompson from sailing in partnership with Oliver Cloberry and George Lewine, a Huguenot merchant, for the Guinea coast. Throughout the 1630s, Maurice Thompson and Sir William Courteen worked hard to break their monopoly as well as the East India Company's. After Courteen's bankruptcy and adherence to the royalist cause, Thompson continued to trade with the Far East, but also saw fit to join the East India Company—a classic case of poacher turned gamekeeper.

After the peace of Nijmegen, which brought the long war between France and the United Provinces to an end in 1678, the Dutch decided to strengthen the tiny Cape settlement, but the problem was to find suitable Dutch emigrants. A number of Germans were sent out to augment the existing settlers, but the solution was found among the Walloons and Huguenots who, after 1670, were fleeing to Holland in ever-increasing numbers from the persecution of Louis XIV. Some went to Brandenburg, some to the Low Countries, others fled to England and the English colonies of North America. In the Netherlands they were organised as branches of existing Dutch congregations, but there were so many of them that they became an embarrassment. With their knowledge of wine, brandy and vinegar manufacturing, the Netherlands East India Company thought that some of them, and more especially their daughters, would do well at the Cape. Those who were prepared to take an oath of allegiance to the Company were offered free passage and advances for equipment, which were to be repaid as soon as the immigrants were well enough established. Their contracts required them to stay for at least five years at the Cape, unless released sooner, when they might pay their own way home if they wished. They were never very numerous, never more than 200 souls altogether, but their influence was out of all proportion to their numbers. They were of a better social class than the Dutch and Germans who accompanied them; some of them were skilled vine and olive dressers or artisans; they were nearly all young and married.

The Huguenots in England and Brandenburg made no secret of their desire, given the chance, to return to France. The Dutch at the Cape, knowing this, thought it doubtful that they would resist their fellow-countrymen, should the colony ever be invaded by the French in a future war between France and the Netherlands. They were therefore settled in 'colonies' in the Berg River Valley and 23 families were given land at Drakenstein and French Hoek, near Stellenbosch, among the Dutch and Germans, something the Huguenots greatly resented. But the Dutch were determined not to have a French Quebec at the Cape, and so French, Dutch and German colonists were spread down the Berg River Valley to Paarl in 1688, to Wagenmaker's Valley in 1698 and to the Land of Waveren in 1699.

The bulk of the Huguenots, however, settled at French Hoek and Drakenstein. Difficulties soon arose between them and the neighbouring Dutch. Paul Roux, the parish clerk and schoolmaster, could speak French and Dutch, but Pierre Simond, the pastor, only his native language, French. Simond was given a seat on the Stellenbosch consistory, but this did not satisfy his followers, who wanted a consistory of their own. Although the local Dutch governor indignantly refused, this request was granted by the Company in Holland, so long as the French undertook to educate their children in the Dutch language. It was also decreed that the French should integrate with the Dutch and to this end services at Stellenbosch and Drakenstein were held alternatively in French and Dutch. During the 17th and 18th centuries the Dutch Reformed Church was the only officially recognised denomination in South Africa and practically all the white population of the Cape was obliged to belong to it. The earliest baptismal, marriages and death registers in the keeping of the Dutch Reformed Church Archives date from about 1665. Photocopies of the original registers are in the keeping of the Transvaal Archives. Wills were registered with the board of the so-called orphan masters from 1689 until its abolition in 1833.

Because recruitment speedily came to an end, amalgamation steadily took place, for no more Huguenots were sent out after 1700. This means that today most South Africans of French descent come from the Afrikaans-speaking section of the population. In 1708 the Drakenstein consistory was told that henceforth all official correspondence must be in Dutch, but as late as 1724, on the death of Paul Roux, Amsterdam gave permission for the appointment of another French parish clerk for the sake of the 20 or so old people who knew no Dutch. Thereafter such a concession was unnecessary for French simply died out. French influence, however, lives on in the Afrikaans language, which turned 17th-century High Dutch into something distinctive and different from the Netherlands Dutch of today.

Chapter Four

PLANNING AND ORGANISING A RESEARCH PROJECT

SOME PEOPLE will be aware of their Huguenot descent because of the traditions and history that have been handed down from one generation to another. Some will be better informed than others because they have inherited documents, paintings and other memorabilia in addition to the oral tradition. Yet others may be able to establish a direct link with their immigrant ancestor. Because many Huguenot refugees left their mark on the life and times of their country of adoption, there are biographies and histories telling of their achievements. On the other hand, those who descend from families of artisans and working men will have nothing more than a vague tradition that their family name was French, and little or nothing to connect them firmly with the distant past of France. If the surname has retained its original form this will undoubtedly have kept the tradition alive, but for those families whose name has been anglicised, the problems become more difficult and the memory of the refugee ancestry is lost. Yet again, there is the case of families who at some time in the past have married a woman with an unusual surname, where, perhaps, the fact that it was foreign and vaguely French is the only remaining clue they have of their remoter Huguenot ancestors. In many cases these family traditions include information about the part of the country with which the family was associated since its arrival as refugees, and this will be of great help when it comes to starting a search in local and national archives. But for those who have no idea of the district in which their Huguenot ancestors settled, all is not in vain for logical, progressive research may well provide the answer in the end.

The first step in all family history research is to collect all possible information from the family itself. Parents and grandparents can usually provide a considerable amount of material, though not always of complete accuracy, but which can provide clues upon which to base further research. The grandmother of one of the authors—a lady with some social pretensions, it must be said—claimed that her husband was descended from the Percy dukes of Northumberland. On investigation, the ancestry proved to be nothing like so aristocratic, for the family had been ironmongers in Alnwick for several generations, and may well have provided nuts and bolts for the ducal household, though they never intermarried with them, or, for that matter, had any contact with them. However, the Percy clue led directly to the discovery of the family's origins.

Uncles, aunts and cousins, too, may have inherited records from earlier generations which are of equal importance and interest, and which will help to supplement what has been obtained from parents and grandparents. But don't confine the search to known relatives: if the surname is an unusual one, it is nearly always worth the

trouble of writing to strangers of the same name in case they turn out to be distant
kinsmen with information unknown to you. If you can, a visit to such people can be
most rewarding, for better results can generally be achieved by talking to people
rather than by correspondence. If this is impossible or unusually difficult, then a
short letter explaining that you are undertaking a family history research project,
and including in it a family tree of that part of the family you already know about,
often produces a ready response, especially if you ask your correspondent to make
additions and alterations to the pedigree from his own knowledge. (But a word of
warning: never trust someone else's work. Always check such information to make
sure it is really accurate.) It is hardly necessary to add that a stamped, addressed
envelope should always be enclosed as a matter of courtesy.

For those with few or no family contacts, an advertisement in the personal column
of the local paper of the districts known to have been associated with the family can
sometimes yield good results. To find the name and address of these local newspapers
you should consult the *Newspaper Press Directory,* which is to be found in most
county libraries. Head the advertisement in bold type with the surname in which
you are interested and follow this with a brief outline of your research project. Most
people stop to read anything about their own surname or that of someone closely
connected with them, and this approach has frequently produced contacts which
have led to a positive contribution to family research. Do not, however, be surprised
if this produces anomalies in forenames, dates, ages and places, because much of
this kind of information is from memory, which is not always reliable. In regard to
forenames, every family tends to give its members nicknames, and someone generally
known as Georgie or Bill may have been christened Algernon or Hereward, but didn't
like either name. Provided you bear this in mind, these anomalies are not critical at
this stage, as most of the information can be checked and documented later. You will
often be shown old photographs, and whenever possible try to get copies of them, as
they will be of great value and interest when you come to write up your notes as a
family history. Indeed, this applies to all documents, deeds, certificates and the like.
Having got everything you can from this source, it is time to find out if any work
has been done by others unknown to you and to those you have managed to contact.
If so, where might it be?

There are two important books to consult as a start: G. W. Marshall's *The Genealogist's Guide* and J. B. Whitmore's *A Genealogical Guide,* which is a continuation of
Marshall. Both are alphabetical indexes by surname of pedigrees which have been
published in books, periodicals, journals and learned papers. Both Marshall and
Whitmore are of fundamental importance to anyone embarking on genealogical
research. To get the best out of them it is essential to read the preface, introduction
and list of abbreviations to understand the entries after each surname in the index.
Even if the information they contain doesn't seem to be of interest or relevance at
this point in your research, it may well turn out to be so later, when you have taken
your own pedigree back a few generations. It may then be possible to establish a
connection with an existing pedigree, which will provide valuable information about
earlier generations.

In addition to Marshall and Whitmore there are two more recent works: *The
Genealogist's Guide,* by G. B. Barrow, and *A Catalogue of British Family Histories,*

by T. R. Thomson. In addition to these books it is worth checking the general catalogue index of the British Library or, if it is more convenient, of the National Libraries of Wales, Scotland and Ireland, to see what is listed under the surname in which you are interested. There may be manuscript and privately produced works about the family which would not be included in the books we have just mentioned, for those are exclusively concerned with published works. The libraries of the Society of Genealogists at 14 Charterhouse Buildings, London, EC1M 7BA and of the Huguenot Society of London at University College, Gower Street, London, WC1 6BT do, in addition to their specialist collections of books, have large collections of family histories and related material, much of it in manuscript form. The Huguenot Society library is not open to the public, and has no full-time staff. To use it, you must first become a Fellow of the Society, and then write to the administrative assistant to obtain permission to visit the library. If a member of the family in which you are interested was prominent in national life, then there may be an article about him in the *Dictionary of National Biography,* which can be found in most public libraries. All these sources are worth examining before embarking on your own line of research.

Try to find out if there is anyone else currently engaged in research on the family name. You can do this by consulting the *National Genealogical Directory*, edited by Michael Burchall. This is at present published annually and contains a long list of surnames being researched and the name and address of the persons or societies undertaking the work. There are also many lists of 'Members' Interests' published in the periodicals of family history societies up and down the country affiliated to the Federation of Family History Societies. Finally there is the Guild of One-Name Studies which publishes a register of surnames that are being researched in considerable depth. If you are lucky in finding your surname included in their list, it is worthwhile contacting those doing the research as their archives may be extensive and could be relevant to your own investigations. Don't forget, however, that research is expensive, and that it is unreasonable to expect to receive information for which others may have had to spend a great deal of time and money, without offering to pay for it. This is a matter to be arranged mutually, but far too many people expect to be given information without offering anything in return, and this is apt to cause resentment.

Families of Huguenot descent, for the most part, enjoy a certain advantage over those of native origin because their surnames are likely to be unusual ones in a British or Irish context. As already mentioned, some Huguenot names were anglicised and if the original Le Blanc or Charpentier were turned into White and Carpenter, then you may well have lost all sight of your French origin. But for those whose surnames have remained more or less unchanged, it repays to extract all entries under it in the telephone directories of the British Isles, for this could provide a list of contacts which is helpful in defining the present-day distribution of the surname, and this in turn might indicate the original area of settlement associated with the family. To supplement this the electoral register of the most promising areas can be searched. This would certainly elicit further names and addresses. From this investigation a list can be compiled of people to whom letters of enquiry can be sent in the hope of discovering more about contemporary kinsmen and possible ancestors. All public libraries have complete sets of telephone directories and the major county libraries will have the electoral registers of the areas they serve.

Finally, a word about the spelling of French and Dutch names. Don't forget that most of the records you will be consulting, especially those more than 150 years old, will be public documents in which the surnames will have been written down by clerks and not by those who bore them. This means that they will often have been spelt phonetically, since it is possible that the people concerned may have been illiterate and could not spell their own names. During the first years of Huguenot immigration, the refugees, even when they were highly educated, would have spoken English, if they spoke it at all, with a foreign accent, and the clerks would have written down what they thought was the closest approximation to what they heard. In the case of French names, this can lead to considerable confusion. Take, for example, half a dozen of the most famous Huguenot families—Coligny, d'Olbreuse, d'Aubigné, Pinot, Crommelin and de Liques. In French these names are pronounced Colleenyi, Dolbrerze, Doebeen-yay, Peeno, Crommlang (omitting the final 'g' sound) and De Leek. Englishmen ignorant of French pronunciation would pronounce them Colligny, Dolbrooze, Dorbigny, Peenot, Crumlin, and Deleeks or Delicks. Furthermore, the children and grandchildren of the first refugees ceased speaking French as their first language, and in many cases forgot the original pronunciation of their surnames. By the third generation the sound of the name may have changed out of all recognition—especially among Huguenots who emigrated to the American colonies, where, to give two examples, d'Aubigné became Dabney and Tagliaferro became Tulliver, though in the latter case the original spelling still persists to this day.

Therefore, before embarking on Huguenot research we recommend a short course in French pronunciation and spelling, since there are several vowel sounds in French (especially the nasals -an, -en, -in, -on, and -un) and the 'u' and 'é' which have absolutely no standard English equivalent, although Scots English uses a 'u' sound very close to the French. Genealogically speaking, the 'u' is especially tricky because it is pronounced by making an 'ee' sound with the lips rounded as if you were saying 'oo', and it consequently very often gets transliterated into English as 'ee'. Thus the name Dumas, for instance, sounds to English ears more like Deemah than Doomass, which is what it looks like. Another pitfall is the vowel combination 'au' or 'eau' as in Beaufort or Beauchamp. The French pronounce these names Bowfor and Bowshong (omitting the final 'g' sound), but American pronunciation of the former is Byoofort and English pronunciation of the latter is Beecham.

There are similar difficulties over Dutch names, where vowel sounds such as 'uj', 'ij' and 'oe' have no exact English equivalents, though the consonants are close enough to English to present few difficulties, except that 'v' in both Dutch and German is pronounced like the English 'f'. This can mean that when you are searching for a Dutch name, such as Vermujden, you might find it under the letter F in the index rather than V. 'W' in German is pronounced like the English 'v', so that Wagner in German sounds to English ears like 'Vagner'. The Huguenot family of Wagner, of course, has retained the original spelling, but pronounce the name as in Waggoner, which is the literal translation.

Where French names have been rendered first into Dutch or German and then into English there is additional confusion and obfuscation. Let one example suffice: the

French name Quisingre is pronounced in French (as near as it is possible to transliterate it) Keesangr. In German it became Kissinger with a hard 'g' as in singer. When it crossed the Atlantic the 'g' was softened till the name sounded as the famous Dr. Henry pronounced it—Kissinjer.

Need one say more? Only that you have to dig deep and try to get under the skin of those who may have recorded your French ancestor's name. And if this were not enough, do not forget that 17th-century writing with its long 's's' which can often be misread as 'f's', and its 'y's' which stood for 'th's' only add to the confusion. But cheer up! There is always an expert somewhere to give you help and advice, and no matter how far-fetched and improbable a spelling may appear, if you sit down and try to work out what it sounds like, you may be able then to guess how it ought to be spelt.

Once you have got as much information as you can from your family, existing pedigrees and from others engaged in research into the same surname, it is time to organise your own records into a proper filing system, analyse the results you have achieved so far, compile a preliminary pedigree and then decide the next appropriate line of research.

Normally there are two basic types of pedigree used by family historians. The first is known as a 'birth brief' and shows the genetic ancestry of an individual. It includes details of the parents, grandparents, eight great-grandparents, 16 great-great-grandparents, and so on, and includes all the family surnames from which the individual descends. It is not, therefore, really appropriate for someone tracing their Huguenot descent unless, of course, they are searching for some very remote ancestors in the female lines who were of Huguenot stock.

Assuming, therefore, that you or your mother bear a Huguenot surname and wish to confine your research to this line only, the second type of pedigree, known as a 'drop line' chart is best for your purpose. An example of this type of pedigree can be seen in Figure 4. The fold-out pedigree shows the Huguenot ancestry of Prince William and Prince Henry of Wales and is a combination of birth-brief and drop-line, since the Princes' patrilineal and matrilineal Huguenot ancestry is shown. But if you are working backwards from a person with a known Huguenot surname, then the pedigree you require is a simple arrangement of that ancestry generation by generation through the male line only. On the other hand, if you need to work back through a few generations of other families, as in the princes' case, until a connection is made with a Huguenot surname or surnames, then the layout will display whatever male or female surnames are involved along the way, as in the example, where the princes' most recent Huguenot ancestors are underlined. In their case, they descend from 30 different Huguenot families. Through their grandfather, the Duke of Edinburgh the princes are descended through 19 generations from Louise de Coligny and through 12 generations from Catherine de Rohan. Through their grandmother, Queen Elizabeth II, they are descended through 15 generations from Charlotte de Bourbon-Montpensier; through their great-grandmother, Queen Elizabeth the Queen Mother, and their grandfather, Earl Spencer, they descend through 13 generations from Rachel de Massue. Through their great-grandmother, Lady Fermoy, they descend through seven generations from Susannah Charlotte Guinand. Through their great-great-grandmother, Margaret Baring, they descend from the Thelusson and Bulteel families.

'DROP LINE' CHART EXAMPLE

Fig. 4

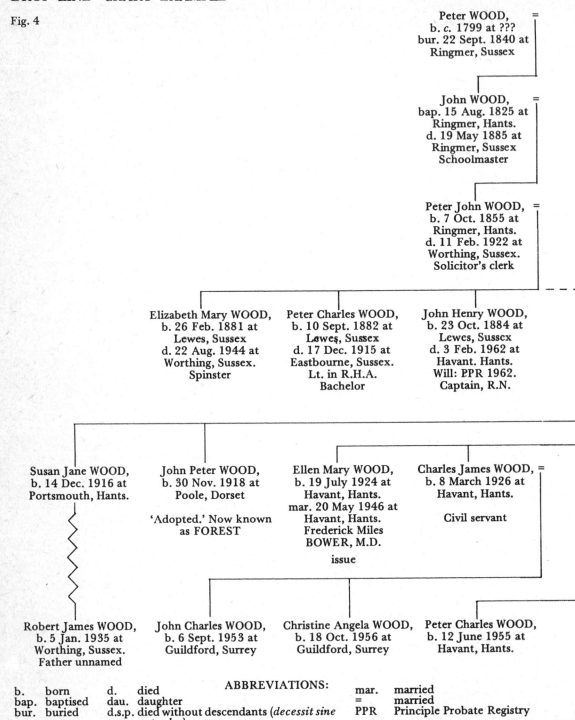

Peter WOOD, =
b. *c.* 1799 at ???
bur. 22 Sept. 1840 at
Ringmer, Sussex

John WOOD, =
bap. 15 Aug. 1825 at
Ringmer, Hants.
d. 19 May 1885 at
Ringmer, Sussex
Schoolmaster

Peter John WOOD, =
b. 7 Oct. 1855 at
Ringmer, Hants.
d. 11 Feb. 1922 at
Worthing, Sussex.
Solicitor's clerk

Elizabeth Mary WOOD,
b. 26 Feb. 1881 at
Lewes, Sussex
d. 22 Aug. 1944 at
Worthing, Sussex.
Spinster

Peter Charles WOOD,
b. 10 Sept. 1882 at
Lewes, Sussex
d. 17 Dec. 1915 at
Eastbourne, Sussex.
Lt. in R.H.A.
Bachelor

John Henry WOOD,
b. 23 Oct. 1884 at
Lewes, Sussex
d. 3 Feb. 1962 at
Havant. Hants.
Will: PPR 1962.
Captain, R.N.

Susan Jane WOOD,
b. 14 Dec. 1916 at
Portsmouth, Hants.

John Peter WOOD,
b. 30 Nov. 1918 at
Poole, Dorset

'Adopted.' Now known
as FOREST

Ellen Mary WOOD,
b. 19 July 1924 at
Havant, Hants.
mar. 20 May 1946 at
Havant, Hants.
Frederick Miles
BOWER, M.D.

issue

Charles James WOOD, =
b. 8 March 1926 at
Havant, Hants.

Civil servant

Robert James WOOD,
b. 5 Jan. 1935 at
Worthing, Sussex.
Father unnamed

John Charles WOOD,
b. 6 Sept. 1953 at
Guildford, Surrey

Christine Angela WOOD,
b. 18 Oct. 1956 at
Guildford, Surrey

Peter Charles WOOD,
b. 12 June 1955 at
Havant, Hants.

ABBREVIATIONS:

b.	born	d.	died	mar. married
bap.	baptised	dau.	daughter	= married
bur.	buried	d.s.p.	died without descendants (*decessit sine proles*)	PPR Principle Probate Registry

Mary

Elizabeth,
b. *c.* 1830
d. 12 Mar. 1890 at
Lewes, Sussex

Catherine Mary,
b. 19 Jan. 1860 at
Brighton, Sussex
mar. 2 Mar. 1880 at
Lewes, Sussex
d. 5 Oct. 1916 at
Lewes, Sussex

= (1)   = (2)

| Susanne Jane, dau. of Jacob FIELD and Mary BARROW, b. 12 July 1883 at Portsmouth, Hants., mar. 6 June, 1916 at Portsmouth, Hants. Ended by divorce; mar. secondly 2 Apr. 1919 George Arthur FOREST | Amelia Frances, dau of Arthur GLADE and Ellen BANKS, b. 15 Feb. 1894 at Southampton, Hants. mar. 8 Aug. 1923 at Portsmouth, Hants. | Charles Philip WOOD, b. *c.* 1888 at ??? d. 3 Jan. 1928 at Worthing, Sussex | = | Mary Rose b. *c.* 1893 at ??? mar. ??? at ??? d. 9 Mar. 1958 at Worthing, Sussex |

d.s.p.

| Angela Constance, dau. of Samuel BROOK and Christine BANKS b. 14 Apr. 1927 at Chichester, Sussex mar. 27 Mar. 1950 at Chichester, Sussex | Peter Henry WOOD, b. 21 Sept. 1927 at Havant, Hants. Lientenant, R.N. | = | Ellen Mary, dau of John HILL and Susan DALE, b. 16 Aug. 1930 at Portsmouth, Hants. mar. 21 Aug. 1951 at Havant, Hants. | Elizabeth Ann WOOD, b. 18 Aug. 1929 at Havant, Hants. d. 3 Mar. 1932 at Havant, Hants. |

| Elizabeth Ellen WOOD, b. 21 June 1957 at Gosport, Hants. | Susan Amelia WOOD, b. 11 Mar. 1960 at Gosport, Hants. | Christine Mary WOOD, b. 22 Apr. 1962 at Gosport, Hants. |

The broken line to Charles Philip WOOD indicates a probable link, but requires confirmation.

As Figure 4 shows, the basic information displayed consists of the full name and title of each individual, with details of their date of birth or baptism, marriage, death or burial, and where, so far as possible, each event took place. In the case of the royal pedigree where all this is easily accessible elsewhere, some of these details have been omitted for the sake of brevity. In most families, of course, there will be many fewer entries than there are on a royal pedigree because sooner or later, alas! a line will peter out if you have the misfortune to come upon an ancestor with an exceedingly common name such as Jones, Evans, Smith, or Brown.

It is customary to display the marriage details under the wife's name, and to balance this, many family historians like to show the occupation or distinctions under the husband's name. It is important to remember when first roughing out a pedigree to allow enough room to show all the brothers and sisters (as far as practicable in age order with the eldest on the left) so that collateral family groups can be shown. It is also important, as the princes' pedigree shows, to place all members of the same generation on the same line. This is not always possible, especially in cases of very large families where the youngest may be 20 years and more junior to the eldest, and could well marry into the next generation of a family or even their own first or second cousins once removed. If a neat and logical layout is not strictly adhered to, the resulting confusion is bound to present problems when it comes to analysis. By displaying the full family groups in this way it not only makes your work as complete as possible, but provides an alternative line of enquiry to push the pedigree farther back if the records for one individual are missing or incomplete.

Organising records into a filing system is a matter of personal choice. Either a loose-leaf A4 or A5 ring-binder system, or a 6in. by 4in. or 5in. by 3in. card index is generally considered the most suitable. Both systems allow for easy expansion and revision. Some family historians keep a separate record of every person shown on their charts and separate sections for information got from, say, civil registration, census returns, probate records, parish registers and so on. All this is really up to the individual, but to avoid confusion, not to mention chaos, some kind of filing and index system is essential. A very useful guide to the type of record sheets used by many researchers is published by the Federation of Family History Societies called *Aids for the Genealogist*. If, in addition, you wish to keep a very detailed archive, you can add separate albums for photographs, letters, mementoes, copies of original documents and suchlike.

Before setting out to do research in official records you will need a research notebook. This can be the ready-punched type of A4 or A5 format, which will enable you to file sheets away into your binders. On the other hand, a reporter's notepad, if you can write shorthand and wish to type up your notes later, is just as useful. You must get used to making notes in pencil because most record offices do not allow the use of pens of any sort. Always take a note of the type of record you are examining, i.e., civil registration, census return and so on, and the date the research was undertaken. This is important because you may need to re-examine such records when you have more knowledge of the family, and important clues can be missed if, when you read your notes years after they were made, you may not be quite sure whether the first examination of the records revealed everything of significance. Greater familiarity with the subject of your research and subsequent information could make a re-examination worthwhile, for entries which meant nothing on the first occasion can assume great significance later on when you know so much more than you did then.

Always make a note of the official reference number of the documents you are looking at, or, in the case of books, the name of the author, date and place of publication, volume and page number, as these are important if you ever need to refer back, and they add authority when quoted in support of statements you make in your family history when you come to write it. You should also make a note of the years you have covered in your search, for it is just as important to record a 'nil' return as a positive one, and it avoids the possible need for a duplication of work in the future. In this connection it is important to note any missing periods in the originals when you are taking notes from printed or typescript transcriptions, in case you can cover these by using other records. This is especially the case in parish register transcripts, where bishops' transcripts can sometimes fill in gaps in the registers themselves. Whenever there is a doubt try to get a sight of the original document, or at least a xerox copy. This is particularly true of computerised records such as the Mormon microfiche indexes.

If you come across references to the surname you are researching which do not appear relevant at the time, take a note of them all the same: they may become significant later. Copy all entries in full and exactly as written or printed, except, perhaps, in the case of wills, where it may not always be necessary to copy all the repetitive legal phraseology, or the declaration of faith with which so many ancient wills begin. If there is no declaration, however, this may be significant, as it might indicate religious nonconformity and its absence should therefore be noted. Wherever possible get very lengthy documents photocopied so that you can study them at leisure at home.

Finally, each step in your research will require analysis so that you can determine what is known and unknown, and hence the direction of your next line of enquiry. Try to resolve each problem by using the records available at the appropriate record office. If you are starting your search from yourself your earliest known ancestor may be your grandfather or great-grandfather. For those born since 1945 this means that you are likely to be looking for the birth of someone born between 1860 and 1900. Usually his age at death will be known approximately—say seventy to eighty. The date of birth of his children is more likely to be known with accuracy, so one has an indication of when he might have married from the date of his eldest child. If the maiden name of his wife is also known, then it should not be too difficult to obtain a copy of their marriage certificate, from which his age may be accurately discovered (though often it is given just as 'of full age') and this enables you to trace his date of birth and obtain his birth certificate. Having got this, search the years before and after to see if you can find any brothers and sisters. By repeating this process you can take the pedigree back, with luck, to people born during the first half of the 19th century. After that you move out of the realm of centralised records into that of local records and parish registers become your primary source.

A further word of advice: do not make your searches too limited; spread them if necessary to five or ten years either side of the year in which you expect to find the entry to ensure the maximum chance of success. It is not unknown for elderly gentlemen to marry and beget children in their 50s, 60s and 70s, and this could explain why an entry cannot be found in the year that you would expect.

Chapter Five

BRITISH RESEARCH SOURCES

THE THIRD STAGE of any genealogical research project is by far the most complex and time-consuming, and consequently requires a separate section to itself. Once all possible information has been obtained from private, family sources and some official archives, it is probable that you will have been able to reconstruct a four- to six-generation pedigree taking your ancestry back to the early years of the last century. Although we have already briefly mentioned official archives, by which we mean the civil registration of births, marriages and deaths and census returns, we must now consider these a little more closely before passing on to other research sources in Britain. Official leaflets are obtainable from the appropriate record office describing the records available, the fees involved for examining them, and, in some cases, useful hints and advice for users. The chief record offices are: for England and Wales, the General Register Office, St Catherine's House, 10 Kingsway, London, WC2B 6JP; for Scotland, the General Register Office for Scotland, New Register House, Edinburgh, EH1, 3YT; for Northern Ireland, the Registrar-General's Office, Oxford House, Chichester Street, Belfast, BT1 4HL; and for the Irish Republic, Oifig An Ard-Chláraitheora, Custom House, Dublin 1.*

Civil registration for England and Wales started on 1 July 1837 and the registration districts were based on the Poor Law Unions. Maps showing these boundaries for the periods 1837–1851 and 1852–1946 can be obtained from the Institute of Heraldic and Genealogical Studies, Northgate, Canterbury, Kent, CT1 1BA, or the Society of Genealogists in London. The original certificates are kept locally and copies sent to London where indexes are compiled covering England and Wales which can be examined free of charge. It is possible to obtain copies of original certificates from the local Superintendent Registrar's Office or copies of the copy certificate from London. At first sight this may seem ridiculous, but it is not unknown for errors to occur in the copies deposited and indexed in London, and in cases of doubt a sight of a photo-copy of the original might be helpful. In each case appropriate fees are payable.

The indexes are divided into years and sub-divided into quarters, so that events registered between 1 January and 31 March are in the March quarter and so on. The four sub-divisions are known as March, June, September and December quarters. Don't forget that the events are listed in the quarters according to the date of registration and *not* the date of the event. Confusion and frustration can result if the searcher does not bear this simple fact in mind. It was not unknown during the two World Wars

*Note that both Belfast and Dublin offices have records for the whole of Ireland up to 31 December 1921, but from 1 January 1922 the records in Dublin only cover the republic and those of Belfast the six counties of Ulster.

for registration of births and deaths to be long delayed, and cases are known where children born during the blitz were not registered until many years afterwards. These, of course, are extreme cases, but if you cannot find an expected event in the quarter in which you believe it occurred, you should search in several subsequent and previous quarters to make sure there has not been an error in your information or a delay in registering the event. Entries are arranged alphabetically by surname and each surname alphabetically by the first forename. Only the first two forenames are usually shown, with any others indicated by initials. In all entries the surname and forename(s) are followed by the name of the district in which the event was registered, and that is followed by the volume and page numbers. So to get a copy certificate you need to note the year, the quarter, the surname, the forename(s), the district, the volume, and the page numbers, as these must be included on the application form. For genealogical purposes full certificates are required for they contain more information than the short ones which one needs for passports, pensions and the like. Further details about civil registration can be found in the authors' *Debrett's Family Historian*, published in 1981.

In addition to records of births, marriages and deaths, there are other records which should be mentioned, as they can prove useful in certain circumstances. These are Records of Still-Births registered in England and Wales since 1 July 1927; Records of Births and Deaths at Sea since 1 July 1837 (Marine Register Books); Records of Births and Deaths in Aircraft since 1949 (Air Register Books); Service Records of Births, Marriages and Deaths of members of the armed forces and certain other persons (army registers date mainly from 1881, but some registers extend as far back as 1761; Royal Air Force returns date from 1920); Consular returns of Births, Marriages and Deaths since July 1849; Miscellaneous Records of Births, Baptisms, Marriages, Deaths and Burials; and Records of Adoptions from 1 January 1927.

For those who need to look for divorce records, these are kept at Somerset House in London and go back to 1857. They are not indexed, so it is necessary to know the full name of at least one of the parties and the approximate date of the divorce. The officials will then check their records and will provide a copy of the decree nisi and absolute for a fee. Before 1857 divorce was only obtainable by special act of Parliament. Since this was extremely expensive, only the rich could afford it. Consequently most couples who could no longer stand living together just parted and lived with their lovers as man and wife, but without going through the formality of marriage. This practice continues to the present day, which is why it is sometimes impossible to find any record of a marriage for a couple whose names appear on the birth certificates of their children. Although it is strictly illegal to give the names of both parties in cases where the children are illegitimate, this deception has frequently happened in the past, and is likely to happen again in the future. In addition to divorce, couples could ask the Church to have their marriage annulled on grounds of non-consummation or consanguinity, but as this was extremely difficult very few marriages ended in this fashion in Britain, though in Catholic countries it was much more common.

In Scotland civil registration began on 1 January 1855, and in Ireland on 1 January 1864, though registers of Protestant marriages started there in April 1845. Civil registration records in the Isle of Man are housed in the General Registry, Finch Road, Douglas, Isle of Man, and for the Channel Islands applications should be made to: The Clerk to the State, Court House, Alderney; The Greffe, Royal Court House, St Peter Port, Guernsey; State Offices, Royal Square, Jersey; The Greffier, Sark.

Although the records we have been considering are official, errors, as we have already mentioned, do creep in. This is something of which those of Huguenot descent with non-English names must be aware. Errors can be due to bad hand-writing, deaf vicars, and carelessness, not to mention deliberate falsification, as in the case of unmarried parents, such as we have just described. You must therefore use your ingenuity to the full, and check every possible variant of the names in which you are interested. The story of the vicar who christened twins Steak and Kidney when he should have baptized them Kate and Sidney is no doubt apocryphal, but by no means impossible.

Another pitfall concerns ages. People are notoriously sensitive about their age, and many an ageing bride has pretended to be younger than she was. If, after searching far beyond the expected date, you can still find no record of the event, there remains the possibility that it took place abroad outside British jurisdiction. Jobs often take people overseas, where they meet and marry natives from the country in which they are stationed.

Finally, always make a note of the addresses shown on certificates, for these will come in useful when you begin to search Census Returns. You should also note religious denominations on marriage certificates as this will help you when you come to search in parish records. Likewise keep a note of witnesses, who may perhaps be close kinsfolk, and help to lead you to the discovery of related families.

Census Records

In 1750 it was first proposed to hold censuses every 10 years, but, as so often happens in Britain, it took another 50 years before the first one was held in 1801. Since then censuses of ever-increasing inquisitiveness have been held every 10 years, except in 1941, when the country had its back to the wall in World War Two. The censuses of 1801, 1811, 1821 and 1831 are of no use to genealogists, for they only included the number of people resident in districts and towns, and not their names or any details about them. Because they are subject to closure for 100 years, the most recent census to which the researcher has access is that of 1881, so, in practical terms, the genealogist has, at the time of writing, only five returns from which he can gain useful information about his family, namely those for 1841, 1851, 1861, 1871 and 1881. The dates on which these censuses were taken can be of importance in family research, so it is as well to state them. They are 7 June, 1841, 30 March 1851, 7 April 1861, 2 April 1871 and 3 April 1881. The original returns are at the Public Record Office in London, but to prevent their deterioration they have been microfilmed and it is these which we now consult. The P.R.O. search room is at present in the Land Registry Building in Portugal Street, behind the Law Courts in London, conveniently close to the General Register Office in Kingsway, and no reader's ticket is required, as is the case for the rest of the public record collections in Chancery Lane and the Public Record Office at Kew. However, most, if not all county record offices, and many of the chief public libraries up and down the country, have copies of the returns for their locality, which is handy for those who live far from London. A useful guide to these local holdings is a small book by J. S. W. Gibson entitled *Census Returns 1841–1881 on microfilm*.

Not all these returns are of equal genealogical value. The 1841 census required information about where people lived, their names, profession or trade, but the age of all those over 15 was rounded down, so that those aged between 15 and 19 were shown as 15, those aged 20 to 24 as 20, and so on. For those under 14 the age to the nearest year was given. People were asked whether they were born inside or outside the county, in Scotland, Ireland or 'Foreign Parts'. Thus the precise parish was omitted, so the returns are of little or no help in tracing the place of origin of those whose names appear in them. This omission was corrected in 1851. In addition to the address and name of each person living in the house, their relationship to the head of the household is given, their 'condition', i.e., whether married, unmarried, widowed and so on, their age to the nearest year, profession or occupation, and place of birth. These particulars were required in 1861, 1871 and 1881.

As with all records, there are a number of points to watch for when using census returns. The final returns which you will see were made up from schedules completed by the householders themselves, and because many of these were illiterate in the 19th century, the enumerator had to complete them from verbal information which might or might not be accurate. For instance, ages are often incorrect; so are forenames, for very often the one used by an individual is different from the one he was given at baptism. There are also copying errors.

The returns for small towns and villages are not only easier to examine, but they may well reveal the existence of other families of the same surname or trade; for London and the large industrial towns of the North and Midlands, this factor is less important and much more difficult to elucidate. There are street indexes for London and the major cities, which are linked to enumerators' districts, and it is as well to examine these before embarking on what will otherwise be a long and possibly frustrating search. If you have an idea of the precise address of the people you are looking for, this examination will save you a great deal of time, for it frequently happens that in a long street in a large city, the task of enumerating will have been allocated to several enumerators, and the houses on one side or end of a street may not be found in the particulars of the other side or end of it.

If you do not find your family in the parish registers of the place named in the census returns, you should examine those of the neighbouring parishes, because some people gave the name of their nearest market town as their birthplace. For example, people in Sewards End or Wendens Ambo might say they came from Saffron Walden.

Although the addresses of members of a family can usually be obtained from documents kept by the family or from civil registration certificates, it may be worth consulting local directories, of which large numbers were published in the 19th century, for families have a habit of moving house at fairly frequent intervals, even if they do not move out of the town. Most county record offices and public libraries have collections of the directories of their own areas, and the Guildhall Library in London has a very large collection covering most of the country.

If you think it essential for your search to obtain information from census returns later than 1881, you can get them by writing to the G.R.O., *not* the Public Record Office, and paying a fee, though you must show that you are a direct descendant of the person you are looking for, and you must give his or her precise name and address.

You will be asked to sign a declaration stating that the information will not be used for purposes of litigation.

We hardly need to say that when examining census returns that you should note the reference number of the microfilm reels, the name of the village or town, the schedule number, page number and the names of all the other people in the house on the night the census was taken. You should also make a note of negative results to avoid wasting time at a later stage, when you might otherwise forget that you have already searched the records of that particular town or village many years before. Finally, you should be aware that some family history societies in Britain and overseas have started to index census returns, and although this is far from being a complete coverage, you may wish to find out what is so far available. If so, you should consult J. S. W. Gibson's booklet entitled *Marriage, Census and Other Indexes*.

The census returns for Scotland available for public inspection were held on the following dates: 7 June 1841, 31 March 1851, 8 April 1861, 3 April 1871, 4 April 1881, and 5 April 1891. These are to be found at the General Register Office in Edinburgh. Almost all the Irish census returns were destroyed in the troubles of 1922, but the surviving records up to 1911 can be seen in Dublin at the Irish Public Record Office. Census returns for the Channel Islands and the Isle of Man are to be found at the P.R.O. in London, or the Manx Museum in Douglas.

Probate Records

Before we look at parish records, it might be as well to examine wills and testaments, since these are probably the most valuable family records there are, because those who make wills usually know a good deal about the people to whom they leave bequests. Originally a will indicated the way a person wished to dispose of his real estate after death, and a testament related to his goods and chattels, moveable and personal objects. Under the Statute of Wills of 1540 the legal disposal of people's estates was codified, and from that time onward the will and testament became a single document. On the death of the testator the executors named in the will were responsible for proving it in the appropriate ecclesiastical probate court. In the case of those dying intestate, this function was carried out by an administrator, usually the next of kin. It is not appropriate in a book dealing mainly with the search for Huguenot ancestors to go into the question of probate records in great depth, for this has been dealt with extensively elsewhere, and especially in the authors' former work on family history mentioned above. All we need to do here is draw the reader's attention to two vitally important reference books to help him find the wills of his ancestors. These are *Wills and their Whereabouts*, by A. J. Camp, and *Wills and Where to Find Them*, by J. S. W. Gibson. To these we might add the latter author's *Probate Jurisdictions* which is a useful additional guide.

Since 12 January 1858 all wills in England and Wales have been proved and kept in the Principal Probate Registry at Somerset House, where the indexes are, and where the documents themselves can be seen. Before this date the proving of wills and the granting of administration lay with the ecclesiastical courts and some manorial courts. The factors determining in which court a grant of probate should be made depended on the size and location of the estate as much as upon the place where the person died, so anyone searching for a will proved before 1858 has to decide in which court the grant was made and where the records of that court are now kept. Broadly speaking he must look in the diocesan records of the district in which the person lived and died, in the records of the Prerogative Courts of Canterbury and York and in the records of a miscellaneous collection of ecclesiastical and manorial authorities where wills were proved. Luckily the majority of these records have now been indexed and the records in question deposited either at the P.R.O. in London, the Borthwick Institute in York, or the various county and diocesan record offices up and down the country. The records of the Prerogative Court of Canterbury (P.C.C.) cover the period from 1383 to 1858 and are to be found in the P.R.O. in London. Printed indexes exist up to the end of the 17th century, and those for the 18th are in the course of production. Manuscript indexes, however (PROB 12) are on the open shelves at the P.R.O. and can be consulted there, but it must be realised that they are arranged year by year, so a long search involves the examination of many volumes of index.

Until 1782 it was obligatory for executors to return an inventory of the deceased's goods. These are sometimes attached to the wills, but more often they are kept separately. In some cases inventories have survived where wills have not, and they can provide useful additional information, though little of it of a directly genealogical character. Where wills were contested there may remain records of the resulting litigation. These, if any, are to be found in PROB 29 and PROB 33. The Death Duty Registers (IR 26 and IR 27) are useful as a means of finding out where a will was proved or administration granted. They also give additional information about estates and legatees, the latter being especially useful when the will only contains a vague phrase such as 'to my surviving children' as the registers list them all by name. These registers start in 1796 and continue to 1894, but they are subject to closure for 125 years. As in the case of the later census returns, information is given on the closed registers to direct descendants or heirs on application to the Capital Taxes Office. A useful work dealing with these public records is *Tracing Your Ancestors in the Public Record Office*, by J. Cox and T. Padfield. A companion work dealing with probate records at the Borthwick Institute of Historical Research, St Anthony's Hall, York, is *A Guide to Genealogical Sources in the Borthwick Institute of Historical Research*, by C. C. Webb.

For the records of the lower ecclesiastical courts you should go first to your county record office for help in finding their whereabouts. Here you will be told where to find them even if they have not been deposited there. Some collections of wills are to be found in the Bodleian Library, Oxford, the Cambridge University Library, and the National Library of Wales at Aberystwyth. Scottish wills can be found by applying to the General Register Office in Edinburgh, and Irish ones by applying to the P.R.O. of Ireland, Four Courts, Dublin 7, and/or the P.R.O. of Northern Ireland, 66 Balmoral Avenue, Belfast, BT9 6NY. For the Channel Islands, some wills are to be found at Winchester, but from 1660 those for Jersey are at the Judicial Greffe, Royal Court, Jersey; those for Guernsey at the Dean of Guernsey, 12 New Street, St Peter Port, and also at the Greffe, Royal Court, Guernsey for some wills proved after 1841. Probate records for the Isle of Man from 1628 to 1846 are kept at the Manx Museum, Douglas, and from 1847 onwards in the Deeds Registry, General Registry, Isle of Man.

Parish Registers

Having exhausted civil registration sources, we have now reached a point where the pedigree has been taken back to people born in the early part of the 19th or later part of the 18th centuries. With luck we shall have discovered the area, and perhaps the parish or parishes in which they were living at that time. This could be the same or close to the district in which your Huguenot ancestors first settled. A clue to this can be found in the frequency with which the surname occurs in the county or city.

One of the best aids to discovering which area is the most likely one is the Mormon International Genealogical Index (I.G.I.), formerly known as the Computer File Index (C.F.I.). This contains over 33 million names for England alone, and has sections for Wales, Scotland, Ireland, the Channel Islands, and the Isle of Man, as well as for many European countries and America. The index is on microfiche and the British part of it contains mostly births, christenings and marriages before 1875 culled from published and unpublished parish registers. The index is arranged county by county and entries are shown alphabetically by surname, followed by the first name or names, father, mother, or spouse; sex, which also covers marital relationship; type of record being dealt with; event date, with entries arranged in chronological order within each surname and forename; town or parish, which may also give the name of the church and/or denomination; and the source from which the record was taken into the computer. Useful as the I.G.I. undoubtedly is, we must stress that it is a finding aid only, and all entries must be checked against the original parish register entries. You should also be aware of the fact that it is by no means a complete coverage of all parish registers. For fuller details, you should get a copy of J. S. W. Gibson's guide, *Where to find the International Genealogical Index.*

Generally speaking, however, the I.G.I. can be found at Mormon branch libraries in Bristol, Huddersfield, Loughborough, London, Southampton, Sunderland, Merthyr Tydfil, and Belfast. Some county record offices and a few family history societies have the whole or part of the I.G.I. (often for their own and immediately neighbouring counties). The I.G.I. is available for examination at the Society of Genealogists for members. Print-outs can be obtained for sections or specific frames of the I.G.I. for a fee from either the Society of Genealogists, the Birmingham and Midland Society for Genealogy and Heraldry, the L.D.S. Church Genealogical Society, and also from the British Isles Microfilm Ordering Centre, Huddersfield. All enquiries should be accompanied by a stamped addressed envelope for the reply.

We have already mentioned the value of unpublished family histories. Many of these may be found in county record offices, and it is at this stage of your search that you should start to study the local history of the district from which your Huguenot ancestors came, or more precisely, where they settled once they had come to Britain. Parish registers are not, of course, the only parish records which have survived, although they are the most important for ancestry research. The earliest start in 1538, but not all of them have survived from that date. As the bulk of the Huguenot refugees did not arrive in Britain until more than a century later, this is not a problem which greatly affects those in search of Huguenot ancestry. Nevertheless, for those whose families migrated before the Revocation of the Edict of Nantes, it should be pointed out that the period between 1645 and 1660 presents problems, since during the Commonwealth period many of the clergy were forced to leave their parishes, and the keeping of registers was often temporarily abandoned. Justices of the Peace were appointed to perform marriages, and were theoretically responsible for recording births and burials as well. But where the parish priest had taken the registers with him, these were not entered into the parish books, with the result that many have been lost.

In 1678 an Act requiring the dead to be buried in woollen shrouds resulted in a temporary decline in the number of burials recorded, for the poor were unable to afford what amounted to a tax on funerals, and disposed of their dead illegally and privately. In 1694 a tax was imposed on all entries in parish registers, which meant that baptisms and marriages declined in number.

After this Act was repealed in 1702, however, some families brought all their children to be baptised in a group, and in such cases their ages were not always given so that their years of birth are hard to determine. On 1 January 1752 the Gregorian (New Style) calendar was introduced. We shall deal with this problem in more detail in Chapter Seven. All we need to point out here is that 2 September 1752 was followed immediately by 14 September, and that any document dated from 3 to 13 September 1752 is an obvious forgery, for these dates never existed in Britain.

In 1753 Lord Hardwick's Marriage Act was introduced under which printed marriage registers were instituted from 1 January 1754. These included not only the names of the parties, but their abodes, marital status, and sometimes their occupations. They also show if the banns had been read, whether a licence had been obtained, and the name of the officiating minister. The Act also laid down that all marriages, except those of Quakers and Jews, must be performed in the parish church and must be by banns or licence.

In 1783 a duty was once more imposed on parish register entries, but as previously, it was soon (1794) repealed. In 1812 George Rose's Act introduced printed registers for baptisms and burials, bringing these into line with the marriage registers. These registers give much the same information as we now find on birth certificates.

We should mention a few further points regarding banns and marriage licences. Banns were called in one parish church if both parties lived in that parish, but if they were from different parishes, the banns were called in both, and a certificate was taken from the parish where the marriage was *not* held to the one where the ceremony was to take place. It was the usual custom for the marriage to take place in the bride's parish, though the couple often returned to the bridegroom's parish to live and work. Consequently it is usual to find the baptisms of the children in the father's parish, though many couples took their first child to be baptized in the bride's parish.

Marriage licences avoided publicity, did not require the three weeks' waiting period as with banns, and were much favoured by nonconformists. The documents of greatest use to the genealogist are not the marriage licences themselves, but the allegations and bonds which preceded the granting of the licence. The date of the allegation was normally not more than a few days before the marriage, and it gives a considerable amount of information not available in the marriage register entry, such as age, occupation, father's name, and so on. It often gives a clue to the parish in which the marriage took place, if this is not otherwise known.

As a result of the Parochial Records Measure of 1 January 1979, a considerable number of old parish registers have now been deposited at the appropriate record office. It is therefore necessary to enquire there before writing to the priest in charge of the parish itself. If the county record office does not hold the register in question, it will know where it is, and may have copies of it such as Bishops Transcripts or more recent transcriptions. There are a number of books and guides to help searchers find parish registers, the best of which is the *National Index of Parish Registers,* by D. J. Steel, of which Volume I covers sources for births, marriages and deaths before 1837 and Volumes IV to XI inclusive will give details of what is available for every parish in each county. Some of these books are already in print, though the series is still far from complete. Books showing the location of registers entitled *Original Parish Registers* have been published by Local Population Studies, and other useful guides are N. H. Graham's 'Parish Registers, Copies and Indexes' for the London area, and the *Phillimore Atlas and Index of Parish Registers,* edited by Cecil Humphery-Smith, which consists of county parish maps which show the pre-1832 parochial boundaries together with a topographical map of each county in 1834 and an index of the where-abouts of the records to which the maps relate. To determine the location of a parish Lewis's *Topographical Dictionary,* though published in the last century, is still an essential tool for the ancestry researcher. Finally, we should mention J. S. W. Gibson's guide to *Bishops' Transcripts and Marriage Licences* which helps to locate them county by county.

There are a number of marriage indexes available, the best known of which is Boyd's, though this is only available to members of the Society of Genealogists. There is also the Pallot Index owned by the Institute of Heraldic and Genealogical Studies in Canterbury, and several family history societies are compiling their own marriage indexes. Once more we refer readers to a Gibson guide—*Marriage, Census and Other Indexes for the Family Historian.* The Society of Genealogists also publishes guides to its holdings.

In Scotland parish registers, or Old Parochial Registers as they are called, were introduced in 1558 and most can be found by enquiring at the New Register House in Edinburgh. Irish registers were introduced in 1634, but a great many perished during the troubles in 1922, and enquiries should be made to the Public Record Office in Dublin. Isle of Man registers can be traced by enquiring at the General Registry in Douglas, and in the Channel Islands by writing to the rectors of the island parishes, who charge a fee for the information required.

In addition to the paper records of parishes much useful information can be gleaned from monumental inscriptions. There are comparatively few monuments dating from before 1700 outside the church building themselves, and of those that survived from after this date, many have been rendered hard to read by weathering, by their removal to the edges of churchyards, and by vandalism. A good deal of work has been done of late by family history and local history societies in attempting to record the inscriptions in churchyards and cemeteries, and the indexes they have compiled can be found in county record offices or with the relevant family and local history societies. Big city cemeteries on the whole keep good records, and where these are still open, it is usually not too difficult to locate the exact plot from the cemetery plan. For those that have been closed, information may be obtained from the local town hall, so a preliminary letter to the town clerk would help you to find out where they are. A useful guide to this subject is Patricia Wolfston's *Greater London Cemeteries and*

Crematoria which is of considerable help to those who want to find where ancestors who lived in London were buried during the 19th and early 20th centuries. It is available from the Society of Genealogists. If you experience difficulty in locating the burial place of an ancestor, it is sometimes worth consulting obituaries in the local newspapers for the district and period. These can be seen at the British Library Newspaper Library at Colindale in north-west London.

So far we have considered the parish registers of the Established Church, but records were kept by other denominations, and since our Huguenot ancestors were for the most part Calvinists, it is quite possible, indeed probable, that their records can be found among those of the nonconformists. It is true that many Huguenot families were absorbed into the Anglican Church within two or three generations of their arrival in Britain, but many preferred to associate with one of the dissenting sects whom they considered to be more in sympathy with their doctrines. Religious toleration was unknown before 1650, and it was not until the Declaration of Indulgence in 1672 and the Toleration Act of 1689 that Protestant dissenters secured licences to worship according to their own rites. They had met privately for many years before these Acts were passed, and in some cases had kept baptismal registers (birth registers in the case of the Quakers). Details of the many nonconformist denominations and their registers can be found in Volume II of Steel's *National Index of Parish Registers,* and of Roman Catholic and Jewish congregations in Volume III, though this volume is unlikely to be of much, if any interest, to those in search of Huguenot ancestry. Over 9,000 nonconformist registers were transferred to the custody of the Public Record Office in the last century, and a useful guide to them is the *List of the non-parochial registers and records in the custody of the Registrar-General* published in 1859. They can be consulted free of charge at the Public Record Office today. For those who may need to consult later nonconformist records, you should ask at the relevant county record office for details and whereabouts.

At the same time the headquarters of the various sects have large collections, and these should be contacted. Those in London are: the Baptist Union Library; the Congregational Union of England and Wales; the Huguenot Library at University College; the Jewish Museum; the Presbyterian Society of England; the Society of Friends (Quakers); the Unitarian Church Headquarters; and, outside London, the Methodist archives at the Rylands Library in Manchester, and the Roman Catholic records at Archbishop's House, in Westminster, if you have reason to think that your Huguenot ancestors may have returned to the old faith. In addition to these there is the Dr. Williams' Library at 14 Gordon Square, London, W.C.1, which has excellent records on nonconformist history. This library does not hold records of births, marriages and deaths, however.

Among the non-parochial registers at the P.R.O. are some that belonged to conforming bodies including the Chapels Royal, Greenwich Hospital (naval), Chelsea Hospital (army), the Lying-in Hospital and the Foundling Hospital. There are also marriage registers for the Mayfair chapel, the Mint in Southwark, the Fleet Prison and the King's Bench Prison. These total some 300 registers and are very often overlooked by searchers, who may not be aware of their existence. Furthermore, there are the registers of some 19th-century cemeteries, including those for Eccelsall in Sheffield,

Leeds, Liverpool, Walworth in London, Bunhill Fields in London, and Victoria Park cemetery, London.

Records of the Poor

Parishes were administered by the priest and churchwardens, the latter serving for a year at a time unless re-elected. Their records, known as the Vestry Minutes and Churchwardens' Accounts give an insight into the administration and social life of the parish. An important part of these records is concerned with the care of the poor and the rates levied on the more wealthy parishioners for their benefit. Many of the acts governing the relief of poverty date from the Tudor period before the mass of Huguenot refugees reached Britain, but these records repay examination for the information they reveal concerning the settlement of the poor and their movement from one parish to another. Throughout the 18th century, for example, there was a lot of litigation between parishes concerning who should be responsible for the relief of individuals and where their proper parish of abode was, so that these records can, and often do, provide a great deal of information about people who moved about the country in search of work and shelter. This system came to an end with the passing of the Poor Law Reform Act of 1834, after which the whole question passed to the responsibility of the Poor Law Commissioners. This system lasted until 1929.

　　Another concern of the parish was the care of illegitimate children, which produced a corpus of documents known as Bastardy Papers. The churchwardens were concerned to establish these children's paternity so that the father could be made responsible for their maintenance, hence there is a better chance of finding out the name of an illegitimate child's father through these records than through those of civil or parochial registration.

　　Finally, there are other parish records which can sometimes throw light on ancestors, such as those of the Waywardens, or Overseers of Highways, of the Parish Constable, and of the Sexton. Likewise, workhouse records and charity records can also be useful. Enquiries about all these should be made in those record offices which have the custody of their accompanying parish registers.

Miscellaneous Records

Before the Education Act of 1872 schooling for the majority of working and middle class children depended on the provision made by the churches or certain charities. With the establishment of the Local School Boards in that year, schools were built throughout the land, and the records they have left are interesting and informative, though they may only concern the parents and grandparents of people living today. For the upper classes of society there were the public and grammar school, many of which are very ancient foundations, and have records of alumni going back many centuries. Before Durham University and London University were founded in 1832 and 1836 respectively, there were only Oxford and Cambridge Universities in England and Wales, and St Andrews, Aberdeen, Glasgow and Edinburgh Universities in Scotland. All of them have lists of alumni which give varying amounts of biographical information. Most of these can be examined in any fair-sized public reference library.

For those who entered the Law there are the Law Lists and the records of the various Inns of Court, which include admission registers. While on the subject of lawyers, it is useful to remember that Quarter Session records can be a useful source of information about one's forebears, as can the records of the various law courts, of which the Courts of Chancery, the Exchequer and the High Court of Admiralty are the most fruitful. Here we should mention in passing that the depositions of witnesses as well as the formal statements of complaint and the replies thereto by defendants are a mine of useful information. Assize records, Gaol Delivery records, Debtors' Rolls and the like can produce valuable material, and you should ask your local record office for details of what they possess, as well as visiting the P.R.O. for national law records.

Many Huguenots were professional men, so the records of doctors are worth consulting. The records of the Royal College of Physicians and the Royal College of Surgeons go back in the first instance to the 16th century and in the second to its foundation in 1800. Many doctors in earlier times were licensed by the Church, and records of the Archdeacons' Courts can be helpful here. Those who were licentiates of the Society of Apothecaries are recorded in its records, now lodged at the Guildhall Library in London. They date from 1670. Before that time apothecaries were licensed by the Grocers' Company, whose records are also to be found at the Guildhall Library along with many of the records of the London Livery Companies to which a very large number of Huguenot merchants belonged in the 17th century and more recently.

Apprenticeship by deed indented was required for many trades and professions from early times, but it was not until 1757 that a properly stamped deed was recognised as legally binding. Sometimes before that date, and often after, a great many poor children were bound by agreements which were entered into the vestry minute book, and occasionally in the parish register. Most were to learn husbandry and housewifery, but some were apprenticed to a trade, and many of the poorest were sent to the nearest manufacturing town to enter industry. A good genealogical source is the record of tax returns from apprenticeship indentures which was introduced in 1710, and which resulted in a central register being kept. The original registers are to be found in the P.R.O., from which an Apprentice Index was compiled covering the years 1710 to 1774. Two classes of apprentice were, however, excluded from these lists, namely those paying less than one shilling for their indenture and parish apprentices.

In addition to the more usual trades, professions such as banking, the railways and merchant navy all have their own records and it may be useful to consult the *Dictionary of British Associations* at some stage to find out the names of many professional bodies, of whom not a few have extensive records of former and present members. For the majority of traders and shopkeepers it is worth consulting the series of printed directories that have been published over the years. The first London directory was published in 1677, but regular up-dates do not begin until well into the 18th century. All known editions are described in two books: *The London Directories, 1677–1855,* by C. W. F. Goss, and the *Guide to the National and Provincial Directories of England and Wales before 1856* (excluding London), by Jane E. Norton. Both of these works give the location of known copies, and most country record offices have good runs of those appropriate to their county. There is also a very extensive collection in the Guildhall Library in London.

Poll books are another useful source, for they contain lists of those entitled to vote at elections when suffrage was limited to those with certain limited property qualifications. They can be seen in county record offices and the Society of Genealogists has a large collection.

In 1641 all adult males were required to take an oath of allegiance to the crown and to the Protestant religion. The Protestation Oath Rolls give names only, but as they are arranged by parishes they can be useful in locating families. The full records are kept in the House of Lords Record Office, but a number of county record offices have copies of their appropriate section. The Recusant Rolls of 1677 are useful for the names and residence of people who were found guilty of nonconformity either as Roman Catholics or Protestant dissenters. They are in the P.R.O., but there is a useful return of all recusants who were convicted, giving their quality and place of residence, in the British Library Manuscript Department.

Another useful 17th-century record is the Hearth Tax which was levied in 1662 and 1674. These returns give lists of householders in each village, showing residents rather than absent owners, and include exemption certificates for those too poor to pay the tax. They, too, are kept at the P.R.O. though many county record offices have copies for their area. A less valuable source is the Window Tax returns. The tax was levied between 1695 and 1851, but it is not as complete as the Hearth Tax returns. Two excellent books dealing with these subjects are *The Parish Chest,* by W. E. Tate, and *Enjoying Archives,* by David Iredale.

Many Huguenots served in the navy and army, whose records are extensive. These have been fully described in the present authors' *Debrett's Family Historian,* already mentioned. British military records before 1900 are for the most part kept in the P.R.O. at Kew, but naval and regimental records are also found in the appropriate museums and libraries. The book *Tracing your Ancestors in the Public Record Office,* by J. Cox and T. Padfield, is very useful, for apart from a general description of the records available, it gives lists of records and the P.R.O reference numbers and bibliographies. Another useful book is *In Search of Army Ancestry*, by Gerald Hamilton-Edwards.

Newspapers and magazines can be very helpful if used in conjunction with the other records for the period being researched. At the British Library in London newspapers before 1800 are catalogued under *Periodical Publications*. The main collection from 1801 onwards is kept at Colindale. *The Times* is the only newspaper to have published an index, and although it does not include the births, marriages and deaths, Palmer's *Index to The Times*, which appeared quarterly from 1791, is invaluable for tracing events in the lives of those listed. *The Gentleman's Magazine* which started in 1731 and ran till 1868 contains a large number of marriage and death notices. In addition to the annual index there are consolidated indexes of all names mentioned by surname for the period 1731–1818. Enquiries about local newspapers should be made at the appropriate record offices for the districts they serve.

Maps are an important aid in ancestry research. Demographic research has shown that nearly half the population during the 17th and 18th centuries in Britain died in different parishes from those in which they had been born, and lived for many years in yet other parishes. Apart from the flow of refugees from Europe to Britain, and within these islands from country districts to London, practically all movement was restricted to a fairly limited distance, less than 20 miles, and a great deal of it took place in an area less than 10 miles. Studies in France, Italy and Hungary, amongst other societies of very different structure, have shown similar movements of population from as early as the 15th century. Of course the Industrial Revolution increased movement of this kind, especially in England where it began earlier and continued longer.

This movement has caused some family historians to give up their research, but it is at this point that real detective work is needed, and every piece of evidence should be used. Among the most useful tools at this stage are maps. The study of local maps will show the growth of local industries, the increase of enclosures and the growth and decline of local communities. Estate maps, which date from about 1570 and continue to the 1860s are useful for showing the layout of towns and villages at any given time and show the progress of urban growth. Enclosure Awards record the terms of enclosure and the disposition of common land; Tithe Commutation maps arising from the Act of 1836 were drawn up to show every parcel of land, path, garden, shed, outhouse, factory and apportionments set out with the names of owners and occupiers. And finally the Ordnance Survey maps are vital for showing the whereabouts of addresses obtained from census returns and civil registration certificates. As we go into this subject in some detail in *Debrett's Family Historian* we do not propose to repeat ourselves here, but we would stress that county record offices have excellent collections of local maps for their areas, as do the Archives Départementales in France. Britain, however, is better served with local and national gazetteers than France, though the Berger-Levrault *Dictionnaire des Communes* is useful so far as it goes, but it stops short at Communes, as its title implies, and does not include geographical features such as rivers, valleys, plains and so on, nor does it mention hamlets, châteaux and farms. The British Library Map Library and the Map Room of the Cambridge University Library have two of the world's major historical map collections, which include charts, plans and topographical views as well as comprehensive collections of modern maps for all countries in the world. The Public Record Offices in London, Edinburgh, Belfast and Dublin, as well as the Royal Geographical Society have their own unique collections.

The Institute of Heraldic and Genealogical Studies, Canterbury, publishes a very useful series of parish maps for each county in England and Wales. These show the ancient parochial boundaries, the Probate Jurisdictions and the dates from which the original registers have survived. These can be got separately, or bound in atlas form together with a detailed index from Phillimore and Co. Ltd., Chichester.

Specialised Sources for Huguenot Ancestry Research

There comes a time when specialised archives have to be consulted. Much will depend on whether the original Huguenot ancestor arrived in Britain in the 16th century or following the Revocation of the Edict of Nantes in 1685. As we have shown, there was a steady trickle of immigrants in the period between the two great upheavals of the Religious Wars and the Revocation, so some will find that their ancestors were recorded in the French Church records of the 18th century, while others will have to use traditional British sources back into the 17th century.

It must be said once again that many Huguenot families were absorbed fairly quickly into the Anglican Church, but those who were originally Calvinist tended to join one

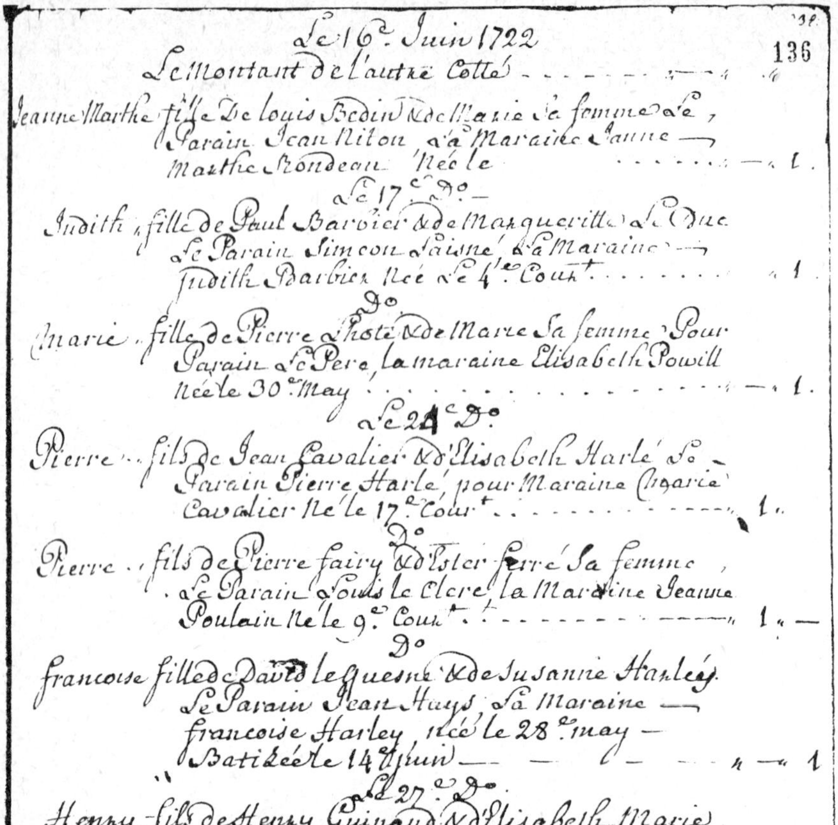

Le 16e. Juin 1722 136

Le Montant de l'autre Cotté

Jeanne Marthe fille De louis Bedin & de Marie Sa femme Le Parain Jean Nilon & la Maraine Jeanne Marthe Rondeau Née le ... 1.

Le 17e. Do.

Judith, fille de Paul Barbier & de Marguerite Sa ... Le Parain Simeon Laisné & la Maraine Judith Barbier Née Le 4e. Court ... 1

Do

Marie, fille de Pierre Lhoté & de Marie Sa femme Pour Parain Le Pere, la maraine Elisabeth Powill Née le 30e. May ... 1.

Le 24e Do.

Pierre .. fils de Jean Cavalier & d'Elisabeth Harlé Sa Parain Pierre Harlé, pour Maraine Marie Cavalier Né le 17e. Court ... 1.

Do

Pierre . fils de Pierre fairy & d'Ester ferré Sa femme Le Parain Louis le Clerc, la Maraine Jeanne Poulain Né le 9e. Court ... 1.

Do

francoise fille de David le Quesne & de Susanne Harlée Le Parain Jean Hays Sa Maraine francoise Harley née le 28e. may Batizée le 14 juin ... 1

Le 27e. Do.

Henry . fils de Henry Guinand & d'Elisabeth Marie Hamelott Le Parain & Maraine, Le Pere & la Mere, Né le 26e. May ... 1.

Do.

Jaques . fils de Jean Rouztier & d'anne Sa femme Le parain Jaques Gent, la Maraine Jeanne Rouztier, Batisé Le 3 Juin, Né le 6 May Dernier ... 1.

Le 1er. Juillet

Pierre, fils de Pierre Mordant & de Marie Launey Le Parain Isaac le Hay, la maraine Susanne Le Blond Né le 10e. juin ... 1.

Do.

Jacob . fils de Jacob Sardent & de Susanne Havy Sa femme Le Parain Jacob Sardent Son grand Pere, pour Maraine Marie Havy Né le 15e. juin ... 1.

Do. Le 8e.

Jeanne . fille D'Etienne Leleu & de Marguerite Chevalier Le Parain abraham Paris, Maraine Jeanne Vautier, Né Le 1er. juillet ... 1

Fig. 5 Baptismal entries from the register of the Walloon and French protestant church in Threadneedle Street, London, and the chapel of the hospital at Spitalfield, an appurtenance of the church.

EGLISE FRANÇAISE DE LONDRES,

THREADNEEDLE-STREET,

Fondée par EDOUARD VI. 1550.

MONSIEUR *Hautot* Collecteur,

Vous mettrez *Rachel Dupuy* sur votre Catalogue, si *elle* vous présente ce billet avant trois mois expirés ; l'Eglise ne se croyant obligée de reconnaître pour Membres, que ceux qui sont munis de ce certificat.

Et vous *Rachel Dupuy* si vous voulez continuer d'être Membre de l'Eglise Française de Londres, vous aurez soin, en cas que vous changiez de demeure, de donner votre nouvelle adresse au Collecteur.

Fait en Consistoire, le *24e Aout* 18 *23*

Ch. Jn. Boiceau Pasteur.

Jn. Jh. Battus Ancien.

J.L. Leber

Fig. 6 Témoignages enclosed in support of a petition for admission to the French Hospital, 1843.

of the nonconformist sects, especially the Congregationalists, Unitarians and Methodists, and the importance of noting the religious group to which your Huguenot ancestors belonged must be stressed. As your research takes you back in time there will come a period when traces of the family vanish from Anglican and nonconformist records into those of the French Churches. Even when you do establish your family's connection with a French Church you will still need to use the Anglican Church records to discover their burials which were nearly always in the parish churchyard. Consequently, there will be a considerable number of spelling variants between names found in French-speaking and English-speaking archives.

Having reached this stage of your research, you should consider joining the Huguenot Society of London if you have not already done so, for its library and archive collection are of great use to you. You should begin by making sure whether anyone has worked on your family before you, and for this purpose you should consult *Huguenot Pedigrees,* by C. R. Lart (two volumes) and the Wagner and other collections of pedigrees in the Huguenot Library. A copy of the Wagner collection is available on microfilm at the Society of Genealogists, whose list of family histories should also be checked. All known Huguenot and Walloon registers were surrendered under the Non-Parochial Registers Act of 1840 and are now at the P.R.O., but since all of them have been printed by the Huguenot Society in their Quarto Series, and are indexed, it is much easier to use these. The registers mainly contain records of baptisms and marriages, and some include banns or marriage contracts and deaths, but as already stated, burials must be sought in the appropriate parochial registers. Irish Huguenot registers do include burials, however. The following is a complete list of the 56 volumes of the Huguenot Quarto Series to date:

Volume

I	The Walloons and their church at Norwich, 1565–1832.
II	Les Actes des Colloques des églises françaises et des Synodes des églises etrangéres refugiées en Angleterre, 1581–1654.
III	Register of the Protestant church at Guisnes, 1668–1685.
IV	Registre de l'église Wallonne de Southampton.
V	Registers of the Walloon church in Canterbury, Parts 1–3.
VI	Despatches of Michele Suriano and Marc' Antonio Barbaro, Venetian ambassadors at the Court of France, 1560–63.
VII	Registers of the French conformed churches of St Patrick and St Mary, Dublin.
VIII	Letters of Denization and Acts of Naturalisation for Aliens in England, 1509–1603.
IX	Registers of the French church of Threadneedle Street, London, Part I.
X	Lists of Aliens resident in London, Henry VIII to James I, Parts I, II, III and Index.
XI	Register of the French church of La Patente, Spitalfields, London.
XII	Register of the Dutch church, Colchester.
XIII	Register of the French church of Threadneedle Street, Part II.
XIV	Registers of the French nonconformist churches, Dublin.
XV	History of the Walloon and Huguenot church at Canterbury.

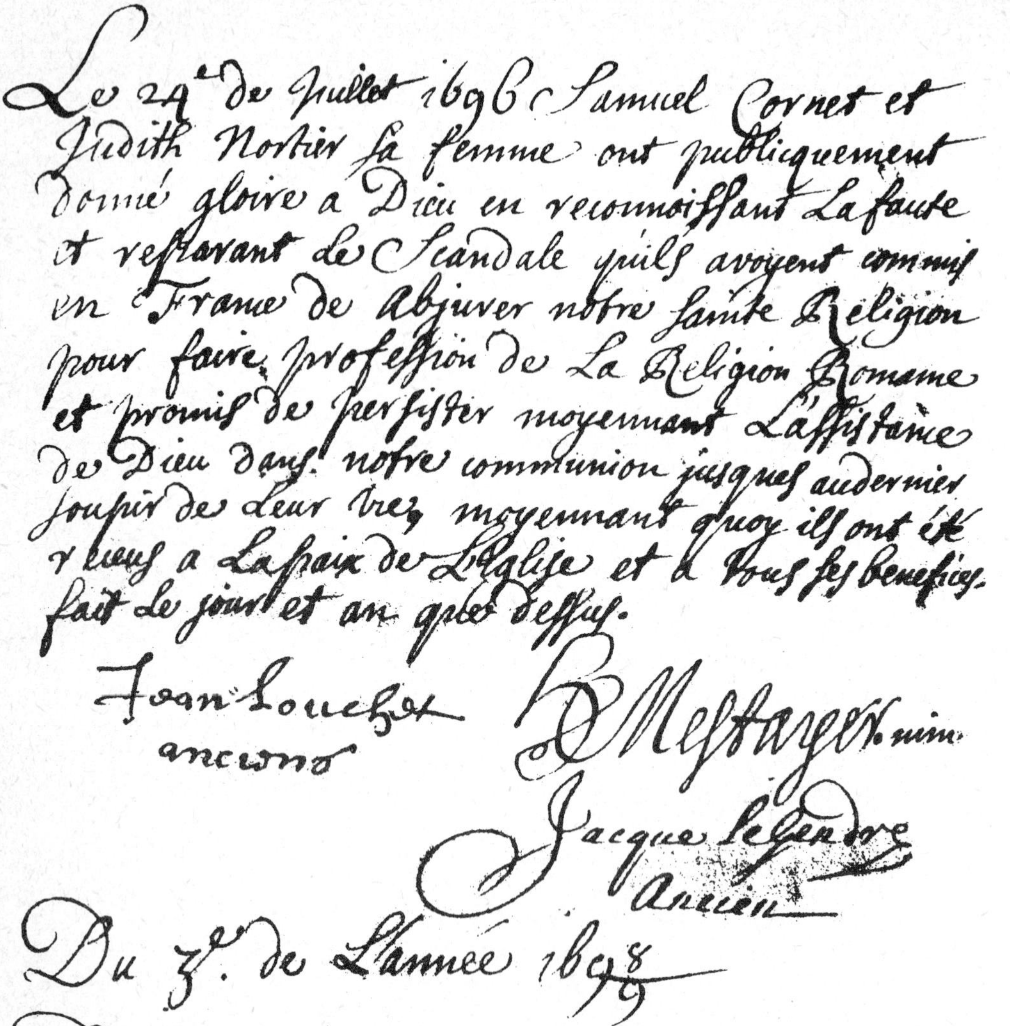

Le 24e de Juillet 1696 Samuel Cornet et
Judith Nortier sa femme ont publiquement
donné gloire a Dieu en reconnoissant La faute
et reparant de Scandale qu'ils avoyent commis
en France de Abjurer notre sainte Religion
pour faire profession de La Religion Romaine
et promis de persister moyennant L'assistance
de Dieu dans notre communion jusques au dernier
soupir de leur vie, moyennant quoy ils ont été
receus a La paix de L'Eglise et a tous ses benefices.
fait le jour et an que dessus.

Jean Loucher
ancien

B Mestayer min.

Jacque legendre
Ancien

Du 3e. de L'anneé 1698

D'autant qu'il y a quelques personnes qui se
sont plaints qu'ils n'avoyent point eu de part aux
deniers qui sont envoyés pour Le soulagement de
ceux qui sont dans La necessité, et que quelques uns mesme qui en avoyent receu ont dit

Fig. 7　Register of 'Les Actes du Consistoire' of the French Church
of Thorpe le Soken, Essex.

XLVII   Registers of Le Mans.
XLVIII   Actes du Consistoire de l'église française de Threadneedle Street, Vol. II,
            1571-77.
XLIX   Relief of French Protestant Refugees, 1681-1687.
L   Archives of the French Protestant church of London: a handlist.
LI   Records in the Huguenot Library: the Royal Bounty and Connected Funds;
            the Burn Donation; the Savoy church.
LII & LIII French Protestant Hospital, Inmates and applications, 1718-1957, and
            applicants for the Coqueau Charity, 1745-1901.
LIV   Calendars and Letter Books of the French church of London, 1643-59.
LV   The Case Book of La Maison de Charité de Spitalfields, 1739-1741.
LVI   Catalogue of Remaining MSS. in the Huguenot Library.

The Reconnaissance of those who joined the congregation with a témoignage from some other church could be found in the registers, and these can establish the approximate date of arrival in Britain. However, when using Huguenot registers it is advisable to check other parish registers for the same period, for individual members of Huguenot families might have left the French church and joined their local parish church, perhaps because of a marriage with an English girl, while other members of the same family remained faithful to their former congregation.

The Actes du Consistoire listed above are the equivalent of the Vestry Minutes, and record the activities of the church. They sometimes contain permissions to marry, marriage contracts, wills and deeds. There are also the registers of the church members, which sometimes show places of birth, their témoignages and the names of those with whom they were living, or the names of those who vouched for their respectability. Those who came of age to be admitted to the sacrament were usually vouched for by their parents, aunts or uncles.

Another group of records are those for the relief of the poor. These are in books entitled 'Cas des Pauvres', 'Livres des Pauvres Refugiés', 'Livres des Pauvres Reglés' and 'Livres des Hardes'. In addition to these there are also 'Passades', which were grants made to refugees in need of help while on their way from one place to another. These accounts show nearly all the names of recipients as well, in many cases, as the names of their dependants. Further records include lists of apprentices, scholars in the charity schools, marriage licences, will extracts, and miscellaneous correspondence.

Some of this material if not in the Huguenot Library can be found in such record offices as those at Canterbury, Norwich or Southampton. There is also a collection of minutes for the French Protestant Hospital, La Providence, at Rochester, Kent, and its register of petitions often gives details of the ancestry of those seeking admission. The registers of the French Protestant School, L'Ecole de la Charité, at Westminster, founded in 1747, give the date and place of birth and baptism as well as the names of the parents, including the mother's maiden name, of all pupils.

The Proceedings of the Huguenot Society of London contain many articles in its 24 volumes to date, which it is prudent to investigate. From this wealth of material most researchers should be able to trace their ancestry back to the original refugee who arrived in Britain in the 16th or 17th century. The next problem is to discover where he came from. There may be some indication of this in the records of denizations and

Fig. 8 The Massacre of St Bartholomew and the assassination of Admiral Coligny, from a contemporary engraving.

Fig. 9 Calvinism on its death-bed (French caricature against the Huguenots).

naturalisations and Returns of Aliens published by the Huguenot Society, but you should also consult *Lists of Foreign Protestants and Aliens from 1618–1688,* edited by W. Durrant Cooper and published as Volume 82 of the Camden Society Old Series. *Protestant Exiles from France in the reign of Louis XIV,* by D. C. A. Agnew, gives a list of naturalisations from 1681 to 1707. There is also an article in the *Genealogist's Magazine,* Vol. 16, No. 5, p. 197, by R. F. Monger, which is an account of the main sources for tracing immigrants.

A final word of advice: before setting out on your research, get whatever guides and leaflets you can find from the archive or record office you intend to use so that you can peruse them before you set out. This will save you a great deal of time and effort, for you will be able to sort out where to go and what to examine when you arrive there. Once you have identified your immigrant ancestor, it will be time to embark on research in France itself. But before you turn to Chapter Six, we have tried to summarise the main British sources available to you. Some of the works listed are in French, and may not be very easily available in Britain, but if you have joined the Huguenot Society, then it is likely you will be able to find someone there to help you.

Alien and Immigrant Sources

The Public Record Office and the Huguenot Society of London are, as already stated, the two major sources of information. The following list contains the chief P.R.O. sources and their class numbers—

Aliens Act (HO 1, 2, 3 and 5) (including Entry Books).
The Bouillon Papers (HO 69).
Calendar of State Papers (Domestic): Vols. I to V (SP 10–12, 14, 15, 29 and 30).
Chancery Close Rolls (C 54).
Chancery Denizations (C 24).
Chancery Depositions (C 97).
Chancery Miscellanea (C 47).
Domestic Entry Books (SP 44/67).
Exchequer Accounts Various (E 101).
Exchequer Extents of Alien Priories (E 106).
Exchequer Subsidy Rolls (E 179).
Oaths of Allegiance (E 169/86).
Original Patents for Denizations (HO 4).
Passenger Lists (BT 26 and 32).
Patent Rolls (C 66 and 67).
Privy Council Papers (PC 1, FO 95).
P.R.O. Lists and Indexes, Vols. XXXV, XLII and XLVI.
Registered Papers (HO 45 and 144).
Swearing or Oath Rolls (KB 24).
Treasury Records (T 93).
Genealogist's Magazine, Vol. XII (1956).

Fig. 10   The Cassini Map of France, drawn on the orders of Louis XV. It is the oldest topographical set of maps of the whole of France. Work on the ground and on the copper engravings of the sheets was begun in 1750 but not completed until 1815.

Guilds and Livery Company Records

Guilds of traders and craftsmen originated in the Middle Ages to regulate admission to their respective trades and crafts. Although based in London their authority often extended beyond the City. Their records of apprenticeships and freedoms are a useful source of information bearing in mind the large number of Huguenot refugees who were craftsmen and merchants. Full lists of Livery Companies and Guilds can be obtained at the Guildhall Library in London, where many of their records have been deposited. On the other hand, most records of the extant Livery Companies, numbering over 70, are still retained at the Halls and offices of the respective Companies. The main sources of information are as follows—

  Apprenticeship Enrolments and Indentures.
  Card Index of Freemen of the City of London, 1498–1679 in the Repertoires of
    the Court of Aldermen. (at the City of London Record Offices.)
  Complaint Books.
  English Provincial, Scottish and Irish Guilds (*see* Guildhall Library G.S.C. 338.6).
  Freedom Enrolment Books.
  Freedom Minute or Declaration Books.
  Guildhall Library lists of Printed Books and MSS. (L 37).
  Lord Mayor's Court Records.
  The Ward Mote Inquest Returns.

Miscellaneous British and French Secondary Sources (including Societies and
    Other Organisations)

  Achievements, Ltd., Northgate, Canterbury, Kent.
  Admiralty records.
  Almanach de Gotha (records of European nobility).
  Bernau Index of Chancery Proceedings: Society of Genealogists.
  Boyd's London Citizens: Society of Genealogists and Guildhall Library.
  Boyd's Marriage Index: Society of Genealogists.
  Calendars of Patent Rolls, State Papers, Colonial, Treasury Books and Papers,
    Venetian Papers (1513–1745): Guildhall and major public libraries.
  Camden Society publications.
  Chancery Proceedings: P.R.O. leaflet 32.
  Court of Orphans records: City of London Record Office.
  Deeds and Property Transfers: P.R.O. leaflet 34.
  Dictionary of National Biography.
  East India Company Registers: Percy Smith Collection, Society of Genealogists.
  East India Company: Hudson's Index: National Army Museum, London.
  Emigrants: P.R.O. leaflet 7.
  Fleet Registers—Clandestine marriages near the Fleet Prison, from 1667: Public
    Record Office.
  Foreign Registers: Public Record Office.
  Germany (West): *How to find German Ancestors and Relatives,* published by
    Family History Association, Mormon Genealogical Libraries at Frankfurt,
    Hamburg and Maiserlautern.

Historic MSS. Commission publications.

House of Lords Record Office, Westminster (*see also* Naylor Collection, Guildhall Library).

Hudsons Bay Company Records (microfilm): P.R.O. Class B.H.

India: Records and Library, 197 Blackfriars Road, London, S.E.1.

Lambeth Palace Library and Archives.

Land Confiscations, Crown and Royalist, 1642–1660: P.R.O. leaflet 54.

Leeson Surname Archive, 108 Sea Lane, Ferring, West Sussex.

National Register of Archives, Quality House, Chancery Lane, London, W.C.1.

Netherlands (*see* Chapter Six and list of Huguenot Society's publications above): Central Bureau voor Genealogie, Nassaulaan 18, The Hague.

Overseas Anglican Records: General Register Office, St Catherine's House, London, WC2B 6JP; Guildhall Library MS. 15,061/1–2; Diocesan Registers, MS. 10,926/1/13.

Pallot Index: Institute of Heraldic and Genealogical Studies, Canterbury

Protestant Returns 1641–2: Royal Commission on Historical MSS. (originals at House of Lords Record Office).

Royalist Composition Papers: P.R.O. Class S.P. 23 (also printed).

South Africa (*see* Chapter Three above): Human Sciences Research Council, Private Bag X41, Pretoria, R.S.A. 0001.

Switzerland (*see* Chapter Six below): Mormon Library, Zurich.

West Indies: V. T. C. Smith Collection: Society of Genealogists.

Chapter Six

RESEARCH IN FRANCE, THE NETHERLANDS, GERMANY
AND SWITZERLAND

OWING TO THE CENTRALISED NATURE of French government dating from the
16th century, there has always been a tendency in France for demographic information
to be concentrated in the chief towns of the provinces and later in the départements.
As in England, parish registers were kept by the parish priests—the earliest date from
slightly earlier in the 16th century than they do in England—but from the 18th century,
and in some cases from the end of the 17th, the curé was obliged to send a copy of
all entries made during the year to the Greffe du Tribunal. These copies, which are
not unlike English Bishops' Transcripts, offer a second chance of finding what one is
looking for in parishes where the original registers have been lost or destroyed. After
the Revolution the job of recording births, marriages and deaths was transferred to
the Mairie, but as most English people of Huguenot descent will be seaching in
pre-Revolutionary records this will not be of much help. Unfortunately, very few
registers exist for the period before the 17th century, though there are a few excep-
tions, such as the registers of Riom in the Auvergne (63300 Puy-de-Dôme), which date
from 1530. In Paris, all the original registers and their duplicates were lost during the
Franco–Prussian war of 1870-1871. Extracts from some pre-Revolutionary registers
are to be found in the MS. department of the Bibliothèque Nationale in Paris. Such
Huguenot registers as survive are to be found in Archive Départementales, though
there are some copies in the Protestant Library in Paris.

Although the destruction of so many early registers is a grievous loss, this is to some
extent offset by the fact that the notaries and their records, which include wills, are
much better preserved than might be expected. These notarial archives contain a
vast amount of genealogical information, for in addition to wills they contain
information relating to marriage contracts, deeds for the sale and purchase of land
and for its division following the death of owners. The inheritance laws of France
differ radically from those of England, it being the law that real estate is to be shared
among all members of the family. In cases where siblings wish to renounce their
rights—as they often do—these transfers had to be made by the notaries, and the
evidence of title they contain is of the greatest genealogical value. Notarial records
are to be found either among the papers of their successors or in the Archives
Départementales in the provinces or in the Minutier of the Archives Nationales in
Paris. The volume of records and minutes are usually indexed. Many notarial trans-
actions were taxed, and summaries of these had to be entered in registers and handed
to the Service de l'Enrégistrement et du Timbre, which is part of the Ministry of

Finance. The archives of the Comté de Nice were handed over to the kingdom of Savoy when the territory was ceded after the fall of Napoleon, and so there are extensive notarial records dating back to 1600 in Italy, in the archives of Alpes Maritimes at Nice (06088) as well as in the Royal archives of Monaco.

As we have shown in the first part of this book, some Huguenot refugees were of noble descent, and France is fortunate to possess three extensive works on noble genealogy, plus an incomplete work—*Liste des Familles Francais,* by G. Chaix d'Est-Ange, which only covers the letters A–Gau. All of these are of immense value for those in search of aristocratic ancestry. Probably the most valuable is the massive work of Père Anselme, which he produced between 1726 and 1733, entitled *Histoire de la Maison Royale de France.* This work does not, as its name implies, confine itself to the royal family exclusively, but includes much information about those families who were related to the ruling house by marriage with their daughters, and also the ancestry of important officers of state, such as the Marshals and Constables of France. Up-to-date xerox copies of this vast work can be found in the University Library at Cambridge and in the British Museum and other British libraries. Copies are more widely available in France.

The second work, by de Courcelles, and published in 1824, is entitled *Histoire Généalogique et Héraldique des Pairs de France* and is confined to those families who were given grants of nobility before 1400 and who were considered equals or peers of the king, whom they acknowledged as their feudal overlord. These are known as the feudal families.

The third work is the *Dictionnaire de la Noblesse Française,* by de la Chenaye-Desbois and Badier, published in 1844. It deals with the quasi-feudal families who can prove an uninterrupted descent from 1560—provided that this descent is coupled with a fief—but which lack a known grant of nobility. The descendants of such families were known as gentlemen of rank, birth or blood, and they could assume titles at will, which demonstrates one of the main differences between the French and English nobility. The English received their titles from the sovereign, which then descended through the operation of primogeniture through the senior male line (except in the rare cases of special remainder such as, for example, the dukedom of Marlborough and the earldom of Mountbatten of Burma).

In England the lowest rank of the peerage is the baron, though not of the aristocracy, for the lowest inheritable title is that of baronet, a 17th-century creation devised by James I to bring in cash to the royal treasury. In France the lowest rank of the noblesse is the écuyer, or esquire. The term seigneur, which is usually translated 'lord', more nearly equates to the English term 'Lord of the Manor'. It is heritable only in the sense that it could be taken by whichever member of the family happened to be the owner of a particular seigneurie, and did not necessarily descend to the eldest son. It could, of course, be assumed by a daughter, who might be known as the Dame de Quelquechose, even after marriage. Take as an illustration this medieval example: Robert de Courtenay, the grandson of King Louis de Gros was Seigneur de Champignolles, de Château Renard and de Charny. His son, Pierre de Courtenay was Seigneur de Couches and de Charny and de Tanlay. The seigneuries of Charny and Tanlay in later generations descended to two families, the former to Ponce de Mont-Saint-Jean, the latter to a branch of the de Joinville family. Mont-Saint-Jean had earlier been a seigneurie of the de Vergy family, and is now a seigneurie of the kings of Italy, having come to them through the marriage of a descendant of the de Vergy and de Charny family to a younger son of one of the counts, later dukes, of Savoy.

Regardless of whether you were a seigneur or a duke you owed your nobility to the fact that you were an écuyer. In one sense an écuyer was the lowest rank of nobility, but on the other hand unless you were an écuyer you couldn't be noble. Whether you called yourself baron, viscount, count, marquis or duke depended on the number of seigneuries you owned, and each seigneurie differed in size and importance, and could range in size from the smallest manor to a fair-sized city or tract of land. Thus your rank reflected the size of your property, with the result that in any given family, some could apparently bear senior titles to their fathers. Let us take a hypothetical example. The Faurieux family might own 20 seigneuries, ranging in size from marquisates to baronies. The senior member of the family may have elected to live in one of them, which happened to be a marquisate—and call himself the Marquis du Maine-Foucaud. His youngest son married an heiress who owned a dukedom, and his eldest son married one who only owned a large number of counties, thus the sons would call themselves the duc de Lusignac and the comte de Fayol respectively. Their family name, of course, would remain de Faurieux. However, after several generations, the descendants of the duc and the comte might become known as de Lusignac and de Fayol, more through usage than anything else. This, of course, is quite different from England, where the family names of the dukes of Grafton, for example, remain Fitzroy, or of the earls of Devon, Courtenay. Francis I, king of France, is reported to have said, 'Je suis né gentilhomme et non pas roi', meaning that his nobility depended upon his being born a gentleman.

Below these great feudal families, some of whom were almost sovereign rulers of the vast territories they owned, and who owed the king military support—l'impôt du sang—there was an entirely separate class of nobleman who were granted titles of nobility by letters patent or through the exercise of certain offices—the governorship of certain provinces or cities such as Paris, Rouen, Niort, Angers, Bordeaux and so on. Such high officials obtained successively either nobility at the first degree or nobility at the third generation, and were known as the noblesse de robe and the noblesse de cloche.

Thus there were several ways of acquiring 'noblesse'—seven, in fact. First was by 'extraction', where the origins of nobility were so old they had been forgotten. Several of such families could trace their ancestry to the time of the Merovingian kings of the fifth and sixth centuries. Next came 'noblesse uterine', which was especially confined to certain provinces, mainly in eastern France and especially Champagne, where descent could be traced through the female line. Noblesse uterine was of four kinds: royal descent; feudal dignity—where, for example, an ancestor had been a Maréchal de France, a Seneschal or a Porte-Oriflamme (a post which literally meant standard-bearer, but which was not unlike the English Earl-Marshal); by letters patent; and by provincial custom. A few of these families held the rank of prince and had held fiefs under the Holy Roman Empire, but later became subjects of the kings of France. It was maintained that a noble mother could transmit nobility, even if she married beneath her, though there were many disputes under this claim. The third was 'par chevalerie' and was not unlike knighthood in England and was conferred on the field of battle by the king on men of non-noble rank. Like knighthood, it could also be conferred for services rendered in the field of civil affairs. The fourth was by letters patent registered in the Cour de Comptes on the payment of a fee. (Note that the Cour de Comptes should be translated as the Court of Accounts, not the Court of Counts.) The fifth was 'par fiefs' which meant the acquisition of nobility by the investiture of a noble fief. The sixth was 'par office' and applied to the noblesse de robe. It was conditional on the family living for three generations in 'noble fashion' and failing this could be forfeited. Finally there was 'noblesse militaire' which was granted to men whose fathers and grandfathers had served in the army for 20 years as a captain, lieutenant or ensign.

The mere acquisition of noblesse, did not, of course, raise the family to an equal social status with the old families. There were a host of Court duties and privileges, such as the right to have daughters presented, to hunt with the king and in the royal forests, to ride in the king's carriages and the like which were reserved to the members of families who could trace unbroken descent from someone ennobled before 1400.

It cannot be too strongly emphasised that titles under the *ancien régime* derived from land, which was deemed to be a barony, county, marquisate or duchy, not from the individual who possessed it. Up to the end of the 17th century there were no personal titles such as there were and continue to be in Britain, though in the 18th century they began to be assumed. There were a few instances where the king made a man a duke, but this was more like a life peerage in modern Britain, and the title could not be transmitted to his sons or daughters. Usage tended to differ from province to province and, as already stated, it did not follow that the son of a marquis was a count or the son of a count a viscount. For example the son of the Marquis de Thouars was called Louis Jacques de Cougnée (his family name), Marquis of Puissar, the name of his seigneurie. In the hypothetical example given above, if the seigneurie of Maine-Foucaud—a marquisate—was subdivided through several generations of inheritance, and was reduced in size to, say, a barony, then the holder in that generation might call himself Baron du Maine-Foucaud, or, if it was divided in such a way that it fell below the extent deemed worthy even of a barony, the owner or owners could not bear any title at all. The composition of marquisates and baronies varied from period to period and province to province, but generally speaking a barony comprised three parishes or manors.

This linking of names to land generates much confusion when it comes to tracing French ancestors, for the whole question of surnames is one that differs considerably from the practice in England. Let us begin with one extremely important difference, that concerning the names and titles by which women were known. The title 'Madame' to designate a married woman only dates from the 17th century, and even then was only gradually adopted throughout all strata of society. Before that time the title was reserved for women of a certain rank, just as 'Lady' is in Britain today. The parallel is almost exact, for even today one refers to all women below the rank of duchess and above that of an esquire's wife as 'Lady'. It is perfectly correct to refer to the Marchioness of Londonderry as Lady Londonderry, or to the Countess Bathurst as Lady Bathurst, or to the wife of Sir Ablative Absolute as Lady Absolute. Women below that rank are called Mrs., short for Mistress.

In France the title Madame was given to the daughters of the king, wives of princes of the blood, wives of marshals of France, certain of the very highest nobility not

covered by these classes and to the wives of *chevaliers des ordres*. It was also given to
abbesses and prioresses, especially of the bigger convents. For other women, whether
noble or bourgeoise, married or single, 'Mademoiselle' was the only title in use, just as
in medieval England all women not entitled to be called 'Lady' or 'Milady' were
addressed as 'Mistress' or 'Goodwife'. 'Mistress' was later abbreviated to 'Mrs.' and
'Miss' to denote whether or not the woman was married. In the case of the French
bourgeoisie the husband's or father's family name was used; noblewomen almost
always used a territorial name with the prefix 'de'. For example, Mademoiselle Lefevre
would almost certainly be a bourgeoise, whereas Mlle. de Ganages would be noble,
and her father's name could be, and often was, quite different. Montaigne protested
against this confusing custom. 'It is a vile habit', he wrote, 'and one fraught with evil
for France for people to be called after their estates, and one that breeds more
confusion of families than any other thing. A cadet of good family, who receives as
his portion an estate whose name he bears with credit, cannot abandon it with honour.
Ten years after his death the land passes to a stranger, who in his turn bears the name.'

Every child, girls as well as boys, might bear a different name and much of the
significance of historical events can be lost by those who fail to realise relationships
through this maze of names. Take the Montmorency family as an example. During the
early 16th century there were five Montmorency brothers, known respectively by the
names Montmorency (the eldest), Damville, Montbéran, Méru and de Thorè. But it
didn't end there: these were the sons of the Constable de Montmorency. His nephews,
his brother's sons, were known as the de Châtillon brothers, but are known to history
as Admiral de Coligny, whose first name was Gaspard; Cardinal de Châtillon (Odon);
and the Sieur d'Andelot (François).

In the same way the sons of every little squire with a small property or two to divide
among his children were each known by a different name. Take for example the
Huguenot family of Mornay: the eldest was de Buhy; the second de Plessis Marly;
the third de Beaunes; their uncle was d'Auberville, and his son de Villarceaux, and so
on throughout the entire French nobility. Furthermore, as Montaigne complained,
when the property was alienated to a stranger, the name went with it, so that a man
could change his name several times in a lifetime if he happened to move from one
property to another, either because he inherited it, bought it, or married it. A whole
class of bourgeois proprietors arose, who bought the rights to use the name along
with the land to which it belonged, thus giving themselves spurious titles of nobility
by the simple device of using the prefix 'de'.

On marriage an English woman loses her maiden name and henceforth in legal
signatures, as in everyday use, she uses her husband's surname. This did not happen in
France to anything like the same extent until the Revolution. In the 16th and 17th
centuries a woman never legally lost her father's surname, and would sign all legal
documents with it even after her marriage. She might be known as Madame la
Duchesse de Montmorency or Madame La Maréchale d'Ancre, or if she were of lesser
rank as Madame or Mademoiselle de Buhy or de Plessis Marly (but almost certainly
not as Madame or Mademoiselle de Mornay, the family surname) in everyday parlance,
but her name till she died would be Madeleine de Bec Crespin or Charlotte d'Arbaleste
whenever she signed a letter or legal document. In the latter's case her first husband
was Monsieur de Fequères and her second Philippe de Mornay, Sieur du Plessis Marly,

but regardless of this, her legal name remained the one with which she was born. It is of vital importance for anyone tracing Huguenot ancestry to be aware of this matter, for otherwise one can be mightily misled and confused.

There are two main categories of heraldry: familial and individual. The latter is practised throughout Europe, while the former pertains to a family, whereby all male descendants of the original grantee bear the same family arms undifferenced, in much the same way as all the children of a count of the Holy Roman Empire would be counts and countesses themselves. Such a system is only practical where there are a great many surnames, though it is a mistake to think that there is a coat of arms for every surname. The first thing to be said about the use of arms in France is that it has never been so tightly controlled as it is in Britain. For centuries French families chose their own arms, and though attempts were made from time to time to regulate the use of arms, no body like the College of Arms existed. Heralds were used in medieval France in much the same way as they were in England but only in their military and diplomatic roles.

The nearest we come to a register of arms in France is in 1696, when Louis XIV instituted a General Armorial to register all the coats of arms of gentlemen, as well as those of the noblesse de robe, ecclesiastics, burgesses of free cities and of all those holding public offices. It contained over 40,000 coats, both of nobles and non-nobles, but its purpose was not to control the use of arms to avoid duplication, as the College of Arms does in England, but to raise money by taxing those who used arms. Since the collection of these taxes was farmed out, some of the farmers sought fit to 'impose' arms on those who did not, or did not want to bear them so that they might be taxed. It was not unlike the practice of Charles I in England of fining people for refusing to be knighted. In France, such arms were turned out by the dozen. Over 60,000 coats of arms are recorded in the 69 volumes of the MS. *Grand Armorial de France,* known as Hozier after the man who undertook the office of judge of arms, and which is housed in the Bibliothèque Nationale in Paris. In addition to Hozier there are thousands of manuscript volumes containing the papers of the judges of arms from the reigns of Louis XIV, Louis XV and Louis XVI, though generally speaking, only those of the reign of Louis XIV are of use to people of Huguenot descent. There are also 680 volumes known as 'dossiers bleus', 600 'carrés d'Hozier', 350 'cabinet d'Hozier', 350 'nouveau d'Hozier' and 220 'Cherin' filled with genealogical tables and copies of documents submitted to the judges of arms by people who wanted to prove their right to nobility. The best index to these papers is the *Repertoire des series généalogiques.*

Printed inventories of the contents of Archives Départementales and Archives Communales can be consulted in the reading rooms of the Bibliothèque Nationale and of most Archives Départementales. Series E in the Archives Départementales contains many documents relating to individual families.

A letter of introduction from the embassy of the searcher's country is required before admission can be gained to the Bibliothèque Nationale, Archives Nationales and to naval and military archives. In the Archives Départementales admission is less strictly controlled.

Huguenot records have been lost in many parts of France, and the situation varies greatly from department to department. Few records start before 1660, but those at Caen, La Rochelle, Rouen and Nîmes are very extensive and begin at the end of the 16th century and continue up to the Revocation of the Edict of Nantes. Most are to be found in the Archives Départementales, some at the Mairie among parochial registers, and a few in private hands. There are a few stray volumes of church records in the Archives Nationales, Serie T.T. and some copies in the Protestant Library. French Protestant registers also contain entries for English, Scottish and Irish families living in France and especially for merchants and seamen trading between Britain and France. The Huguenot registers of Caen, Angers, Saumur, Tours, Nantes and Bordeaux have numerous references to English and Scots residents.

The following is a list of the Départements of France, with the name and postal code of the chief town in which the Archives Départementales are usually to be found.

Ain	Bourg-en-Bresse 01000	Jura	Lons-le-Saumier 39570
Aisne	Laon 02000	Landes	Mont-de-Marsan 40000
Allier	Moulins 03000	Loir-et-Cher	Blois 41000
Alpes-de-Haute-		Loire	Saint-Étienne 42000
Provence	Digne 04000	Haute-Loire	Le Puy 43000
Hautes Alpes	Gap 05000	Loire-Atlantique	Nantes 44000
Alpes-Maritimes	Grasse 06130	Loiret	Orléans 45000
Ardèche	Privas 07000	Lot	Cahors 46000
Ardennes	Charleville-Mezieres 08000	Lot-et-Garonne	Agen 47000
Ariège	Foix 09000	Lozère	Mende 48000
Aube	Troyes 10000	Maine-et-Loire	Angers 49000
Aude	Carcassonne 11000	Manches	Saint-Lô 50000
Aveyron	Rodez 12000	Marne	Reims 51000
Bouches-du-Rhone	Maresille 13001–13016 (consult telephone directory)	Haute Marne	Chaumont 52000
		Mayenne	Laval 53000
Calvados	Caen 14000	Meurthe-et-Moselle	Nancy 54000
Cantal	Aurillac 15000	Meuse	Bar-le-Duc 55000
Charente	Angoulême 16000	Morbihan	Vannes 56000
Charente-Maritime	La Rochelle 17000	Moselle	Metz 57000
Cher	Bourges 18000	Nièvre	Nevers 58000
Corrèze	Tulle 19000	Nord	Lille 59000
Côte d'Or	Dijon 21000	Oise	Beauvais 60000
Côtes-du-Nord	Saint-Brieuc 22000	Orne	Alençon 61000
Creuse	Guéret 23000	Pas-de-Calais	Arras 62000
Dordogne	Périgueux 24000	Puy-de-Dôme	Clermont Ferrand 63000
Doubs	Besançon 25000	Pyrénées-Atlan-	
Drôme	Valence 26000	tique	Pau 64000
Eure	Evreux 27000	Hautes Pyrénées	Tarbes 65000
Eure-et-Loir	Chartres 28000	Pyrénées-	
Finistere	Quimper 29000	Orientales	Perpignan 66000
Gard	Nîmes 30000	Bas Rhin	Strasbourg 67000
Hante-Garonne	Toulouse 31000	Haut Rhin	Colmar 68000
Gers	Auch 32000	Rhone	Lyon 69000
Gironde	Bordeaux 33000	Haute-Saône	Vesoul 70000
Hérault	Montpellier 34000	Saône-et-Loire	Mâcon 71000
Ille-et-Vilaine	Rennes 35000	Sarthe	Le Mans 72000
Indre	Chateauroux 36000	Savoie	Chambéry 73000
Indre-et-Loir	Tours 37000	Haute-Savoie	Annecy 74000
Isere	Grenoble 38000	Seine-Maritime	Rouen 76000

Seine-et-Marne	Melun 77000	Vaucluse	Avignon 84000
Deux Sèvres	Niort 79000	Vendée	La Roche-sur-Yon 85000
Somme	Amiens 80000	Vienne	Poitiers 86000
Tarn	Albi 81000	Hauts-Vienne	Limoges 87000
Tarn-et-Garonne	Montauban 82000	Vosges	Épinal 88000
Var	Toulon 83000	Yonne	Auxerre 89000

Note.—French telephone directories are arranged by towns, villages and streets. To obtain the address or telephone number of the Archives Départementals in the chief town of any department, you should consult the Department Directory (e.g., 24 Dordogne), look up under Périgueux—Archives Départementales, 2 pl Hoche (53) 53.49.66.

Other reference books and repositories in France include: La Société du Grand Armorial de France, 179 Bvd. Haussmann, 75008 Paris; L'Association d'Entreaide de la Noblesse Française, 9 rue Richepance, 75000 Paris; Société d'Heraldique et de Sigillographie, 113 rue de Courcelles, 75017 Paris; *Armorial Générale de France,* by H. Jougleade Morenau; *Nobiliaire Universel de France,* by M. de St Allain.

Readers who have attempted to trace their English ancestry will be familiar with the works of P. H. Reaney and others on the subject of surnames. The French equivalent is the *Dictionnaire étymologique des noms de famille et prénoms de France,* by Albert Dauzat, published in 1951 by Larousse. There are no specifically Huguenot surnames or families since one finds both Catholic and Protestant members of most families, especially among the nobility. There was, however, a tendency among Protestants in France, just as there was in Britain and the colonies, to give their children Old Testament names. Enquiries made to the Société Française de l'Histoire du Protestantisme, 54 rue des Sainte-Pères, Paris 75007, and to the Société Française d'Onomastique, 87 rue Vielle-du-Temple, Paris 75003 should elicit helpful information on the subject of surnames and their origins and places of distribution.

There are numerous biographies of Huguenot notables in both French and English, many of which can be consulted in the library of the Huguenot Society in London. On the other hand it would be as well to consult the *Bibliographie annuelle de l'Histoire de France,* published by the C.N.R.S., for new works are appearing all the time, and by consulting this one is able to keep up to date.

The French Research Organisation for Genealogical Services (F.R.O.G.S.), of 37 rue La Quintinie, 75015 Paris, offers the publication of your surname(s) in its information sheet to user members; searches in France by professional genealogists of known competence; translations and correspondence for an annual subscription if you are a professional genealogist. For the amateur, this is an Anglo-French research organisation of standing able to help you with research in France.

The following is a list of books and articles, mostly in French, from the *Bibliographie annuelle de l'histoire de France* of 1982, which may be of help to those familiar with the language.

General Studies

Catalogue de l'exposition Présence protestante en Alsace, 1530–1980: Strasbourg, Faculté de Théologie protestante, 1980.

Séguy, Jean: The French Mennonites: tradition and change, *Religion and Change,* Hull, 1981.

16th Century

Audisio, G.	Le massacre des Vaudois du Lubéron en 1545. *B. Soc. aixoise Et. hist.,* 1982, a. 12, No. 82.
Boy, M.	Liste des émigrés protestants d'origine auvergnate à Genève (le Refuge de 1549 à 1587). *A Moi Auvergne!,* 1982, a. 5, No. 22.
Colombet, A.	Les temples en Bourgogne. *Pays Bourgogne,* 1982, a. 29, No. 118.
Flaugères, J.	L'expansion de la Reforme protestante dans le diocèse d'Uzès au XVIe siècle. *Rhodanie,* 1982, No. 2, and No. 3.
Joxe, R.	Les Protestante du comté de Nantes au XVIe siècle au début du XVIIIe siècle. Marseilles, 1982.
Koch, G.	Pasteurs dans la région de Phalsbourg vers la fin du XVIe siècle. *Mélanges offerts à J. Rott, 1980.*
Maurice, M.	Un ancêtre de Benjamin Constant, le pasteur Antoine de Chandier (1534-91), originaire du Mâconnais. *A. Acad. Mâcon,* 1980-81, Series 3, Vol. 57.
Raitt, Jill	Theodore Beza (de Bèze), 1519-1605. *Shapers of religious traditions, 1560-1600,* 1981.

17th Century

Aubert, J-C.	Tribulations de Guillaume de Guyon de Geys de Pampelonne (Protestant émigré after the Revocation of the Edict of Nantes). *R. Vivarais,* 1982.
Boucher, M.	French speakers at the Cape: the European background. Pretoria Univ. Press, 1981.
Causse, M.	Audibert Durand, ministre apostat en Saintonge, 1678-98. *B. Soc. Hist. Prot. franc.,* 1982, Vol. 128, Oct.-Dec.
Coyne, P-L.	Liste alphabétique des familles protestantes de Bordeaux au XVIIe siècle. *Cah. Centre Généal. protestants,* 1982, No. 18-19.
Delormeau, C.	Les cimetières protestants de Nîmes. *B. Scéances Acad. Nîmes,* 1981, n. série, No. 82.
Hickel, M-A.	Les Korn, protestant obernois de la Contre-Réforme. *Soc. Hist. Archéol. Dambach-la-Ville,* 1982.
Kiefner, T.	Hugenotten und Waldenser in Pforzheim (1700-1767). *Z. F. Gesch. d. Oberrheins,* 1981, Vol. 129, n. series, Vol. 90.
Maillet, Nelly	Les Protestantes de Tours au XVIIe siècle. From the author, 81 rue Michelet, Tours, 1981.
Maurel, Lydie	Les Français de la religion réformée émigrés au Danemark (Le Refuge) *Généal, Sud-ouest,* 1981.
Perocheau, Joël	Les protestants sablais (des Sables-d'Olonne) au XVIIe siècle. *Olona,* 1982, No. 99.
Poujol, J.	Jean Cavalier, *B. Soc. Hist. Prot. Franc.,* 1982, Vol. 128, July-Sept.
Rousseau, R.	Les cimetières protestants de Coulon (Deux-Sèvres), Bessines (Deux-Sèvres) et Saint-Symphorien (Deux-Sèvres). *B. Soc. Hist. sci. Deux-Sèvres,* 1981, Series 2, Vol. 14, No. 1.

Ruiz, Alain	Une famille huguenote du Brandebourg au XVIIe siècle: Les Théremin (Issue du pasteur languedocien Etienne Théremin, XVIIe siècle). *Hommage à P-P. Sagave. R. Allemagne,* 1982, Vol. 14, No. 2.
Sambuc, J.	Religionnaires fugitifs du canton de Dieulefit (Dauphiné, Drôme); Sources notariales. *B. Soc. Hist. prot. franc.,* 1982, Vol. 128, April-June.
Van Leouwen-Kerkhof, J-M.	Les artistes huguenots émigrés aux Provinces Unies et leur influence sur l'art des XVII et XVIIIe siècles. *Revue de Culture Néerlandaise* (Rekkem), 1982, a. 11, No. 3.

18th Century

Blanc, J.	Sète, terre d'asile des Protestants au XVIIIe siècle? *B. Soc. Et. sci. Séte,* 1980.
Krumenakre, Yves	Les Protestants de la sénéchausée d'Angoulême dans la deuxieme moitié du XVIIIe siècle. *A. Groupe Rech. Et. Hist. Charente saintongeaise,* 1981, No. 3.

By Subscription

Index des noms cités dans les cahiers du Centre de Généalogie Protestante (1ère Série) (Index of names mentioned in the leaflets of the Protestant Genealogical Centre).

This index comprises 8,000 names mentioned in the 21 issues making up the first series of the C.G.P.'s leaflets, and will greatly assist historical and genealogical research, giving rapid access to relevant texts. Current subscription rate is 65 francs (from 15 November 1984), rising to 95 francs. Details from the French Research Organisation for Genealogical Services, 37 rue La Quintinie, 75015 Paris, France.

Huguenots in Germany, Switzerland and the Netherlands

Because so many Huguenot families emigrated to Britain and the colonies in two stages, we must now trace their pilgrimage through Germany, Switzerland and the Netherlands, for it is possible that those in search of Huguenot ancestry will at some stage need to look into the records of these countries.

Research in Germany is made difficult by the fact that the country was for so long divided into many sovereign states, and the religious divisions into Protestant and Catholic add further complications. Broadly speaking the states of southern Germany were Catholic, so need not concern us here, for it was to the northern ones that French refugees fled from persecution. The most usual asylums for Huguenots were Brandenburg/Prussia, Hanover, Mecklenburg, Nassau, and some states in Westphalia. To make confusion worse the German Protestants were divided into Lutherans and Reformed Churches. The Protestant states consisted of the following: the kingdom of Prussia

(Brandenburg), capital Berlin; the kingdom of Saxony, capital Dresden; the grand duchies of Hessen (Darmstadt), Mecklenburg (Schwerin and Neu–Strelitz), Sachsen-Weimar (Weimar) and Oldenburg (Oldenburg). The less important duchies included Anhalt, Sachsen-Altenburg, Sachsen-Coburg-Gotha, Brunswick (Braunschweig), Sachsen-Meiningen, and Schleswig-Holstein (which was sometimes in Denmark). Principalities were even smaller and the Protestant ones included Lippe-Detmold, Lippe-Biesterfeld, Bückeburg, Gera, Rudolstadt und Sondershausen—this list is far from complete. There were also the staunchly Protestant Hanseatic cities of Hamburg, Bremen, Lübeck and Danzig.

There has been little attempt to centralise German records, mainly for historical reasons, since every city of any size possesses its own archives and every province and land its Staatsarchiv. For this reason it is important for the genealogical enquirer to know something about the area to which his ancestor fled from France, but initial enquiries can be made to Der Herold Verein für Heraldik, Genealogie und Verwandte Wissenschaften, Wiesbaden, Dieselstrasse 24. There are likewise many genealogical societies concerned with the particular regions of Germany, and for those with ancestors from West Germany there is a society called the Deutsche Arbeitsgemeinschaft de Genealogischen Verbander (Union of German Genealogical Workers) at Hanover, am Markt 4.

Each of the German Protestant churches had similar, though different systems of registration. The earliest surviving fragments of a German register date from 1390, but the majority of those that have survived in whole or in part date from the end of the 16th century. During the 15th and 16th centuries it became fashionable to latinise names in some parts of Germany, as for example Curtius for Kurz and Piscator for Fischer. In the 17th century French Huguenot names were likewise germanised so that Quisingre became Kissinger and Lefevre, Schmidt. Unlike most other European countries, in Germany copies of wills are not deposited in local record offices. Testators file their wills with the local court if they wish, but there appears to be no compulsion in the matter.

It was not until 1848 that the Swiss Confederation was formally turned into a politically-unified state. Each of the Swiss cantons has its own government and the country as a whole has four official languages—German, French, Italian and Romansch —and two religions—Catholic and Protestant. Of the 25 cantons, the following are Protestant (the name of the chief town and the language is indicated in each case: G = German, F = French, R = Romansch. There were hardly any Huguenot refugees in the Italian-speaking cantons).

Appenzell (Inter-Rhoden)
   Herisau (G).
Aargau
   Aarau (G).
Basel-stadt and Basel-land
   Basel (G).
Berne
   Bern (G).

Geneva (Genf)
  Geneva (F).
Glarus
  Glarus (G).
Grisons (Graubünden)
  Chur (G and R).
Neuchatel
  Neuchatel (F).
Schaffhausen (Schaffhouse)
  Schaffhausen (G).
Thurgau (Thurgovie)
  Frauenfeld (G).
Vaud
  Lausanne (F).
Zurich
  Zurich (G).
All the rest are Catholic cantons.

The Reformation preached by Zwingli and Calvin found fruitful soil for growth in Switzerland. It spread widely, but confederated cantons, anxious to avoid disastrous schisms, took care to refrain from religious strife. This gave substance to Swiss neutrality, which was formally recognised by the signatories of the Treaty of Westphalia in 1648. The cantonal structure of the country is reflected in the way its archives are kept. There is no central organisation or National Archive as in other countries. Before 1848, civil registration was a matter for each canton, with the result that the date for the beginning of registration differs from canton to canton. Before it was taken over by the cantonal governments, it was, as elsewhere, the responsibility of the church. Cantonal records are found at police headquarters, the departments of Communal Affairs of the Chancelleries of each canton in the chief towns, and enquiries should be made there.

By the middle of the 16th century the Netherlands were ruled by the Hapsburg kings of Spain. Because the Reformation had taken so firm a hold over the minds of the Dutch, the imposition by the Spanish of the Inquisition provoked a rebellion in 1566 which resulted in 80 years of bitter warfare. During this war, in 1579, the northern and southern Netherlands were separated from each other, but in 1588 the Republic of the United Netherlands, with the princes of Orange as Stadtholders appointed by the States General, was founded. It lasted until 1795, when Napoleon replaced it by his kingdom of Holland.

Church registers are kept by the ministers of the different denominations. Between 1588 and 1795 the Dutch Reformed Church was the state church and, as in England, people who dissented from it had to marry there, or before a magistrate, as well as in their own churches. The vast majority of the ancient registers were handed over to the civil authorities in 1796 and are now in the custody of the Gemeentearchieven (Municipal Archives). A guide to the whereabouts of Dutch parish registers before

1796–the Reportorium D.T.B.–with English explanations, was published in 1969 by the Central Bureau for Genealogy, Nassauplaan 18, The Hague.

Wills, transfers and divisions of property, marriage contracts, tax rolls, and the administration of orphans' estates were all matters dealt with by notaries, just as they were in France. The language, of course, is Dutch, so it is necessary for those who do not speak and read it to employ local, professional genealogists. A general survey of the contents of notarial records has been published in *De Rijksarchieven in Nederland* (1973). Wills in Holland are generally notarial deeds and are to be found in bound volumes of notarial deeds executed by a particular notary. These volumes are housed in the various record offices up and down the country. The names of the notaries and the towns where they practised are to be found in the *Register der Protocollen van Notarissen in Nederland,* by F. L. Hartong (1916). The list covers the period from 1550 to 1916. In places where there were no notaries, such as Groningen, notarial duties were carried out by the leading functionary of the town, such as the mayor.

Holland is particularly fortunate in having set up a central bureau for genealogical studies 40 years ago. It is located in The Hague at 18 Nassauplaan, and here are housed the national genealogical collections and documents of many kinds relating to family history. There is information on more than 15,000 Dutch families, and a card index of nearly two million baptisms, marriages and deaths, as well as details of membership of Walloon churches in France and Germany in addition to the Netherlands. One of the most valuable sources of information about English and Anglo-Dutch merchants in the 17th and 18th centuries is to be found in the lists of freemen burgesses of Rotterdam and other cities published in *Gens Nostra,* the organ of the Dutch Genealogical Society. A list of university towns appears in the *Genealogisch Repertorium,* by Jonkheer van Beresteyn, which contains information about alumni and graduates of the universities concerned. In these lists are to be found many Huguenot names, but not all of them appear as French ones. A number of Huguenots, who later settled in England or the colonies, went, as we have already seen, first to the Netherlands, and so their names appear in a Dutch form.

A most valuable collection of Huguenot data is at the Bibliothèque Wallonne at Leyden. This comprises copies of baptismal, marriage and death entries to do with refugee families taken from the registers of churches in France before the Revocation of the Edict of Nantes, of the Walloon churches in Holland itself, and of Huguenot churches in Germany. Enquiries should be written in French to the Secretaire de la Commission de l'Histoire des Eglises Wallonnes, Pieterskerkhof 40, Leyden, Netherlands.

The following are the addresses of the chief record offices in Holland. For fuller details of the type of records they contain, reference should be made to *Gide voor de Archieven van Gemeenten en Waterschappen in Nederland* (van de Koning, The Hague, 1945) or *Repertorium van Inventarissen van Nederlandse Archieven* (van de Kamp, Groningen, 1947).

Rijksarchief in Drenthe, Brink 4, Assen.
Rijksarchief in Friesland, Turfmarkt 13, Leeuwarden.
Rijksarchief in Gelderland, Markt 1, Arnhem.
Rijksarchief in Groningen, St Jansstraat 2, Groningen.

Rijksarchief in Limburg, St Pietersstraat 7, Maastricht.
Rijksarchief in Noord-Brabant, Waterstraat 20, 's-Hertogenbosch.
Rijksarchief in Overijssel, Sassenpoort, Zwolle.
Rijksarchief in Utrecht, Alexander Numankade 201, Utrecht.
Rijksarchief in Zeeland, St Pieterstraat 38, Middleburg.
Algemeen Rijksarchief, Bleyenburg 6, 's-Gravenhage (The Hague).

Most Belgian parish registers have been transferred to provincial archives, though some are kept in the state archives and a few still remain in the hands of the incumbents. As these are Catholic registers, they are unlikely to contain many references to Huguenot families, although forced conversions meant that some records of their existence might be found there. The addresses of the various state archives are as follows:

Antwerp: 5 Door Verstraeteplaats; Antwerpsche Kring voor Familienkunde, 25 Moonsstraat; Service de Centralisation des Etudes Généalogiques et Démographiques de Belgique, 26 rue aux Laines.
Arlon: Place Lépold.
Bruges: 14–18 Akademiestraat.
Brussels: Archives Générales du Royanne (Het Algemeen Rijksarchief), 78 Gallerie Ravenstein; L'Office Généalogique et Héraldique de Belgique, 36 rue Bosquet. Le Conseil Héraldique, 85 rue du Prince Royal; L'Association de la Noblesse du Royaume de Belgique, 96 rue Souveraine.
Ghent: Geeraard Duivelsteen.
Hassalt: Bampsplaan.
Liège: 8 rue Pouplin.
Mons: 23 Place du Parc.
Namur: 45 rue d'Arquet.

Chapter Seven

RECORDING THE RESULTS

RESEARCH IS FUN: unfortunately, writing up the results is hell! But undigested material is of no interest to those who have not collected it, and sooner or later it will become necessary to record the results of one's labours, not only for one's own satisfaction but for the edification of one's descendants and others interested in genealogy and family history. This chapter attempts to set down some do's and don'ts for those embarking on the writing of their family history, and to offer suggestions which may help with the recording of information gained by research which might have covered many years.

The *Oxford English Dictionary* defines genealogy as the *account* of a person's descent from an ancestor or ancestors. A pedigree, on the other hand, is defined as the table which genealogists draw up to illustrate descent. Family histories, however, are usually confined to the record of individuals sharing a common surname, though not necessarily all descending from a common ancestor, so the creation of pedigrees is an essential stage in the process, and is merely the framework upon which the history itself can be hung. The history of a Huguenot family, like that of any other, is more often than not the history of the localities in which it settled. It can thus embrace the histories of French villages, Dutch cities, and London suburbs. It follows, therefore, that once a pedigree has been established, the sources for the writing of the family history will be in several languages, and in several cities, towns and villages.

It is often said, with some truth, that the only records the majority of us leave behind us are those which stem from contacts with bureaucracy, the Church and the law. In the case of Huguenot families, brushes with the law loom large, for many were accused of, and imprisoned for, heresy, and once they arrived in their land of refuge, they became enmeshed with the local bureaucracy and local lawyers. On the whole, then, there may well be more material for the Huguenot descendant to use in the compilation of his family history than for those whose ancestors were law-abiding conformists who never strayed far from home.

The first and most important rule for the amateur genealogist and family historian is this: check all sources at first hand. Never trust the printed word. Always make sure that translations are accurate, and wherever possible get a sight of the original documents themselves. This, of course, is a counsel of perfection, but as a general rule it is not advisable to take anything on trust. Our 19th-century ancestors were fiends for constructing false pedigrees. It is hard for us to understand the hypnotic power with which the image of the middle ages obsessed the minds of men and women at the beginning of the 19th century. Until well on into the reign of Queen Victoria the romantic charm of the medieval period was felt throughout the country. And not only throughout Britain—throughout Europe as well. During the 18th century interest in heraldry and grants of arms almost vanished, and, sadly, until about 1760, many medieval privileges were discontinued, and disappeared unnoticed. Before the accession of George III there were few works on peerage and pedigree available to the ordinary reader—Dugdale's *Baronage* of 1676 and Collins' *Peerage* of 1709 were just about the only ones. By the time Queen Victoria came to the throne there were at least 20 different peerages, many of which were plagiarised miniatures of existing publications. Then arose Samuel Egerton Brydges, whose passion for all things Gothic amounted to mania.

Samuel Egerton Bridges (Bruges—Burges—Brydges as the name was spelled from time to time), was the eighth child and second surviving son of a Kentish family. He liked to believe that he came from a 'line of great nobility and antiquity which had come to England with William the Conqueror from Bruges. At the age of 24 he claimed kinship with the family of the first Lord Chandos, a peerage created in 1554, and thereupon changed the spelling of his name from Bridges to Brydges to prove it. The barony of Chandos having become vacant, Samuel Egerton persuaded his elder brother to claim it. The proceedings which followed were perhaps the most farcical that have ever wasted the time of the College of Arms and the House of Lords. When the claim was turned down for lack of evidence, Samuel set to and produced some more, and when this, too, was pronounced inadequate, he began to forge it. He found little black boxes full of documents in remote attics, which mysteriously vanished when anyone lifted their lids. He quoted entries from parish registers, which had recently been destroyed by fire or damp. He even went so far as to produce a crinkled piece of parchment, on which there appeared to be nothing but a coat of arms and some arcane squiggles, and called upon a Mr. Lemon (who gave his address as the Tower of London), to apply a magic liquid to revive the invisible ink with which it was written. This was done, but, if any ink had ever been applied, the writing could not be seen. After 13½ years in which the Committee of Privileges sat 22 times, they gave as their opinion that Samuel and his brother had not made out. their claim to the barony.

Undaunted, Samuel spent the next six years compiling a new edition of Collins' *Peerage,* a gigantic work which is still consulted, but since its aim was to establish his family's antiquity and claim to the Chandos barony, must be regarded with some degree of caution. As if this were not enough, he published an enormous tome called *Stemmata Illustria* in which with a great shield showing 360 quarterings he proved in over 300 pages to his own satisfaction his descent from the Merovingian kings in the fifth century, and showed in more than 250 different pedigrees that more of Charlemagne's blood flowed in his veins than in those of the royal family. In doing this he spent more than £100,000, and all it earned him was a baronetcy for his work on Collins' *Peerage,* and the doubtful honour of being lampooned in Disraeli's novel *Sybil.*

But Samuel was not alone; a close-run rival was Sir Richard Broun [*sic*] who tried to prove that the baronetcy was of medieval origin, and to bolster this fantastic claim produced Broun's *Baronetage* in which he filled the preface with 20 pages of argument and gave his own family four times as much space as anyone else.

Others less elevated took a different line and simply changed their names from Smith or Brown to what they supposed they might have been in France in the middle ages by adding the particle 'de' in front of them. De Burghs, de Veres, de Brownes and de Beechamps multiplied like weeds in a wet summer. A family called Mullins became de Moleyns, and one called Wilkins decided their name was really de Winton. Thackeray's character, the footman, James Plush, appeared in *Punch* as Jeames de la Pluche and announced that he was descended from Hugo de la Pluche who came over with William the Conqueror.

But enough of all this. The point we must make is that a French or medieval origin has always been thought desirable by certain sections of society, and even a Huguenot ancestry has been forged to impress the Joneses next door. Undoubtedly, the work of people like Samuel Egerton Brydges and Sir Richard Broun have some merit, for not everything in them is fraudulent, but the point we must make is that these are secondary sources, and that to produce a valid family history or pedigree one should always go back to the original sources, and every statement in a published account of the ancestry of a family, especially if written during the period we have just been talking about, should be examined with the greatest possible care.

But it is possible to take this to too great a length, and an equally frequent error is to quote in full every single document, no matter how slightly relevant. Too many family histories are made unreadable by the inclusion of such quotations. Take, for example, wills: many are written in a verbose, legalistic manner, and contain a great deal of stuff of no relevance to the matter in hand. Until the early 19th century they began with a set-piece declaration of faith, which can nearly always be omitted, or at least drastically abbreviated. Many legal documents, such as those dealing with the transfer of property, or depositions in lawsuits are full of unnecessary words. If you feel that these documents contain valuable material, it is always possible to quote them in full in an appendix, but to do so in the body of your text makes that text almost unreadable.

Don't make claims to Huguenot, noble or medieval descent unless you can substantiate them. Where any doubt exists, admit it. Much material you will obtain in the course of your research will be circumstantial. It is quite legitimate to make a well-informed guess so long as you say so. The final proof is often lacking simply because the relevant document has been lost, or you haven't been able to find it. The important thing is to indicate to your readers what can be substantiated by documentary evidence, what is probable, and what is possible. There will always be someone ready to shoot you down, so the more authentic your statements the greater the fun you will have in proving such people wrong.

Don't be afraid to open cupboard doors and of letting out skeletons. Most families have sired bastards, both of the genetic and moral kind, so there is nothing to be afraid of. After all, we cannot be held entirely responsible for the sins and omissions of our ancestors. One of the present authors was once asked to write the history of a family which had produced at the end of the 19th century a very successful engineer and businessmen. His descendants aspired to a knighthood or baronetcy, and were also very pious Catholics. In the course of the investigations it was discovered that the engineer's mother had been married twice, and that her first husband, a Polish aristocrat, had deserted her at the time of the Crimean War, and had not communicated with her for many years. Meanwhile, she met the engineer's father, and they fell in love, but because she was already married to the Polish count, she refused to marry him. The law of Britain allows one to assume death if, after seven years, nothing has been heard of the person who had vanished, and so in due course, she agreed to the marriage. To her dismay her Polish husband turned up within a year of her second marriage, and after the birth of her first child, the engineer. Although neither party had acted either illegally or immorally, the mother was, in fact, married bigamously. Rather than let this family secret slip out, the engineer's grandson, who had commissioned the work, insisted that all copies of the book which had been written about the family should be burnt. Luckily the author had been given half a dozen copies as part of his fee, and these are now safely deposited in the copyright libraries. Unless one is prepared to tell the truth about one's family, then there seems no point at all in setting out to explore its history.

Always make sure your geography is accurate. Check all place names in a good gazetteer: there are 25 places called Broughton in England, and 23 Kilbrides in Scotland and Ireland. As for 'Saints' in France, there are 47 Saint-Sauveurs, not to mention 249 Saint-Martins. Bartholomew's *Survey Gazetteer of the British Isles* is an extremely useful one to have on your shelves. In France there is nothing quite like it, but a useful next-best is the *Dictionnaire des Communes*, published by Berger–Levrault. Departmental gazetteers do exist in some parts of the country, but there is nothing so thorough as Bartholomew's gazetteer.

It is often helpful to include maps and illustrations of places in a family history. Knowledge of the topography of a district can be helpful, especially in France, when searching for spouses. Until the 19th century, the rivers of France were the main highways, so it was often very much easier to find a wife 20 miles downstream than it was to trudge five miles over a range of hills. Whenever possible, therefore, try to visit the district from which your ancestors came. Not only may you have the satisfaction of seeing the hills and valleys they saw, but there is no substitute for getting the 'atmosphere' of a place, which can very frequently tell you more than you might at first think possible.

The problem of dates before 1752 is one of particular importance for people of Huguenot descent, for the Catholic countries of Europe, which effectively meant almost all except Britain and Russia, adopted the Gregorian calendar in 1582. Before 1752 the official English calendar reckoned the year as beginning on 25 March (Old Style), and from 1752 the year was reckoned from 1 January. The English colonies used the official English calendar, though Scotland adopted 1 January as New Year in 1600, although retaining the Julian calendar. Britain and its colonies were therefore 10 days out of phase with Europe from 1582 to 1700, and 11 days out from 1700 to 1752. When writing a family history it is necessary to be consistent with dates. You should state at the outset whether you propose to use New Style or Old Style dates, and indicate this quite clearly. If you decided to use Old Style, then everything you wish to record as having taken place between 1 January and 24 March should be double-year dated, thus 17 February 1624/5 or whatever. When it comes to deciding the year and the date of arrival of a Huguenot ancestor do not forget that a refugee leaving France on what he would think of as 1 March 1686 would arrive in Dover the same day and find it was 10 March 1685. Untold confusion can arise from a lack of awareness of this problem.

Some family histories are spoilt by their authors writing large chunks in olde englisshe. Itte is a dredfulle bore. When quoting from original documents confine antique spelling to a minimum. It is better to transcribe the documents into modern spelling than labour your readers with long, difficult passages in the original. If the document is so important, then xerox it and publish it in facsimile. It is exceedingly tedious to have to wade through even modern legal documents, many of which are little better than gobbledegook; just because a will or a deed is 300 years old doesn't make it any less turgid or boring. Lawyers used to be paid by the length of the documents they produced—to read some modern examples, you might think they still are—so get down to the nub of the matter in question, and only quote those passages which are really important, and more especially, those that have a close bearing on your narrative. And while we are on the subject of olde englisshe, do remember that the letter that looks like a 'y' is really shorthand for 'th'. People never actually said 'ye olde bunne shoppe', they spoke very much as we do today, and the sound we indicate by 'th' was never pronounced as 'y' in yet or yes. Final 'e's' are linguistic relics and have not usually been pronounced during the last 300 years, which is why they have tended to fall out of the written language.

Remember, too, that the French language has also changed, though somewhat less than English during the past 400 years. The main difference between modern and 16th- or 17th-century French is in the introduction and increasing use of accents to indicate missing letters—more often than not the letter 's'. The circumflex accent (ˆ) almost invariably indicates the former presence of 's' after the vowel over which it is placed. For example, château used to be written chasteau or chastel; Evêque was evesque; cf. the Latin episcopus = English bishop. Ignorance of the way in which accents have come into use can lead to confusion when it comes to identifying French surnames, so many of which among the nobility were also place-names. Any elementary French language primer is worth studying to ensure familiarity with accents, even if you have no other familiarity with the language.

There is another point to remember in connection with France and the French language: until well into the 17th century, some would say even later, people living south of the River Loire spoke a very different kind of French from those who lived north of it. The langue d'Oc and the langue d'Oil were much more than a mere difference of accent such as one finds in Britain, where someone living in Kent is perfectly intelligible to someone from Caithness or Ulster. This difference exists even today, so that a recent film shot in Périgord about a peasant boy who went to the First World War, in which all the characters spoke the local dialect or patois, had to be dubbed with sub-titles in French when it was shown in Paris. Because many Huguenot families came from the south-west, this is a matter you should bear in mind, for some documents relating to them might be written in langue d'Oc rather than French. In translating them do not be tempted to render them in Mockswold English.

Remember that the process of research is itself great fun, and that when you come to write your family history it would interest your readers to know how you made your discoveries. Too many family histories read as if everything had been known from the start. It wasn't. Obtaining the material can be as exciting as the solving of a crime, and as the information itself. Your readers' interest will be held if you impart this excitement to them by telling how you came across the evidence supporting your story.

It is also worth remembering that lateral genealogy is often as interesting as vertical. Who married whom, and the interconnection of families is as important and just as interesting as tracing a patrilineal line back to Noah. We live among friends and relations, not among our ancestors—each individual is just as, if not more interesting than his grandfather and great-grandfather.

Finally, there are two chronological approaches to the writing of a family history. You can either begin by describing your own and your parents' families and then work back generation by generation, or you can start with your earliest-known ancestor and work forwards to the present day. Whichever method you choose doesn't really matter so long as you are consistent. It is a mistake to jump from period to period, though sometimes this is unavoidable if you decide to follow the history of one branch and then move on to another.

Always include the year when you give dates. It is very easy to forget to do this if you are describing a series of events in a given period of time. Phrases like 'In the following year such and such happened' or 'Three years before, he went to Paris to see the king' are all very well, but frustrating for the reader when the last date you mentioned was 20 pages back. He wants to know if it happened in 1563 or 1565.

To end on a dogmatic note: don't forget that even the best family history can be ruined if it doesn't have an index. Tedious though the compiling of indexes can be, their value is beyond price to those who come after, and who want to derive all they can from your work. Unhappily, family histories, containing as they do so many names, require large indexes, but the time spent on compiling them, whether for publication or just for ease of access to the unpublished part of your records, is well worth the effort. Let us give thanks to God that He has given men the intelligence to devise the computer, for henceforth the task of family historians will be much easier.

CHRONOLOGY

1455   First printed edition of the Bible

c. 1500 Erasmus (1467–1563) begins to write and preach reform of the church

1512   Jacques le Fevre (Jacobus Faber) writes *Sancti Pauli Epistolas*

1515   Accession of Francis I of France

1516   Concordat of Bologna

1523   First French translation of the Bible

1526   Tyndale's English version of the New Testament printed in Antwerp

1529   Louis de Berquin burnt at the stake

1534   Protestant placard campaign in Paris. Calvin settles in Basle

1535   Edict banning all heretics in France. First refugees leave France. Publication of Tyndale and Coverdale Bible in English in Hamburg

1538   Foundation of first French Protestant church at Strasbourg

1539   Bernard Palissy settles at Saintes

1540   First substantial Huguenot settlements in Kent and Sussex

1541   French forts established near Quebec

1545   Jean de Maynier, baron d'Oppède orders massacre of Waldensians at Mérindol and Cabrières

1547   Death of Henry VIII of England; accession of Edward VI. Death of Francis I of France; accession of Henry II. Protestantism established officially in England. Increased immigration of Huguenots to Kent, especially Canterbury. Chambre Ardente established in Paris

1548   First Huguenot congregation established at Canterbury by Jan Utehove and François de la Rivière of Orleans

1550   Temple of Jesus licensed, earliest foreign Protestant church in London

1551   Edict of Chateaubriant

1553   Death of Edward VI; accession of Mary I of England. Dispersion of London Protestant refugees; persecution of English Protestants begins

1555   First Huguenot consistory at Paris

1556   First Protestant church in Paris founded. Philip II succeeds to throne of Spain

1558   Death of Mary I; accession of Elizabeth I

1559   Treaty of Cateau-Cambresis. Synod of Paris at which 15 Protestant churches are represented. Death of Henry II; accession of Francis II of France

1560   Conspiracy of Amboise to kill the king of France fails. Edict of Romorantin lays interdict on Protestantism. Meeting of States General at Orleans. Death of Francis II; accession of Charles IX of France

1561   Edict of July. Meeting of States General at Pontoise. Beginning of influx of refugees to Kent from Low Countries, Picardy, Artois and Flanders. Colloquy of Poissy attempts to bring about a *modus vivendi* between Catholics and Protestants in France

1562	Edict of Saint-Germain assures religious liberty to Huguenots. Massacre of Vassy. First battle of civil war at Dreux. Siege of Rouen
1563	Assassination of Francis, duke of Guise. Pacification of Amboise
1564	French settlement at Fort Caroline, Florida, founded. Treaty of Troyes
1565	Spanish attack on Fort Caroline
1567	Siege of Saint-Denis. Death of duke of Montmorency
1568	Treaty of Longjumeau. Fort Caroline recaptured
1569	Battle of Jarnac. Death of Condé. Battle of Montcontour. Peace of Saint-Germain
1570	Henry of Navarre affianced to Marguerite de Valois
1572	Anglo-French Treaty of Blois. Death of Jeanne d'Albret, queen of Navarre. Marriage of Henry of Navarre and Marguerite de Valois. Attempted assassination of Coligny. Massacre of St Bartholomew begins in August and lasts till October. Civil war resumed
1573	Duke of Anjou elected king of Poland. Edict of Boulogne
1574	Death of Charles IX; accession of Henry III of France. Huguenot settlement at Winchelsea moved to Canterbury. Truce with Huguenots in France
1575	Confederation of Milhaud
1576	Formation of the Holy League. Peace of Monsieur and defeat of Henry III. War renewed
1577	Peace of Bergerac
1579	Peace of Fleix. Ordonnance of Blois
1584	Death of duke of Anjou; Henry of Navarre becomes heir to the throne of France. Duke of Guise proclaims Cardinal de Bourbon heir apparent. Treaty of Joinville
1585	Henry III forced to surrender to the League and the Guises. Treaty of Nemours. Outbreak of the War of the Three Henrys
1586	Truce of Saint-Brice
1587	Execution of Mary, queen of Scots. Battle of Coutras. Battle of Auneau
1588	Day of Barricades. Spanish Armada. Edict of Union. Duke of Guise and cardinal of Guise assassinated at Blois
1589	Henry III assassinated; accession of Henry of Navarre as Henry IV of France. Death of Catherine de' Medici. Battle of Arques. Death of Cardinal de Bourbon (Charles X)
1590	Battle of Ivry. Siege of Paris
1592	Battle of Aumale
1593	States General meet in Paris to elect a king. Henry IV converted to Catholicism
1594	Henry IV crowned at Chartres. Henry IV enters Paris
1595	Defeat of Spanish at Fontaine-Française
1596	Conference of Notables at Rouen
1597	Spanish capture Amiens. French recapture Amiens
1598	Peace of Vervins. Death of Philip II of Spain. Promulgation of the Edict of Nantes. End of Franco-Spanish War. Sable Island colony off Nova Scotia founded
1600	Tadoussac on the St Lawrence founded. Spanish defeat at Nieuport
1603	Death of Elizabeth I; accession of James I of England

1608   Champlain founded Quebec
1609   Disputed succession to the duchy of Cleves
1610   Assassination of Henry IV; accession of Louis XIII. Duke de Rohan becomes
        leader of the Huguenots. Alliance with Evangelical Union of Swabisch
1615   Sir Thomas Roe lands at Table Bay en route for India
1616   Treaty of Loudon
1618   Richelieu publishes *Principal Points of Faith of the Catholic Church*
1619   Huguenot church in Béarn rejects Decree of Restitution. La Rochelle supports
        Béarnais resistance to Louis XIII
1620   Sieges of Montauban and Montpellier. Death of duke of Luynes. Defection of
        Sully, La Force and Châtillon to the Catholics
1621   Jesse de Forest's request to settle in English colonies turned down by Sir
        Dudley Carleton
1622   Archbishop Laud attempts to compel refugees to conform to Anglican
        liturgy. Siege of Montpellier abandoned and peace signed
1623   *Nieuw Nederlandt* sails for America
1624   Richelieu given seat on royal council and appointed chief minister to Louis
        XIII
1625   Soubise seizes Ile de Ré and Ile d'Oléron. Death of James I; accession of
        Charles I of England
1626   Siege of La Rochelle begins. Manhattan Island bought from the Indians by
        Peter Minuit
1628   Ineffectual intervention by English fleet at La Rochelle. Siege ends; Richelieu
        takes La Rochelle
1629   Massachusetts Bay Company charter granted. Sir Robert Heath's Carolina
        charter granted. Baltimore decides to settle in the Chesapeake. Peace of
        Alais ends civil war in France. Huguenots cease to exist as political force.
        Baron de Sauce's emigration to Virginia with Huguenot settlers
1632   Baltimore's Maryland charter granted. Kirke brothers capture Quebec. Louis
        XIII bans all Huguenots from Canada
1633   Archbishop Laud appointed to head commission for regulating colonies
1642   Death of Richelieu
1643   Death of Louis XIII; accession of Louis XIV. Louis XIV guarantees Edict of
        Nantes. Mazarin prevents clamour for revocation
1647   Dutch establish refreshment station at Table Bay
1648   Outbreak of Fronde in France. Treaty of Westphalia
1649   Execution of Charles I; establishment of Commonwealth in England
1650   Jan van Riebeck establishes permanent settlement at Table Bay
1654   Beginning of Huguenot emigration on a large scale to North America
1658   New Haarlem founded
1659   Treaty of the Pyrenees
1660   Restoration of Charles II to throne of England
1661   Death of Cardinal Mazarin. Beginning of serious persecution of Huguenots and
        infringement of Edict of Nantes
1662   Jean Touton's colony in Massachusetts founded
1665   First Dutch church registers in South Africa

1677   New Paltz, New York State, founded
1678   Peace of Nijmegen. Attacks on Huguenots increase in France
1681   William Penn receives grant of Pennsylvania. Collections made in England
       for needy French refugees
1682   Pierre Daillé sent to minister to American Huguenots
1683   Dragonnards organised to harrass Huguenots in France
1685   Revocation of Edict of Nantes. Death of Charles II; accession of James II in
       England. Flood of refugees leaves France
1687   Foundation of Huguenot church at Charleston, South Carolina
1689   Deposition of James II; accession of William III and Mary II
1702   Death of William III; accession of Anne in England. Huguenot rising in
       Cévennes. War of Camisards
1711   Huguenot rising put down in France
1714   Death of Anne; accession of George I in England
1715   Louis XIV decrees end of Protestantism in France. Death of Louis XIV.
       First Synod of the Desert at Nîmes
1727   Death of George I; accession of George II
1745   Protestant uprising in France
1754   Protestant risings in eastern and southern France
1789   Declaration of the Rights of Man
1802   Code Napoléon gives full civil and religious equality to Protestants in France
1905   Separation of Church and State in France

BIBLIOGRAPHY

Lord Acton, *History of Freedom & Other Essays*, 1907.
Agnew, D. C. A., *Protestant Exiles from France*, 2 Vols., 1886.
Andrieux, M., *Henri IV dans ses années pacifiques*, 1954.
Anselme, Père, *Histoire de la Maison Royale de France*, 1723-33.
Armstrong, E., *The French Wars of Religion*, 1892.
d'Aumale, H. duc, *Histoire des Princes de Condé pendant les XVIe et XVIIe siècles*, 8 vols., 1863-96.
Baird, C. W., *History of Huguenot Immigration to America*, 1885.
Baird, H. M., *The Huguenots and Henry of Navarre*, 1886.
—— *History of the Rise of the Huguenots in France*, 1890.
—— *The Huguenots and the Revocation of the Edict of Nantes*, 1895.
Barrow, G. B., *The Genealogist's Guide*.
Bartholomew's Survey Gazetteer of the British Isles.
Baxter, Ian, *Brief Guide to Biographical Sources: Far East*.
Benoir, Elie, *Histoire de l'Edit de Nantes*, 1875.
Berger-Levrault, *Dictionnaire des Communes*, 1980.
Berthaut, Jules, *Les Emigrés francais à Londres*, 1904.
Bitton, D., *The French Nobility in Crisis, 1540-1640*, 1969.
Boisset, J., *Histoire du Protestantisme*, 1970.
Briggs, Robin, *Early Modern France, 1560-1717*, 1977.
British Library, Periodical Publications.
Browning, A., *History of the Huguenots*, 2 vols., 1829.
Buisseret, J., *Sully and the Growth of Centralised Government in France*, 1968.
Burchall, Michael, *National Genealogical Directory*.
Camp, A. J., *Wills and their Whereabouts*, 1971.
Capewell, J., *Index of Nonconformist Registers*, 1965.
Chaix-d'Est-Ange, G., *Liste des Familles Francaises*, Cover letters A–Gau only (Incomplete work), 1910.
de la Chenaye-Desbois & Badier, *Dictionnaire de la Noblesse Francaise*, 1893.
C.N.R.S.. *Bibliographie annuelle de l'Histoire de France*.
Coquerel, C., *Histoire des Églises du Désert*, 1841.
de Councelles., *Histoire Genealogique et Héraldique des Pairs de France*, 1824.
Coveney, B., *France in Crisis, 1620-1715*, 1977.
Cox, J. & Padfield, T., *Tracing your Ancestors in the PRO*, 1981.
Cunningham, W., *Alien Immigrants to England*, 1897.
Currer-Briggs, N., *Virginia Settlers & English Adventurers*, 1969.
—— *English Adventurers & Colonial Settlers*, 1970.
—— *English Wills of Colonial Families*, 1970.
—— & Gambier, R. F., *Debrett's Family Historian*, 1981.
Dauzat, A., *Dictionnaire Etymologique des Noms de Famille et Prénoms de France*, 1951.
Denis, P., *Bibliographie de l'Histoire Demographique des Refugiés Flamandes et Wallons en Angleterre, 1558-1625*. (See Bulletin de la Société d'Histoire du Protestantisme Belge, Vol. 6., 1975).
Descendants of the Refugees — The Witnesses in Sackcloth, 1852.
Dictionary of National Biography.
Directory of British Associations.
Doucet, R., *Les Institutions de la France au 16e siècle*, 1948.
Dunn, R. S., *The Age of Religious Wars, 1559-1715*, 1970.

England, S. L., *The Massacre of St Bartholomew*, 1938.

Erlanger, P., *Le Massacre de la St Barthélemy* (Trans. P. O'Brien).

Federation of Family History Societies, *Aids for Genealogists*, 1975.

Federn, C., *Mazarin*, 1934.

Foster, Sir W., *Guide to the India Office Records, 1600–1858*.

Friedrichs, H., *How to find German Ancestors*, 1974.

The Gentleman's Magazine (1713–1868).

Gibson, J. S. W., *Census Returns 1841–1881 on Microfilm.*

— *Marriage, Census and Other Indexes for the Family Historian.*

— *Wills and Where to Find Them.*

— *Probate Jurisdictions.*

— *Where to Find the International Genealogical Index.*

— *Bishops Transcripts and Marriage Licences.*

Gieseler, J. G. L., *Die Protestantische Kirche*, 1935.

Goss, C. W. F., *The London Directories, 1677–1855.*

Goubert, P., *Louis XIV and Twenty Million Frenchmen*, 1970.

Graham, N. H., *Parish Registers, Copies and Indexes, Inner & Outer London.*

— *Nonconformist and Foreign Registers of Inner London.*

Grant, A. J., *The Huguenots*, 1934.

— & Mayo, R., *The Huguenots*, 1973.

Grant, A. J., *The French Monarchy*, 1910.

Grosley, P. J., *A Tour of London*, 1772.

Gwynn, R. D., *Huguenot Heritage*, 1984.

Haag, Eugene, *La France Protestante* (From Lives of French Protestants), 1877–88.

Hamilton-Edwards, G., *In Search of Army Ancestry*, 1978.

Hanotaux, G. & The duc de La Force, *Histoire du Cardinal Richelieu*, 1896, 1947.

Hardy, W. J. & Page, W., *Calendar of Feet of Fines for London and Middlesex.*

Hartog, F. L., *Register der Protocollen van Notarissen in Nederland.*

Heritier, J., *Catherine de Medici* (Trans. C. Haldane), 1963.

Hessels, J. H., *Register of the Dutch Church of Austin Friars, 1568–1872.*

Hodson, V. C. P., *India Office Records.*

Hozier's, *Grand Armorial de France*, 1695.

Hurst, Q., *Henry of Navarre*, 1937.

Iredale, D., *Enjoying Archives*, 1985.

Jackson, Lady C., *The Last of the Valois*, (2 vols.), 1895.

James, G. P. R., *The Life of Henry the Fourth, King of France and Navarre*, (3 vols.), 1847.

Janelle, P., *The Catholic Reformation*, 1949.

Jongla de Morenau, H., *Armorial Generale de France.*

Jones, P. E. & Smith, R., *Guide to the Records of the City of London Record Office & Guildhall Library.*

Kelley, C. G., *French Protestantism, 1559–1562*, 1918.

Kershaw, W. L., *Protestants from France in their English Homes*, 1885.

Kingdon, R. M., *Geneva and the Coming of the Wars of Religion in France, 1555–1563*, 1956.

— *Geneva and the Consolidation of the French Protestant Movement, 1564–1572*, 1967.

Knox, S. J., *Ireland's Debt to the Huguenots*, 1959.

Koenigsberger, H. G., *Western Europe and the Rise of Spain*, New Modern Cambridge History, Vol. III.

Lart, C. E., *Huguenot Pedigrees* (2 vols.), 1924–28.

— *The Huguenot Church in Caen in the 16th century*, 1927.

Lavisse, E., *Histoire de la France*, vols. VI, VII and VIII, 1904–8.

Leathes, Sir S., *Henry IV of France*, Cambridge Modern History, Vol. III.

Lee, Grace L., *Huguenots in Ireland*, 1936.

Lee, Hannah F., *The Huguenots in France and America*, 1843.

Leonard, E. G., *A History of Protestantism*, 1964.

Leclerc, J., *Toleration and the Reformation* (Trans. J. Weston).

Lefroy, J. P., *Loffroy de Cambrai by a Cadet*, 1961.
> NOTE: This is one of many family histories, some of them unpublished or privately printed in the library of Huguenot Society. Available to Fellows and Members only.

Lewis's Topographical Dictionary.

Local Population Studies, *Original Parish Registers*, 4 vols., 1973.

Lough, J. (ed.), *Locke's Travels in France*, 1953.

Mackinnon, J., *Calvin and the Reformation*, 1936.

Mariejol, J. H., *La Reforme et la Ligue. L'édit de Nantes, 1559-1598*, Article in *Histoire de France depuis les Origines jusqu'à la Révolution*, ed. Lavisse, Vol. IV, Pt. 1. 1904.

—— *Henri IV et Louis XIII, 1598-1643*. Ibid.

Marion, M., *Dictionnaire des Institutions de la France au 17e et 18e siècles*, 1923.

Marshall, G. W., *The Genealogist's Guide*.

Medlycott, M. T., *City of London Freedom Registers*, 1976.

Mettam, R., *Government and Society in Louis XIV's France*, 1970.

Mettam & Johnson, *French History and Society: The Wars of Religion to the Fifth Republic*, 1972.

Misson de Valbourg, *Misson's Memoirs and Observations in his Travels over England*, 1719.

Mogen, B., *Die Wallonengemunde in Canterbury von ihrer Gründung bis zum Jahre 1635*, 1973.

Mousnier, R., *Les Institutions de la France sous la Monarchie Absolue*, 1974.

Neale, J. E., *The Age of Catherine de Medici*, 1963.

—— *Queen Elizabeth I*, 1952.

Newspaper Press Directory.

Noguères, H., *The Massacre of St Bartholomew*, 1962 (Trans. C. E. Engel).

Norton, Jane E., *Guide to the National and Provincial Directories of England and Wales before 1856*.

Norwood, A., *The Reformation Refugees as an Economic Force. Studies in Church History*, Vol. V. Chicago, 1942.

Palmer's *Index to The Times*.

Pérouas, L., *Le Diocèse de La Rochelle, 1648-1724*, 1964.

Phillimore, W. P. W. & Fry, E. A., *Index to Changes of Name*.

Phillimore Atlas and Index of Parish Registers.

Poirson, A., *Histoire du Regne de Henri IV*, 4 vols., 1862-67.

Poole, R. L., *The Huguenots of the Dispersion*, 1880.

Public Record Office, *List of the Non-Parochial Registers and Records in the Custody of the Registrar-General.*

Reaman, G. E., *Trail of the Huguenots in Europe*, 1925.

Rocheblave, S., *Agrippa d'Aubigné*, 1910.

de St-Alain, M., *Nobiliaire Universel de France*, 1875.

Salisbury, E., *List of Liverymen and Freemen of the City Companies.*

Salmon, J. H. M., *Society in Crisis: France in the 16th century*, 1975.

Schilling, H., *Niederlandische Exultanten im 16. Jahrhundert*, 1972.

Scoville, W. C., *The Persecution of the Huguenots & French Economic Development, 1680-1720*, Berkeley, 1960.

Sedgwick, H. D., *Henry of Navarre*, Indianapolis, 1930.

—— *The House of Guise*, Indianapolis, 1938.

Seward, Desmond, *The First Bourbon — Henry IV of France and Navarre*, Boston, 1971.

Shennan, I. H., *Government and Society in France, 1461-1661*, 1969.

Sims, S. J., *London and Middlesex Published Records.*

Smedley, B., *History of the Reformed Religion in France*, 3 vols., 1832-34.

Smiles, S., *The Huguenots*, 1866, 1876 and 1880.

Steel, D. J., *National Index of Parish Registers*, 12 vols. Not yet completed.

Stoye, J. W., *English Travellers Abroad, 1604-1667*, 1952.

de Schickler, F., *Les Eglises de Refuge en Angleterre*, 3 vols, 1892.
> NOTE: This is an excellent general history, but not of great genealogical use.

Sully, Duc de, *Memoirs*, 1856.

Sutherland, N.M., *Huguenot Struggle for Recognition*, 1980.

Tapie, V. L., *France in the Age of Louis XIII & Richelieu*, 1975.
Tate, W. E., *The Parish Chest*, 1983.
Thompson, J. W., *The Wars of Religion in France, 1559-1576*, 1909.
Thomson, T. R., *A Catalogue of British Family Histories*.
Treasure, G. R. R., *Seventeenth Century France*, 1981.
Van de Koning, *Gids voor de Archieven van Gemeenten en Waterschappen in Nederland*.
Van de Kemp, *Repertorium van Inventarissen van Nederlandse Archieven*.
Webb, C. C., *Guide to Genealogical Sources at the Borthwick Institute of Historical Research*.
Weiss, C., *History of the French Protestant Refugees from the Edict of Nantes*. Trans. F. Hardman, 1854.
Welch, C., *Register of Freemen of the City of London in the Reigns of Henry VIII & Edward VI*.
Wendel, F., *Calvin*. Trans. P. Mairet, 1963.
Whitehead, A. W., *Gaspard de Coligny*, 1904.
Whitmore, J. B., *A Genealogical Guide*.
Whitworth, R., *Lord Ligonier*, 1958.
Wilkinson, M., *A History of the League or Sainte Union*, 1576-95.
Will, J. S., *Protestantism in France*, 1921.
Wilson, J., *They Came as Strangers*, 1959.
Wolfston, Patricia, *Greater London Cemeteries and Crematoria*.
Zoff, O., *The Huguenots*, 1943.

Periodicals and Journals

Agenda Protestant, ed. F. Puaux, 1880-94; continued as *Agenda Annuaire*, ed. H. Gambier.
Annales.
Annuaire Ecclésiastique à l'usage des Eglises Reformées, ed. P. A. Rabant-Dupuis, 1807.
Annuaire Protestante, ed. T. de Prat, 1862-84.
Bulletin de la Société de l'Histoire du Protestantisme Français.
French Historical Studies.
Handbook of French and Belgian Protestantism.
Proceedings of the Huguenot Society of London.
Revue Historique.
XVIIe Siècle.

NOTE: All English books and all French books were published in London and Paris unless otherwise stated.

SOME LEADING HUGUENOT FAMILIES AND THEIR DESCENDANTS

Samuel Smiles in his work on the Huguenots published a list of refugees and their descendants, to which readers should refer for more information. The following list is based on Smiles' but excludes many of the details he gives, and should be considered as an index to Smiles' list. Smiles collated his list from Haag's *La France Protestante*, Agnew's *Protestant Exiles from France*, Cooper's *Lists of Foreign Protestants and Aliens, 1618-1688*, Burn's *History of Foreign Refugees*, the *Ulster Journal of Archaeology* and private sources of information. This list, which we do not claim to be exhaustive, includes many references from the *Dictionary of National Biography* as well. It does not include some of the names mentioned in the text, which should be looked for in the Index.

Abbadie, Jacques (1654?-1727)
Allix, Pierre (1641-1717)
Amand (or Amyand), Claude (fl. 1700)
Amyot, Thomas (1775-1850)
Amyraut or Amyrott, Paul (fl. 1636-62)
Andreas or André, Bernard (fl. 1500)
Andrée, Jean (1699?-1785)
Angier, John (1605-1677)
d'Arblay, General (husband of Fanney Burney) (fl. 1790)
Aubertin, Pierre
Aufrère, Anthony (1756-1833)
Aufrère, George (fl. 1761-8)
Aurelius, Abraham (1575-1632)
Auriol, Pierre

Bacquencourt (see des Voeux)
Bâron, Pierre (fl. 1575)
Barrallier, Francis Louis (1773?-1853)
Barré, Isaac and William Vincent (1726-1802 and 1760?-1829)
Barthélemon, François Hippolite (1741-1808)
Barttelot, Sir Walter (1820-93)
Batz, Joseph de (fl. 1700)
Bazalgette, Sir Joseph (1819-1891)
Beaufort, Daniel Cornelis de (1700-1788)
Beaulieu, Luke de (d. 1723)
Beauvoir, François de (fl. 1685)
Beek, David (d. 1656)
Belcastel de Montvaillant, Pierre (fl. 1680-90)
Belchier, Daubridgecourt (1580?-1621)
Benezet, Anthony (1713-1784)
Benoir, N. (of Spitalfields, silk-weaver)
Benoist, Antoine (1721-1770)
Berchet, Pierre (1659-1720)
Bernher, Augustine (fl. 1554)
Berniere, Jean Antoine de
Bertheau, Charles (1660-1732)

Bion, Jean François (fl. 1704)
Bizari, Pietro (1530?-1586?)
Blanc, Antoine (fl. 1692)
Blaquière, Jean, Baron de (1732-1812)
Blondel, James Augustus and Moses (d. 1734 and fl. 1621)
Blosset (Sieur de Fleury)
Bochart, François (fl. 1730)
Bodt or Bott, Jean de (fl. 1690)
Bohemus, Mauritius (fl. 1647-62)
Boesmer de la Touche (fl. 1700-6)
Boileau de Castelnau, Sir John Peter (1749-1869)
Boisbelau de la Chappelle (fl. 1685)
Boitard, Louis Pierre (fl. 1750)
Bonhomme (of Ipswich, draper)
Bonnell, James (1653-99)
Bosanquet, David (fl. 1687)
Bosquet, Andrew (fl. 1747)
Bostaquet, Isaac Dumont de (fl. 1650-80)
Bouffard, Sieur de la Garrigue (Garrick)
Bouherau, Elias (fl. 1680)
Bourdillon, Jacob (fl. 1730-80)
Bouveries, Laurent de (fl. 1550-70)
Boyer, Abel (1667-1729)
Briot, Nicholas (1579-1646)
Brissac, Capt. George (fl. 1773)
Brunel, Sir Marc Isambard (1769-1849)
Brunet Family of Saintonge (fl. 1685)
Bucer, Martin (1491-1551)
Buissière, Paul (d. 1739)

Cabanel, Rudolph (1762-1839)
Caesar (Cesare Adelmare) (d. 1569)
Cambon, — (d. 1693)
Capel, Louis (b. 1585)
Carbonel, Jean (fl. 1685)
Cardonnel, Adam de (d. 1719)

Carle, Pierre (1666-1730)
Cartaud, Matthew (fl. 1550-80)
Casaubon, Isaac (1559-1614)
Casteels, Peter (1684-1749)
Caus, Solomon de (1576-1630)
Cavalier, Jean (1681-1740)
Chaigneau, Louis, Jean and Etienne (fl. late
    17th c.)
Chalon, Alfred Edward and John James (1780-
    1860 and 1778-1854)
Chamberlain or Chamberlen, Peter (d. 1631)
Chambré, Sir Alan (1739-1823)
Chamier, Daniel and Anthony (d. 1753 and
    1780)
Champagné, Robillar de, family (fl.
    mid-17th c.)
Chardevenne, Pierre (fl. 1670-1724)
Chardin, Sir John (1643-1713)
Charpentier, John (fl. 1710)
Chastelet, Hippolyte (fl. 1672)
Chatelain, Henri (1684-1743)
Chenevix, Richard (1698-1779)
Chéron, Louis (1655-1725)
Chevalier, Antoine-Rodolph (1507-1572)
Claude, Jean-Jacques (fl. 1710)
Claudet, Antoine, François Jean (1797-1867)
Colignon, Abraham de (fl. late 17th c.)
Collot de l'Escury, David (fl. late 17th c.)
Colomiès or Colomesius, Paul (1638-1692)
Constant, Samuel (fl. 1704)
Corcellis, Nicholas (fl. early 17th c.)
Cornaud de la Croze
Cosne, Pierre de and Cosne-Chaverney family
    (fl. late 17th c.)
Coste, Pierre (1668-1747)
Cotterau, N. ... (fl. 1695-90)
Coulan, Antoine (d. 1694)
Courayer, Pierre François le (1681-1766)
Courtauld family
Courteen, Sir William (1572-1636)
Courteville, Raphael or Ralph (d. 1772)
Cousin, Jean (fl. 1562-80)
Cramahé family of La Rochelle (fl. mid 17th c.)
Cramer, Gabriel and Jean-Louis (fl. 1677)
Cregut, ...
Crespigny, Claude Champion de (fl. 1685)
Crommelin, Samuel Louis (1652-1727)
Cruso, John and Timothy (d. 1681 and
    1655?-1697)

Daillon, James de (d. 1726)
D'Albiac, Sir James Charles (1776-1848)
Dalbier, Jean (d. 1648)
Dalechamp, Caleb
Dansays, François (d. 1787)

Dargent or Dargan, Jean and James (fl. mid
    18th c.)
Dassier, John (1676-1763)
D'Assigney, Marius (1643-1717)
Daubuz, Charles (1673-1717)
Daude, Pierre (fl. 1680)
David, John (fl. 1750)
De Caus, Salomon (1576-1626?)
Decker, Sir Matthew (1679-1749)
De Heere or D'Heere, Lucas (1543-1584)
De Jean, Louis
De Keyser, William (1647-1692?)
Delabar, John (fl. mid 17th c.)
De la Cherois, Nicholas, Daniel (fl. 1690)
De Laine, Pierre (fl. 1681)
De la Mothe, Claude (fl. 1685)
De Lancey, Oliver (1749-1822)
Delattre, Jean Marie (1745-1840)
Delaune, William and Gideon (d. 1610 and
    1565?-1659)
De Lavalade family (fl. 18th c.)
Delemar (de la Mer, Delmer) family (fl. 18th c.)
Delmé, Peter
Deloval, Vicomte de (fl. 1685)
Demainbray, Stephen Charles Triboudet
    (1710-1782)
De Moivre, Abraham (1667-1754)
Desaguliers, John Theophilus (1683-1744)
Desbarres, Joseph Frederick, Walsh
    (1722-1824)
Des Champs, John (d. 1767)
Desmaizeaux, Pierre (1673?-1745)
Des Ormeaux, Colin (family also known as
    Colin) (fl. 1685)
Des Voeux, Vinchen (fl. 1742)
Devaynes, William (fl. 1774)
De Veille, Hans (fl. end 17th c.)
Devisme, Louis (1720-1776)
Dollond, John (1706-1761)
Dorigny, Sir Nicholas (1658-1746)
Drebbel, Cornelis (1572-1634)
Drelincourt, Peter (1644-1722)
Droeshout, Martin (fl. 1620-51)
Du Bois Edward (1622-99?)
Du Bosc, Claude (1682-1745?)
Du Boulay family (fl. 1685)
Dubouchet family (fl. mid-18th c.)
Dubourdieu, Isaac (1597?-1692?)
Dubuisson, Francis (fl. mid 16th c.)
Ducarel, Andrew Coltre (1713-1785)
Du Cros, John (fl. early 18th c.)
Du Jon family (fl. 17th c.)
Du Moulin, Charles (fl. 1542-72)
Duncan, Mark (fl. 17th c.)
Dupin, Paul (fl. 1685)

Du Plessis, Jacques (fl. 1750)
Du Port, James (fl. 1590)
Du Puy, Philip and David (fl. 1685)
Du Quesne, Abraham (fl. 1685)
Durand, David (1680–1763)
Durant, Thomas (fl. 1768)
Durfey, Thomas (1653–1723)
Durfort de Duras, Louis, Marquis de
    Blanquefort (fl. 1650–85)
Duroure, Francis (fl. mid 17th c.)
Dury, Paul (fl. 1688)
Du Soul, Moses (fl. early 18th c.)
Dutens, Louis (1730–1812)
Duval, Claude (1643–70)
Duval, Philip (d. 1709)
Duval, Robert (1644–1732)

Emeris family (fl. 1685)
Espagne, Jean d' (1591–1659)
Evremond, Charles de St Denis de Ste
    Evremond (fl. 1678–1705)
Eynard, Anthony (fl. 1739)

Faber, John (1660?–1721)
Faccio, Nicolas (1664–1753)
Fagius, Paul (1504–1549)
Fargues, Jacques de (fl. late 16th c.)
Fauntleroy, Henry (1785–1824)
Fauquier, Francis (1704?–1768)
Fleury, Louis (fl. 1683)
Fonblanque, John de Grenier (1760–1867)
Fonnereau, Thomas George (1789–1850)
Fontaine, James (fl. late 17th c.)
Forêt, Marquis de la (fl. 1699)
Forrester or Forrestier, Peter (fl. 1708)
Fourdrinier, Peter (fl. 1720–50)
Fradelle, Henry (1778–1865)

Gagnier, John (1670?–1740)
Gambier, James (b. 1692)
Garancières, Theophilus (1610–80)
Garret (Gerrard) Mark (fl. 1618)
Garrick (see Bouffard)
Gastigny, . . . de (d. 1708)
Gaussen, David (1685)
Gautier, N. (fl. 1685)
Goldorp, George (fl. 1611 60)
Geneste, Louis (fl. mid 17th c.)
Gentili, Alberico (1552–1608)
Georges, Paul (fl. 1630) another Paul
    (fl. 1647–89)
Gerbier, Sir Balthazar (1591?–1667)
Gervaise, Louis (1615–1690?)
Gibert, Etienne (fl. 1763–1817)
Gosset, Isaac (1713–1799), Matthew (1684–1744)

Goulard, James, Marquis de Vervans (d. 1700)
Goupy, Louis (d. 1747)
Goyer, Peter (fl. mid 17th c., 1685)
Gravelot, Hubert Francois (1699–1773) (also
    known as Bourguignon)
Graverol, Jean (1647–post 85)
Grostête, Claude, see La Mothe
Grote or de Groot family (fl. mid 16th c.)
Gualy, Pierre de Gineste (fl. 1685)
Guérin (or Geeran) (see Crofts family)
Guide, Philip (fl. 1685)
Guillemard, John (fl. 17th c.)
Guillot (or Gillet) family (fl. 17th c.)
Guyon, Richard Debaufre (1803–1885)

Haak, Theodore (1605–1690)
Harenc, Benjamin (fl. 1765)
Hazard or Hasaert, Peter (d. 1568)
Heemskerk, Egbert van (1645–1704)
Hérault, Louis (fl. early 17th c.)
Hervart, Philibert, Baron de Huningue (d. 1721)
Houblon, Peter (fl. 1568)
Hudel or Udel, . . . (fl. 1680)
Hugessen, James (fl. late 16th c.)
Huysmans (Houseman) Jacob (1636?–1696)

Janssen Sir Theodore (1658?–1748)
Justel, Henri (1620–93)

Labouchere, Henry (1798–1869)
Lacroix, Alphonse Francois (1799–1859)
La Condamine, Andre (fl. 17th c.)
La Melonniere, Isaac de Monceau (fl. 1685)
La Mothe, Claud Grostete (1647–1715)
La Motte, Francis and John (fl. mid 16th c.
    and 1570?–1655)
L'Angle, Samuel de (fl. 1682–3)
La Pierre, Mac-Conrad (fl. 1685)
La Pilonniere, . . . (fl. 1716)
La Primaudaye, Pierre de (fl. 1740)
La Roche, Sir James (fl. 1768)
La Rochefoucauld, Frederic Charles, Comte
    de Roye (fl. 1670–80)
La Rochefoucauld, Francois de Montendre
    (fl. 18th c.)
La Roche-Guilhem, Melle de (fl. end 17th c.)
Larpent, Jean de (fl. 1685)
Laski or A'Lasco, John (1499–1560)
La Tombe, Thomas (fl. 1588)
La Touche, David Digues de (fl. 1685)
La Tranche, Frederic de (fl. 1575)
La Tremouille, Charlotte, wife of James
    Stanley, Earl of Derby
Laval, Etienne-Abel (fl. mid 18th c.)
Layard (or Lajard), Antoine (d. 1681).

La Bas, Charles Webb (1799–1861)

← Le Blanc, Sir Imon (d. 1816)

Le Blon (or Blond), Jacques Christophe (1670–1741)

Le Cene, Charles (1647?–1703)

Le Courrayer, Pierre-Francois (fl. early 18th c.)

Le Fanu, Etienne (fl. mid 17th c.)

Lefevre, Roland (1608–77)

Le Fevre, Nicolas (d. 1669)

Lefroy, Antoine (fl. 1579)

Legard family

Leguat, Francois (1638–1735)

Legoulon, . . . (fl. mid 18th c.)

Le Moine, Abraham (d. 1757)

Lemoine, Henry (1756–1812)

Lesieur, Sir Stephen (fl. 1586–1627)

Lestang, Louis de (fl. late 17th c.)

Le Sueur, Hubert (1595?–1650?)

Lethieullier, John (fl. mid 17th c.)

Le Vassor, Michel (fl. mid. 17th c.)

Ligonier, John Louis, first Earl Ligonier (1680–1770)

Logier, Jean-Bernard (1780–1846)

Lombart, Lierre (1620?–80)

Luard, Robert Abraham (fl. 17th c.)

Maittaire, Michael (1668–1747)

Majendie, Jean-Jacques (fl. late 17th c.)

Mangine, Edward (1772–1852)

Marcet, Alexander (fl. end 18th c.)

Marie, Jean (fl. 1685)

Marion, Elié (fl. mid 18th c.)

Martineau, Gaston and David (fl. 1685)

Masères, Francis (1731–1824)

Massue de Ruvigny, Henri de (1st Earl of Galway) (1648–1720)

Mathy, Matthew (fl. mid 18th c.)

Maturin, Gabriel (fl. 18th c.)

Mauduit Israel (1708–1787)

Maury, Matthew (mid 18th c.)

Mayerne, Sir Theodore Tourquet de (1573–1655)

Mazières de (family) (fl. 17th c.)

Mercier, Philip (d. 1760)

Mesnard, Jean (fl. 1685)

Mettayer, John (d. 1707)

Meusnier, Philip

Misson, Francos Maximilien (1650?–1722)

Missy, Cesar de (fl. 1731)

Molenier, Stephen

Molines, Moleyns or Mullins, James (d. 1639)

Montolieu de St Hippolyte (fl late 17th c.)

Motteux, Peter Antony (1660–1718)

Moulin, Peter du (1601–84)

Nadauld family (fl. 1685)

Ouvry, James (fl. late 17th c.)

Paget, Valerian (fl. 1575)

Palavicino, Sir Horatio (d. 1600)

Papillon, David (1581–1655?)

Papin, Denis (1647–1712?)

Pastorius, Francis Daniel (1651–1719?)

Paul, Louis (d. 1759)

Pechell, Samuel (fl. 18th c.)

Perrin, Jean Baptiste (fl. 1786)

Petit des Étans, Louis (1665?–1720)

Pineton, James de Chambrun (fl. mid 17th c.)

Portal, Louis de (fl. mid 17th c.)

Prelleur, Peter (fl. 18th c.)

Primrose, Gilbert (1580?–1641)

Pryme, Abraham de la (fl. 1625–35)

Puissart, Louis James, Marquis de (fl. 1695)

Pusey (see Bouveries and Pusey, Edward Bouverie (1800–1882)

Raboteau, John Charles (fl. 18th c.)

Rapin de Thoyras, Paul de (1661–1725)

Ravanel, Samuel de (fl. 1685)

Ravenet, Simon François (1721?–1774)

Rebow, Sir Isaac (fl. 18th c.)

Riollay, Francis (1748–1797)

Ritschel, George (1616–83)

Rival, Peter (d. c. 1728)

Robethon, John (d. 1722)

Roche, Louis (fl. late 17th c.)

Roche, Michel de la (fl. 1710–31)

Rocheblave, Henri de (d. 1709)

Romaine, William (1714–1795)

Romilly, Sir Samuel (1757–1818)

Roubillac, Louis-Francois (1695–1762)

Roumieu family

Rouquet, James (d. 1776)

Rousseau, Jacques (1626–94)

Rousseau, Samuel (1763–1820)

Roussell, Isaac (fl. 1699)

St André, Nathaniel (1680–1776)

Saurin, Jacques (fl. late 17th c.)

Say, Samuel (1676–1743)

Schalch, Andrew (1692–1776)

Scheemakers, Peter (1691–1770)

Schomberg, Frederick Herman, Duke of (1615–90)

Simon, John (1675?–1751)

Tascher, Pierre de (fl. 1727)

Teulon or Tholon, Peter and Anthony (fl. 1685)

Textard, Leon, Sieur des Melards (fl. lid 17th c.)
Thelluson, Peter (1737-97)
Thorius, Raphael (d. 1625)
Tovey, De Blossiers (1692-1745)
Trench (see La Tranche)
Tryon, Peter (fl. early 17th c.)
Turquand, Peter
Tyssen, Francis

Vanacker, John (fl. mid 17th c.)
Van Haecken (Vanacken, Joseph) (1699?-1749)
Vanbrugh, Sir John (1664-1726)
Vandeleur, Sir John Ormsby (1763-1849)
Vanderputt, Henry (fl. 1568)
Vanderbank (or Vandrebanc) Peter (1649-97)
Van der Doort, Abraham (d. 1640)
Van de Eyden, Jeremiah (d. 1695)
Van de Gucht, Michael (1660-1725)
Van der Myn (or Mijn), Herman (1684-1741)
Van der Vaart, Jan (1647-1721)
Van de Velde, Willem (1610-93)

Van Diest, Adriaen (1656-1704)
Van Leemput, Remigius (1609?-75)
Van Lemens, Balthasar (1637-1704)
Vanlore, Peter (fl. early 17th c.)
Vansittart, Henry (1732-1770)
Van Somer, Paul (1576-1621)
Van Son, Jan Frans (1668-1718)
Van Voerst, Robert (1596-1636)
Varennes, Jean de
Vassall, John (d. 1625)
Vautrollier, Thomas (d. 1578?)
Vermuyden, Sir Cornelius (?1595-1683?)
Verneuil, John (1583?-1647)
Vicose, Guy de, Baron de la Court (fl. 1718-22)
Vignolles, Charles de (fl. late 17th c.)
Vilettes, Sebastian de (fl. late 17th c.)
Vincent family

Witteronge, Jacob (fl. 17th c.)

Yver, John (fl. 17th c.)